RISE OF THE THINKING COMPUTERS

RISE OF THE THINKING COMPUTERS

COMPUTERS

A science fantasy

Richard M. Weiner

translated from the German by
Tony Bowley

ISBN: 1535095768
ISBN 13: 9781535095761

Thanks

Without the decisive contribution by my wife Nina Uli Weiner, who was always supportive of my writing, this book would never have been finished. I also thank her for input on the cover design. I am very grateful to Monika Lessner, one of the first readers of the manuscript, for her useful comments. And, last but not least, I thank the late Heribert Reitboeck, a pioneer in the field of neuroscience, for his 'realistic' assurance that, what appears here as fantasy and science fiction, will become a reality in less than fifty years. I wish all my readers that they may experience it.

Cover: Marion Malinowski

Motto of a thinking computer:

Sum, ergo cogito

MAIN CHARACTERS

Solange Darboux, computer specialist
George Wilson, psychologist
Laurent Barrois, physicist
Lev Davidovitsch Hochkant, physicist
Jean-Baptiste Levallois, banker
Gerhard Hassler, banker
Hans Marek, TV talkmaster
N.N., TV announcer
Lothar Mingus, Director of Channel One Television
Anton Koppelmannn, President of the Swiss Federal Banking Commission
Gus Bones, founder and chief executive, Doors Inc.
Boris Razoumov, inventor of the Roof operating system
Yogiro Fukuda, Director of Robotics
Martha Issing, chief police commissioner
Wolfgang Peters, head of the Frankfurt airport computer center
Patrick Woods, President of the USA
Felix Lacher, President of the German Anticomputer Party
Naoki Akio Tanaka a.k.a. Suzuki, thinking robot

CONTENTS

PART I

CHAPTER 1

ONCE A YEAR

The question surprised Roland and he finally had to consult the Paris Guide on his terminal. After three years in this job at the front desk of the All Seasons hotel, in an outstanding tourist area like the Latin Quarter, he should have known better. Which is the oldest cemetery in Paris? His first answer, *Père Lachaise*, didn't satisfy the guest at all. She was quite sure there were older cemeteries. She made a very convincing and resolute impression generally. Her French was excellent, although it sometimes sounded slightly strange. But then Roland remembered she had submitted a Swiss passport when checking in. There was also something unusual in her appearance, although he couldn't say exactly what it was. Could it be the regular features of her face; a face you might expect to see in a fashion magazine? Her beautiful, raven-black hair was combed backward to bring her high forehead to full advantage, emphasizing the immaculate white of her skin. Or could it be her expressive eyes of indeterminate color or her perfect figure? Her clothing was distinguished by simplicity; the jeans and leather jacket were almost certainly from Gucci or Saint Laurent. No, all this could not explain why Solange Darboux made such a strange, almost esoteric impression on Roland.

"You're right, there is an older cemetery: *Montmartre Le Calvaire*, from the year 1801. But it's only three years older than *Père Lachaise*."

She seemed surprised. "Isn't there a really old cemetery? In a city that is over two thousand years old?"

Roland had no other choice than to look at the Guide again, this time with success: "The older cemeteries ... didn't survive, if I may put it that way. Some were closed for sanitary reasons in 1786 and the remains were transferred to the catacombs. The old Montmartre cemetery was destroyed during the Revolution."

"And then came a new one, *Montmartre le Calvaire*, in 1801?"

"That's what's written here. But it was already closed again in 1831." Roland continued, reading aloud: "It is next to the oldest Paris church, *Église de Saint Pierre de Montmartre*. That was built in 1147 and still exists today." The exact address is Rue du Mont Cenis 2." Roland began to write down the address, but Solange interrupted him: "That's not necessary. I'll remember it."

"I can show you on the map," said Roland. She was faster again: "It is in the quadrant F1 next to the *Sacré Coeur*." Roland was staggered because a glance at the map showed him this was indeed correct. He looked at her in amazement, and she seemed to enjoy his bewilderment. Then she said: "Metro station Abbesses or bus No. 85, isn't it?"

"Precisely. But there's something else."

"Something else?"

Now, Roland thought, I can surprise you: "According to the Guide the cemetery is only open on one day of the year, namely All Saints' Day. So, if you want to visit it this year, you will have to come back again in six weeks."

"In six weeks?"

"Exactly; November first is All Saints' day."

When he saw her disappointment, he added: "But I can comfort you. Paris is also nice in November. It's not for nothing that our hotel is called All Seasons." He began to hum Sinatra's «I love Paris in the fall».

"Are you sure it isn't the other way round? That All Saints is the only day on which the cemetery is closed?"

"Here; see for yourself," said Roland, showing her his terminal. Solange saw that Roland was right about the cemetery. At the same time, she saw that the catacombs could be visited all year round, Tuesdays to Fridays.

"By the way, I would advise you to reserve a room right now. The Paris computer fair and international conference on artificial intelligence takes place in early November and we are almost fully booked already."

She was on the point of leaving the hotel, but turned suddenly and went back to the front desk: "Did you say international conference on artificial intelligence? How could I forget that?"

"Would you like to have more information about it?"

"Actually, I was already aware of the fact. Can you please reserve a room for me from October 30 to November 5."

"I'll send you the confirmation immediately", said Roland.

CHAPTER 2

AT THE AI MEETING

"**I** am firmly convinced. At this rate of progress computers will achieve a level of intelligence comparable to humans in only a few decades."

With this prophecy Thomas Hawthorne ended his presentation on the role of elementary particle physics in the development of artificial intelligence. The plenary session of the 20th International Congress on Artificial Intelligence (AI) was being held in the main auditorium of the Sorbonne University. The five hundred or so participants, including almost all AI experts of world renown, were electrified and the room hummed like a swarm of bees. The many raised hands showed how much the audience wanted to participate in the discussion that followed. One participant even held up both hands to make it clear how urgent his need to say something was. All questions focused on two main points, which the chairman finally summarized as follows:

"There are two main concerns: The human brain has hundreds of billions of nerve cells or neurons, each of which has thousands of connections called synapses. So, mathematically, it would take millions of billions of conventional transistors to replace one brain."

This argument was confidently rejected by Hawthorne with the remark: "You forget that the integrated circuits and chips of today contain thousands of megabytes, the equivalent of tens of billions of transistors. And experience shows that a tenfold increase in storage capacity of these chips can be anticipated every three years."

The second objection carried more weight: "Computers will never be able to perform such complex operations as the human brain. The brain functions in a completely different way. Computers perform simple arithmetic operations while the brain accomplishes complex operations such as pattern recognition, which are not reducible to simple arithmetic." To emphasize this point, the chairman added: "For me, pattern recognition, among other things, includes hazard identification, food identification and mate recognition. The survival of the species depends on it."

The speaker was not impressed by this argument either: "This is exactly where the new developments in elementary particle physics come into play, as I already mentioned. In recent years we have shown that, what was previously considered as an elementary, punctiform particle, is, in fact, a vast, string-like object. This string exists in ten dimensions, not just three." Pausing to highlight what was about to follow and, turning to look at the chairman, the speaker continued: "And that is why a string is much more like a neuron than a transistor, the basis of today's computer industry. That is why the string is also much better adapted to perform complex operations."

Among the AI experts present, there were a considerable number of physicists. But none of them, not to mention the non-physicists, who were in the majority, were able to follow the speaker's argument. He was the only elementary-particle physicist in the hall. Nevertheless, or perhaps precisely for that reason, most of the participants nodded in agreement. After all, he must know what he was talking about because he had been awarded the Nobel

Prize the previous year for his groundbreaking work in the field of string theory.

One young lady in the audience, however, simply followed the discussion with quiet amusement.

"You seem to be enjoying yourself; don't you find these ideas far-fetched?" her neighbor asked. He had almost constantly been looking at her during the lecture. She had been aware of it but hadn't looked back. This didn't seem to discourage him, however. He had even managed to read her name and affiliation written on her badge, although it was partially obscured by a scarf. The name Solange Darboux meant nothing to him, but he was familiar with the name of her institution, the Swiss Trading Bank.

"Quite the contrary, I even believe he considerably overestimates the amount of time it will take until artificial intelligence reaches the human level."

"So you really expect that computers will be able to think like humans?"

"Yes, certainly. They already do in some fields. Do you doubt it?"

"I am neither a physicist nor a computer expert, merely a psychologist." It sounded like a declaration of poverty. "I wouldn't dare to contradict; incidentally, my name is George Wilson."

"You already know my name from my badge," she replied slightly ironically. But this time she looked him straight in the eye and smiled warmly. He even had the impression that she was encouraging him to keep up the conversation. The chairman had announced a break, so he continued talking.

"I see you are from Switzerland. I would like to ask your advice on an entirely different matter if you don't mind."

"Fire away. What is it?"

"Skiing. What are the conditions in Switzerland like at this time of year?"

"November is not the best season for skiing."

"I know. But I want to take the opportunity. It's only a stone's throw to Switzerland from here. On top of that, I urgently need a break to relax. This is my third meeting in Europe in the last three weeks."

"Bored by so much science?"

"Yes, bored. Doesn't that happen to you sometimes?"

She thought for a moment, but left the question unanswered.

Finally, she said: "Switzerland does have some ski resorts that might be worth considering in November."

"Tomorrow there are no lectures. If you are free and want to do some sightseeing, maybe we could do it together. Then you could tell me something more about these ski resorts."

"Tomorrow is All Saints' Day and I am planning to visit the Cemetery *Montmartre de Calvaire*. It's the oldest cemetery in Paris, and you can only visit it once a year, on All Saints' Day. This is actually why I am in Paris just now."

"So you are not here because of the meeting?"

"No. I'm just an observer."

"Then you must be a very important observer. It is not easy to get hold of an invitation to this exclusive meeting."

"My bank is one of the sponsors of the meeting. So it wasn't difficult to get invited."

"Where is this cemetery you mentioned?"

"In Montmartre, next to the *Sacré Coeur.*"

"May I join you? Montmartre is, I believe, one of the most interesting districts of Paris."

"By all means, if you wish."

"Are you also staying at the All Seasons Hotel?"

"Yes."

"We could meet at breakfast then."

"Agreed. Half past eight?"

"Half past eight."

CHAPTER 3

MONTMARTRE

"I have no experience with buses in Paris," said George. They stood at the bus stop and Solange was taking in its battered timetable.

"In principle it should come every six to eight minutes."

"I believe tourists usually prefer the Metro; the stations are easier to find and it's faster."

"Not always. Anyway, the bus ride is more pleasant."

After they had boarded the bus and even found seats with a good view of the street, George admitted, "It was a good idea not to take the Metro."

The fog was beginning to lift and it looked like it was going to be a nice day. As if she had read his thoughts, Solange said: "Some people claim there is nothing better than a sunny day for seeing the boulevards of Paris."

"Is that your opinion too?"

"I used to think so. But then I became habituated to the beauty."

"So you've spent a lot of time in Paris?"

"I studied here for one of my degrees."

"What did you study here, if I may ask? Economics?"

"That too."

"Too?"

"I studied electronics and then specialized on applications in computer science and finance."

"Computer science; that's very appropriate. So perhaps you can explain to me what they meant with pattern recognition yesterday. And why it is so important."

"That will be a double consultation."

"A double consultation?"

"You're forgetting the skiing!" They both laughed. They were on the Boulevard St. Michel and had just crossed the Boulevard St. Germain.

"Are you impressed?" Solange asked.

George replied with another question: "Have you ever wondered why French poets and singers have developed such a weakness particularly for St. Germain?"

"Some of the most famous Parisian cafes are here. That could have contributed to the boulevard's attractiveness."

"And what makes these cafes so famous?"

"Perhaps because of the many famous writers and artists who frequented them," said Solange. "Even today there are people who rave about them."

"Do you belong to that category?" Coming from a psychoanalyst, it sounded almost as if he was questioning a patient.

Solange hesitated, but then said: "In my college days I didn't have the opportunity to learn about Paris from that angle. I was too busy. But I'm making up for it now."

"It would in fact be interesting to clarify what made these cafes so attractive. The atmosphere maybe?"

"You take the words out of my mouth, although the concept still doesn't say much to me. It obviously has to be 'clarified'," she answered, quoting him with relish. Then, after a brief silence, she continued with a smile: "I was just reminded of a story I read some-where that has something to do with the atmosphere of Parisian cafes, and this in the truest sense of the word."

"A story? I have always been interested in stories, especially when they come from such an attractive story teller."

"Thank you for the compliment. Simone de Beauvoir, Sartre's companion, and quite a great writer herself, discovered the *Deux Magots* cafe here on the Boulevard St. Germain during the war, and made it the meeting place of the existentialist movement. Guess why!"

"No idea."

"In 1941 it was the only heated cafe in Paris."

"That's how history is written, in the truest double meaning of the word, if I might put it that way. It's probably the reason why, by way of compensation, today they even heat the streets!" Although it was quite cold, you could see customers sitting comfortably at the tables on the sidewalk under the cafe's retractable roof. Huge electric heaters made this possible.

A few minutes later, they had left the more elegant quarter and were approaching Montmartre, George said: "Coming back to this issue of pattern recognition, why is it such a formidable challenge for computers?"

"It has to do with the fact that conventional computers and the brain work in different ways. The brain can recognize a certain situation immediately, in an instant as it were, while a computer can't."

"And does anybody know why that is?"

"Current theory contends that conventional computers oper-ate according to the laws of classical physics, while the brain fol-lows the principles of quantum physics. It would therefore need a quantum computer to compete with the brain."

"A quantum computer? What's that?" George's facial expres-sion told Solange that she had lost him.

"In quantum physics, as long as a certain condition, a certain property has not been measured, a state has not been established, you can't be sure if that condition truly exists; whether the situation is real or not."

"What a strange coincidence; I've been invited to speak at a meeting on elementary-particle physics tomorrow. Presumably it's all about quantum physics. I guess yesterday's speaker at the session on artificial intelligence will be there too."

"That sounds interesting," Solange said almost admiringly.

"Interesting is perhaps not the right word; I'd call it funny. You see, physics and especially quantum physics is beyond me. Maybe that's why they invited me! These physicists just have a strange sense of humor. However, it's only a breakfast address."

"And what are you going to talk about?"

"I must confess, I don't even know that myself yet. I hope I can think of something by tomorrow. But to come back to my question; does quantum physics say you can't distinguish between 'yes' and 'no'?"

"That's the way it is. Schroedinger put it in a nutshell: Without verification, the cat is both alive 'and' dead."

"That sounds strange. And what does that have to do with computers, with pattern recognition?"

"Conventional computers and robots operate on the yes-or-no principle, that is to say: true-or-false. To check whether a certain situation, a certain condition exists, whether the facts correspond to a pattern that has been experienced before, the conventional computer must check all the possibilities, one by one. And that takes a very long time because the number of alternatives is tremendous."

"Are you saying that the brain or a quantum computer doesn't have to sift through all these options, one after the other? How can you be sure it comes up with the correct answer then?"

"Even the brain has to consider all options. But it does so in a much more efficient way because it initially works with superposition

13

of 'yes and no' and therefore with a much more limited number of alternatives."

George interrupted her: "and only tests if 'yes or no' at the end! He was seemingly beside himself with excitement. Not only Solange noticed it, but the other passengers on the bus did too. The reason for his arousal was that he thought he had found in Solange's quantum considerations a possible explanation for some strange behavioral patterns in his own field. For the moment, however, he kept his suspicions to himself. He could see that Solange was pleasantly surprised by her partner's rapid progress. She knew from experience that even physicists and computer experts often had difficulty with the topic. Psychologists, and George was the first one she had ever met, are more perceptive, she thought. "That's right," she said, "and that shortens computing time exponentially, or many times if you prefer to put it simply."

"If that's the case, why haven't quantum computers replaced conventional computers yet?" asked George.

"I'm not an expert in this particular field, but as far as I know it's a complicated technical problem. However, the specialists claim it's only a matter of time until they get it under control."

"And once we have quantum computers shall we have solved the problem of pattern recognition?"

George, who, during this conversation, occasionally cast a look outside at the scenery and street activity, now focused exclusively on the woman sitting across from him. At the first opportunity, he had taken a seat facing Solange and was now unabashedly enjoying the direct 'view'.

His interest in old cemeteries was, to put it mildly, limited. What made a young person like Solange so keen on the subject, he wondered? Was it perhaps the atmosphere again? Anyway, under the present circumstances, he would have followed her to even more bizarre places. Nevertheless, he was relieved to learn that she had already been to the Paris catacombs.

For inexplicable reasons, he felt irresistibly attracted to this woman. It wasn't just a physical attraction, even though he was well aware she was really very good looking. She radiated that certain something; exercised a strange fascination over her environment. He could tell by the looks the other passengers gave her; even the bus driver had turned to watch as she passed him. George had met many beautiful and interesting women in his career; many of his patients were well-known actors and his wife was elected Miss Massachusetts before graduating from Harvard Law School. But none of his female acquaintances had made such an impression on him.

The attraction that George felt for Solange was obviously mutual, because the bus driver, whom she had asked to tell them when they should get out, had to call *"pour Sacré Coeur"* twice before she reacted. But after they had descended from the bus, Solange seemed to be in complete control again. While George consulted the map on his phone, which he held in his right hand, she took his free left hand, tucked it under her arm and led him through the maze of narrow streets without looking at the names George had tried to find.

"We don't need the map," she said; "we're in quadrant F1."

"When were you last here that you know the neighborhood so well?"

"Years ago. But I looked at the map in the hotel this morning and made a mental note of some of the landmarks."

They walked on in silence. George was so enchanted by Solange's proximity that he cared for nothing else. It seemed like she felt the same way.

It turned out to be a very small cemetery. That could explain why it had closed after only thirty years. As the guard told them, there were only 87 registered graves there, including those of such famous names as Crillon, owners of the noble Hotel Crillon.

"Crillon, that name rings a bell. I think I might have read about it."

"Between 1947 and 1953, the Hotel Crillon was the seat of the commission that managed the Marshall Plan for Western Europe. But that's all I know."

Soon they came across another well-known personality, Pigalle, a famous sculptor who gave his name to a Montmartre neighborhood. Although the man's tomb was no longer there, a commemorative plaque showed that he had been buried here. Solange and George were surprised to find that many of the graves were well kept, suggesting that the descendants of the deceased were still around. In fact, they also saw some people, mostly elderly, looking after some of them. Their impression was confirmed by another surprising observation when they entered the *Église de Saint Pierre de Montmartre* next door. As the service seemed to be almost over, they waited near the entrance.

"Good timing," said George. Neither he nor Solange was interested in participating; they just wanted to look around. Very small and dark, the church turned out to be rather a disappointment. However, George's interest was aroused when he read that the Church had been built in 1147 on the same ground as a fifth-century Merovingian church, which itself replaced a temple dedicated to the Roman god Mars.

The officiating priest spoke the final benedictions. Then, to Solange's and George's surprise, the members of the congregation began to embrace each other. George turned to Solange and jokingly opened his arms. Solange did the same and they suddenly found themselves in an embrace. But what was merely a conventional gesture for the other churchgoers was for them a true act of love. Solange responded to George's hesitant hug by resolutely pulling him closer and kissing him on the lips. George not only returned the kiss; he couldn't pull himself away. This didn't go unnoticed by the others present, but who cares about that in Paris, even in a church.

It was not long until they both guessed why the parishioners had embraced. Most of them were relatives or good friends and it was customary for them to meet at the cemetery every year on All Saints' Day to take care of the graves of their ancestors. While people at other churches and other religious services generally don't know each other so well and after the service only hold hands, this was different: Every All Saints' Day they celebrated a sort of family reunion at this ancient Paris church. Neither Solange nor George regretted this misunderstanding. It showed them what effect the atmosphere of an old cemetery and an old church could have.

Of the hundreds of tourists they saw after they left the church, many, if not all of them, were oblivious to what had happened inside. Montmartre had many other things to offer, especially on such a beautiful day: the breathtaking views of Paris from the *Sacré Coeur* basilica; the *Moulin de la Galette* windmill immortalized by Renoir; the Cabaret *Moulin Rouge*, whose first posters had been painted by Toulouse-Lautrec; the houses in which the composer Satie or the poet Tristan Tzara had lived; and last but not least, the Montmartre cemetery where Stendhal, Heine, Berlioz, Zola, Dalida, Truffaut and many other celebrities have their final resting place.

Solange and George, however, strolled from one sight to the next, but hardly noticing them. Their attraction for each other held them completely spellbound. They held each other's hands, looked each other almost continuously in the eye and tried to make out what had happened to them and what had transformed them into this trance-like, but wonderful condition. Finally reality caught up with them, when George, who had followed Solange's example and taken only a croissant and coffee for breakfast, felt hungry.

"How about lunch?" He asked.

"A good idea, it's already 12.34."

"How do you know that so precisely?" There was no clock to be seen and Solange wasn't wearing one.

"I have an internal clock," she quipped.

Following Solange's proposal they went to the *Bistro de la Mere Catherine*. While they waited to be served, Solange explained why she had just chosen this one among the half-dozen restaurants on the Place du Tertre.

"This is the oldest bistro, not only in Paris, but the whole world."

"Really? Didn't we pass another, much older one this morning in the Latin Quarter? I think it was frequented by Voltaire, d'Alembert and Marat"

"You mean *Le Procope*. No. *Le Procope* is the oldest cafe in Paris. However, today you can hardly distinguish it from a bistro. I really meant bistro. When Paris was occupied by the Russians in 1814, they wanted to be served quickly, or *bystro* as they say in Russian. That's how the name came about."

"Very interesting. Does that mean the first bistro was a Russian-French invention?" George took a sip from his typically French aperitif, *Pineau de Charente*, which, as Solange told him, comes from the Charente province in the southwest of France, and is prepared from 30% cognac and 70% grape juice. Then he said: "You seem to know Montmartre like the back of your hand. How is it that you didn't visit that old cemetery before?"

"As I said, while I was studying I was too busy. Besides, as far as I remember, I was not interested in cemeteries then."

"And why this interest now? Please excuse my curiosity; it's probably a professional deformation."

"So it looks like I'm lying on the psychoanalyst's couch now," Solange remarked with a smile. "I am also an inquisitive person, although not an analyst. I am interested in everything human, including cemeteries. Also, I've been invited to participate in a television debate on the topic."

In the meantime, the waiter served the appetizer. Both had ordered salmon mousse. George had followed Solange's example again and ordered, contrary to his American habits, a full menu. Solange observed with amusement that he wasn't regretting it. He seemed so preoccupied with his food that he left it to Solange to keep up the conversation. She could do that easily, as she ate very little.

"Don't you like it?"

"Yes, but I never eat more."

"With your figure you could though. Most people find pleasure in eating. Don't you?"

"I find it just as much fun to watch other people indulge. But, to change the subject, there is a question I wanted to ask you yesterday; what does psychology have to do with artificial intelligence?"

"You want to know what I'm doing at a conference on artificial intelligence? That's a good question. Let me answer it with another question: What does psychology have to do with natural intelligence?"

Solange hesitated as if she were thinking. Then she said: "I must confess, I have never asked myself that question. At first sight I would imagine psychology is concerned with intellectual activities and intelligence is a measure of intellectual activity."

"That's true, but it doesn't stop there. Next, you should ask yourself what this measure of intellectual activity really is."

"It's the ability to think ... to think abstractly, right?"

"That's also correct, but there is more to it. Intelligence is a measure of the ability to learn, the ability to solve problems, as well as of adaptability. And this where artificial intelligence comes into play."

"And psychology?"

"Psychology teaches us, among other things, how the learning process takes place. And you, as a computer expert, can then use this knowledge to build intelligent computers."

"Perfectly clear. So, if I may quote Molière, this means I have been producing prose until now without knowing it."

At that moment, George was busy carving his leg of lamb cooked Norman style. He had expected a stew, but this far exceeded all his expectations. "What kind of prose do you produce, then, if I may ask?"

"I'm working on computer security issues in the banking system."

Their discussion and lunch were abruptly interrupted by Solange's cell phone. She had already warned George that she was expecting an important call from her bank. The conversation didn't last long and George's knowledge of French was just enough to understand she had to return to Geneva right away.

"I'm sorry, George, but I have to take the next flight to Geneva. Our computer system has crashed," she told him. George's disappointment at the sudden end to their tête-à-tête, which had been progressing so well, was only eased by the thought that Solange also seemed to regret it. She asked the waiter for the bill, but George insisted on paying. "You may have your turn in Chamonix," he said. He had decided to follow Solange's advice and spend his holiday in Chamonix, where skiing conditions were acceptable all year round. The choice was made all the easier for him because Solange had mentioned her boss had a chalet in Chamonix, where he spent almost every weekend with his family and he had invited Solange to join them on the following weekend. She kissed George goodbye and took a taxi to the hotel to pick up her belongings. George decided to continue his tour to some sights Solange had recommended and that he didn't know.

That evening at the hotel he wrote in his diary as usual what he had done during the day. This time everything centered on Solange. His notes read like a psychoanalytic session with one of his patients. From a purely professional point of view her spontaneity and her excellent memory were remarkable. She knew when almost all of the famous Montmartre painters and writers had lived, not to mention her particular interest in cemeteries. It was so unusual for a person of her age. On the other hand, he found her statements about the atmosphere of boulevard cafes typical for her age. He himself, although much older than Solange, found it hard to think like the post-war Paris generation. There were also many other small details he had noticed during the morning, but he had forgotten what they were by the evening.

On the other hand, he suddenly remembered he had to give a lecture the following day. The organizer of the meeting had allowed him complete freedom in the choice of subject, under the condition that it somehow related to the topic of the meeting, which was 'correlations in particle physics'. After a moment's thought, George decided to speak off the cuff. He thought the proposed term was unspecific enough.

CHAPTER 4

CORRELATIONS – THE BREAKFAST MEETING

They didn't call Paris the city of meetings for nothing. In addition to the conference on artificial intelligence, another meeting was being held in the Latin Quarter at the same time. It was on correlations in particle physics, or CPP for short. The two meetings not only differed in the topic, but also in the numbers and specializations of the participants. The AI conference had attracted a wide range of professions: computer scientists, mathematicians, physicists, psychologists, physicians, pharmacologists, philologists, musicians and even philosophers. By contrast, the CPP meeting had only attracted physicists and, in particular, only ones specialized in particle and nuclear physics. Accordingly the AI conference was taking place in the famous Sorbonne University, while the CPP was in a shabby building of the Paris University on Place Jussieu. The two meetings also differed in that the AI conference traditionally held its banquet at the end of the meeting, while the CPP banquet took place on the morning of the first day. Laurent Barrois, who chaired the CPP meeting, didn't explain the reason for this innovation until the last session, during his closing address. So, except for the Russian theorist Kant, who had guessed why after inspecting some of the restaurants the organizers had recommended, the reason remained a mystery for most. Kant, or Lev Davidovics Hochkant to use his full name, was the star of Russian theoretical physics, which is why his friends called him Kant. He was also a first-class connoisseur of food and wines and an excellent cook.

There was a simple explanation why the CPP banquet was on the first morning. It reflected a deeper, general problem. Nuclear and particle physics were out of fashion. The French science ministry was usually quite generous when asked to sponsor a scientific meeting, especially when it was held in Paris, because it drew a lot of attention from the media. The support usually included banquets in the best restaurants, considered as a specific form of promotion for the country. Recently though, following the widespread anti-atomic movement that had led to the closing of numerous nuclear power stations, the ministry had changed its policy. It no longer considered research in particle and nuclear physics as a priority. Because of its status as a nuclear power, as well as for historical and prestige reasons, France was the only country of the West that had long opposed this trend. But after a member of the Green Party became France's Science Minister, the situation here also began to change. On the pretext of complying with budget cuts decreed by the European Union in Brussels, and following Germany's example of closing its nuclear power stations, the ministry began to limit funds for particle physics. This had an immediate impact on financing for the CPP meeting. Instead of reserving a five-star restaurant for the banquet, the organizers had to move it to a simple bistro without stars.

This change created another problem: The documentation sent to the participants several months beforehand had recommended restaurants where they could eat on their own account. These restaurants were of a much higher standard than the bistro selected at the last minute for the banquet. But to end a meeting in Paris with a culinary decline would have been a disgrace. The organizing secretary came up with the bright idea to hold the banquet on the very first morning at the start of the meeting. In that way, the participants wouldn't be spoiled by better food before the banquet; they would take eating in a bistro for granted, seeing that restaurants didn't open before midday. It also meant the organizers didn't need to serve champagne, wine or other alcoholic beverages, which were a major cost factor under normal circumstances. This CPP meeting went down in the history of scientific meetings under the name 'breakfast banquet meeting'.

Another amendment dictated by the reduction in resources involved the invited banquet speaker. Normally, it would have been a well-known scientist from a related field, who not only had his expenses reimbursed, but was also paid a substantial fee. The only condition for the theme of his presentation was that it had something to do with correlations. Initially, the organizers had intended to invite the developer of the latest potency pill to talk about 'correlations between potency and frigidity'. For years, Barrois had argued with his wife whether he or she was responsible for their unsatisfactory sex life, and had hoped to get some first-hand tips from the inventor of the miracle pill. The invitation had to be withdrawn, however, because the cost of a transatlantic flight in business class was simply prohibitive.

At the suggestion of one of Barrois' colleagues, who happened to be in the organizing committee of the AI meeting, they instead invited a psychoanalyst who was attending the AI meeting anyway. That solved the problem of travel expenses. However, since this change took place at the last minute and the new banquet speaker was already on his way to Paris, there was no time to discuss with him the exact title of his presentation. So it was shown as TBA. The organizers usually only announced presentations in the program as 'to be announced' if the speaker was so famous that his name was enough to arouse participants' interest. It only took a quick look in the Web to convince Barrois that George Wilson belonged in this category. Anyway, it was only on the evening before the meeting that George decided to present some interesting cases from his psychoanalytic practice, in the hope that the listeners, who were all professionals in the field of correlations, would find out for themselves what was being correlated.

In the end, this seemingly naive idea turned out to be extremely fruitful, with far-reaching consequences not only for psychology but also for the whole of society. Many years later in her memoirs, the French science minister claimed that her decision to curb support for the CPP meeting was responsible for the revolutionary developments resulting from this impromptu lecture, as we shall see.

CHAPTER 5

MR. HASSLER, WE HAVE A PROBLEM

Jean-Baptiste Levallois, deputy director general and director of customer services at the Swiss Trading Bank, was always in a hurry and didn't care who was already waiting to see his boss. Usually, he was at least polite enough to apologize. But this time he ignored all those present in the waiting room, including Yvonne the boss' secretary. Though normally the perfect gentleman, this time he didn't greet her at all, in spite of the fact that it was the first time he had seen her that day. Like a rocket he rushed past her desk directly to the door marked 'GERHARD HASSLER DIRECTOR GENERAL' in golden letters. He knocked and stormed into the room. Without waiting, he blurted out: "Mr. Hassler, we have a problem."

Roger Cardot, the director of human resources, who was already in the office, looked embarrassed towards Levallois and Hassler, who turned with a helpless gesture to Cardot and said: "Would you excuse us, please, Mr. Cardot? It really seems to be something very urgent." On this, Cardot had no choice but to leave the room in a hurry.

"Thank God we only have a problem to solve. I thought we must be out of work. What happened, Jean-Baptiste?"

The two men spoke formally only in the presence of other bank employees. When they were alone, they addressed each other by their first names. Hassler had suggested it; he wasn't only the boss, but also a few years older than Levallois. It wasn't absolutely ironic when he said 'out of work' either. There was a danger, or hope, depending on whether you took the position of the employees or the owners, that the planned automation of banking operations would make up to two thirds of the bank's employees redundant. That was also what that Hassler had just been talking about to Cardot.

But Levallois had other worries: "The number of dormant accounts has increased dramatically," he said. "While we only had three of them in the past ten years, the number has increased to sixty-nine in the past nine months."

Dormant or inactive accounts were accounts with no recorded movement in the past five years. They had made headlines during the Swiss banking scandal. Some Swiss banks apparently held money from people who had perished during the Second World War. Not only had they omitted to search for the heirs of those accounts; some of them had even refused to recognize the claims of the few cases that arose, and demanded they provide official death certificates. The fact that the concentration camps of Auschwitz and Treblinka hadn't issued death certificates to their inmates was a regrettable but nonetheless undeniable fact from the standpoint of the banks. The banking laws in Switzerland were subsequently amended as a result of pressure from the United States. Economic relations with America were too important for Switzerland for them to ignore the demands of Uncle Sam. According to the new law, banks were obliged to report any accounts that had been dormant over the past five years to the Swiss authorities. These accounts were then closed and the balance handed over to the authorities, which were obliged to seek the heirs and hold the assets at their disposal for another fifty years. After this, any unclaimed money had to be made available to appropriate philanthropic organizations.

"That really is a problem," confirmed Hassler. "The tax inspectors will start to ask questions again. Is there any common denominator for these accounts, any clue?"

"I'm afraid so: Most of them amount to more than ten million Swiss francs and were opened by the AFQ (ask few questions) procedure."

Hassler's face darkened. This procedure was the successor to the ANQ (ask no questions) procedure that banks had used for anonymous number accounts. Although these had been illegal for many years because of the money laundering laws, it had been easy to get round them in the past. The events of September 11, 2001, however, had forced Western governments to tighten controls on banking activities. Bank executives were now held responsible for complying with the regulations and risked heavy fines or even imprisonment if an illegal account was found. For this reason ANQ was replaced by AFQ.

Several moments passed. There were four wrinkles on Hassler's forehead instead of the usual three and his lips were pressed together, as if he wanted to force them to be silent. He seemed to have forgotten Levallois' presence and focused his eyes on a sheet of white paper lying on the desk before him.

Levallois interpreted his boss' reaction as intense reflection. The issue was obviously giving him more to think about than expected, because the silence lengthened. In order not to cause Hassler even more embarrassment Levallois turned to look at the Miró hanging on the wall behind Hassler's chair. Finally Hassler asked:

"Who besides you knows about these accounts?"
"Nobody"
"Keep it that way."
"So we do nothing?"
"Not for the moment."

Hassler had his reasons for not wanting to report the dormant accounts immediately as prescribed by the law. It was clear to him that he would have to report them sooner or later; the Jewish accounts' affair was still too fresh in the minds of the public, even if it wasn't the center of attention of the authorities. First, he wanted to find out whether other banks were in a similar situation. If that wasn't the case, it meant his bank was enjoying privileged treatment by certain customers who value discretion. Under normal circumstances, every businessman would welcome such preferential treatment. In this case, however, Hassler was worried. Not about the moral aspect. That had never hindered his activities. Rather, it was the legal aspects that caused him a headache. If these accounts were only at his bank, the authorities, as soon as they got wind of the affair, would start enquiring why the bank had failed to ask those questions that were obligatory before opening such accounts. If they accused his bank of being too easy going, wouldn't it blow the whole AFQ procedure to pieces? And even if the authorities didn't ask why had he cultivated his network; wouldn't the other banks ask, if only for competitive reasons? If it really were the case that this problem only affected his bank, it might be worthwhile to retroactively amend the AFQ questionnaire by introducing additional questions. Or, even better, to replace it with the questionnaire of another bank that had been less successful in acquiring dormant accounts.

Suddenly Hassler was haunted by even worse fears. Wasn't this whole affair a Jewish conspiracy, an attempt to compromise his bank? It was no secret that his bank had close relations with Iraq and Libya, and that he himself was chairman of the Swiss-Arab society. His resolute attitude towards Zionism and the current policy of the Israeli government, which he had compared with Nazi Germany, hadn't only brought him new and wealthy clients, but also heavy criticism in the media. No wonder, he thought, considering these media were in Jewish hands. That was a more compelling reason to treat this issue with caution and circumspection.

CHAPTER 6

ADDRESSING THE BREAKFAST BANQUET

"Ladies and Gentlemen, thank you for inviting me to speak to you today. It is a great honor for me for at least two reasons. First, the list of banquet speakers at earlier correlation meetings is a veritable Who is Who. In addition, I have the privilege of being the first psychologist to speak at this series of exclusive meetings. You are perfectly entitled to ask what a psychologist, and in particular a psychoanalyst, has lost at a meeting of world experts on particle correlation. I must confess, I already asked Professor Barrois, the chairman of the meeting, the same question. His response was that physicists, and especially particle correlation physicists, never ask why. At best they ask why not. I find this argument perfectly convincing; I apply the same principle myself in the treatment of 'my particles'. I'm sure you know what I mean when I say my particles." Roaring laughter rang through the hall. "When a patient tells me he has hallucinations, I never ask why. On the contrary, I am surprised when he claims he has none." The audience rocked with laughter. "For the same reason I was pleased to learn that for you as particle physicists, 'yes or no' also means 'yes and no' and that the cat may be alive and dead at the same time. You've guessed it; I mean the Schroedinger cat. In my zoo, pardon, in my field, this happens every day. We call it split personality. And so I get to the serious part of my presentation."

The tension in the room was palpable. With his last two sentences George Wilson had managed to attract the undivided attention of the whole audience.

"I am going to tell you about some recent observations my colleagues and I have made that indicate a significant change in human behavior. From a medical point of view the statistics are convincing: we have about ten thousand cases. Of course I am aware that a statistics with less than a million events is a paltry number for you as particle physicists. Still, for us psychologists it is quite conclusive. I have no explanation for these observations. All I can say is that they are correlated, to use the theme of your meeting. This means we have observed seven different changes relating to the same group of people worldwide in the last decade. In other words, once you define a category of people who are distinguished by a particular new feature, you will most likely find the other six new features in the same category. The first observation relates to human sexuality. What else would you expect from a psychoanalyst? The views of people regarding incest have changed. Today society accepts incest almost as easily as homosexuality. This is reminiscent of the views of the Marquis de Sade. May I take the liberty in this context to quote from his 'boudoir philosophy'? 'I dare say that any government whose basic principles include fraternity should accept incest by law'. It is surely no coincidence that this was written in 1795, only six years after the French Revolution had set out the principle of fraternity as one of its basic principles."

A member of the audience asked: "Don't these observations only refer to China?"

"I know what you're getting at," said George. "You mean because of strict birth control laws in Communist China. They only let each family have one child and many Chinese couples aborted female fetuses or even killed daughters when they were born. Indeed, you might think the resulting deficit in women of marriageable age was the reason for changing the philosophy. However," and here George paused to stress what followed, "this phenomenon is not restricted to China. You see, in order to exclude demographic influences, statisticians compared Chinese data with those from Europe and North America. They found no significant difference. Moreover, the views regarding Elektra complexes go hand in hand with the views on Oedipus complexes. This excludes the imbalance between the numbers of men and women observed in China as a possible cause of a rise in incest. I must stress here that this only concerns views on incest, not actual cases. There are no data on that. Everything indicates that public opinion regarding incest has changed. In the 20th century it characterized the general moral principles of the major monotheistic religions Judaism, Christianity and Islam, but not any more."

"The second observation relates to numbered names. The proportion of names that contain numbers seems to be growing worldwide. What is even more remarkable is that you often see numbers as high as Andrew 356 or Ann 798 among them. It is reminiscent of the kings and queens of England and France such as Louis XVI and Henry VIII. However, in these royal names each number referred to a specific generation: Louis XVI was the grandson of Louis XV, who was the great-grandson of Louis XIV and so on back to Louis I. This is obviously not the case with these new names, because the increase in numbered names has only been observed in the last decade. On top of that, the numbers are a hundredfold higher. Incidentally, the names Andrew and Ann have become very popular in the United States lately. To exemplify this correlation, you find it more often in people to whom the first observation also applies. This preference for numbered names goes hand in hand with a considerable increase of so-called number geniuses; people who can mentally multiply large numbers without difficulty and can easily memorize large numbers in general."

"Now to my third observation. We are seeing an increasing difference in educational levels, although, for the majority of the population, the differences in income have decreased. In a sense, it is like a renewal of class divisions, particularly with regard to some habits, taste or language. Let me give you a language example: The vocabulary that people use has changed. Some now use more abbreviations than in the past, which often leads to confusion. For example, some people use the abbreviation Kg for kilograms as well as for kindergarten. There is another category of people who use synonyms less and less. On average, the number of words that these people know and use has declined over the past fifty years from 2,000 to 200. These numbers apply to the English language. However, my French and German colleagues have confirmed that a similar situation exists in their languages, too. For these people, the use of grammar, for example, having to differentiate between singular and plural, between adjective and adverb or between conjugation and declension, is an unnecessary complication. They know nothing about art or literature, and even if they have heard of it, it doesn't interest them."

"At the same time, the number of people who have a large vocabulary has increased considerably. Among people who speak English, French or German the number of those who know more than 50,000 words is no longer uncommon. These people know Shakespeare's sonnets or Lamartine's poems by heart, and many have even mastered several foreign languages in addition to their own." George himself had never actually read a poem by Lamartine, but he was well aware of the sensitivity of his French hosts to such knowledge deficits. "By the way, with regard to memory, this same privileged group of educated people not only has a much better memory for words, but also for numbers. They not only know specific dates from history as, for example, what king lived when, but also geographical data, such as the area of Nigeria or how long the River Yenisei is."

"My fourth observation relates to travel habits. These have changed too. Fewer people travel, no matter whether for business or for leisure. It's easy to understand how Internet communication, videoconferencing and similar technical advances have reduced the need for business trips. However, it's surprising to learn that people are more likely to use their leisure time, including their vacations, to watch documentaries about foreign countries, rather than go and visit these countries themselves."

"My fifth observation: People sleep less. Twenty years ago, an adult slept on average for six hours a night; today it's only four."

"Observation six: People eat less. Food today costs less than a few percent of the median income, which means you can eat for practically nothing. However, it is not uncommon these days for an adult male to be able to survive on 1,000 kilocalories daily, instead of 1,800. In this context it is also worth noting that there are now people whose hunger can be satisfied merely by reading a restaurant menu."

Barrois, who had not been paying much attention to the talk until now, because he had been busy checking in the list of delegates to ensure that those who were present had paid their fees, perked up. At the next meeting he had to organize, he could use this observation to his advantage.

George looked at his watch and hurried to finish his presentation: "I wanted to convince you that there are not only seven wonders of the World, but also seven new curiosities in our lives. And that brings me to my seventh and final observation: Life is also defined by its opposite: Death. Here something fundamental has changed: Our views about death, and the relationship of contemporary man to death, are essentially different. People today aren't so concerned about dying, they don't even think about it so much. Of course, this is also only another statistical observation. Among people in a given age group there are still some who think about the issue, but their percentage has decreased markedly. Could this oddity have something to do with the duality of Schroedinger's cat? This seventh observation of people's attitude towards death has, according to some of my colleagues, a common denominator with the first, relating to incest. This denominator is the move away from religion, which has dominated the moral principles of mankind until recently. This process had already begun in the Renaissance and reflects in part Spinoza's pantheism, which equates the concept of God with the term Nature. It is an inevitable consequence of the progress of science. For you, as physicists, that is surely not surprising."

CHAPTER 7

DEATH AND IMMORTALITY ON TELEVISION

Hans Marek's late night talk show was one of the most successful programs on Channel One. Audience statistics even considered it to be one of German television's most successful programs. This was because the themes selected were attractive, the invited guests were interesting and Marek's dry humor, what critics called the 'Marek Factor', was rather special. This time, however, even the most benevolent reviewers felt it was too much of a good thing. What had happened?

The title of the program was: 'opposites attract each other'. As usual the announcer introduced the program with: "Here come Hans Marek and his guests." Then, as usual, Marek appeared and presented the invited couples. The first was a pastor and a former prostitute; they were followed by a famous footballer with his ex-wife. The third couple was a banker and a communist member of parliament. The announcement of the final guest, Bertha Seidlitz, caused uproar. She had died six months ago!

Viewers bombarded the television studio with phone calls complaining about what they considered had been one of Marek's tasteless jokes. In fact, it wasn't his fault at all. The mistake was that the announcer had failed to say this was not a live show, but a recording of one broadcast a year earlier.

The story didn't end there, though. When Channel One's director, Lothar Mingus, learned of the incident through the newspapers, he told the announcer N.N. to apologize. N.N. said he didn't understand what the excitement was all about, however.

"Why is it so important that Bertha Seidlitz is dead and the others aren't? Sooner or later they will all die."

"You don't seem to realize that we don't want to be reminded of that."

"We? As for me, I don't care at all."

"You forget the letters of protest."

"There were fifty of them; from five million viewers! Anyway, television, and especially state television, also has to play an educational role."

"What do you mean by that?"

"First, it must prepare the public for death. Secondly, quantum mechanics has taught us that as long as you don't know, as long as you haven't checked..."

Mingus was beginning to realize that N.N. hadn't forgotten to mention it was a recording; he had done it on purpose. "Don't start giving me that nonsense again: 'what the eye cannot see, the heart cannot grieve over'. Mingus knew N.N. was an original; it was one of his quirks to call himself N.N. The interior minister had given him special authorization to use this name on official documents. This quirk, combined with Marek's irony, had so far contributed to the popularity of the program. Protests are a fundamental part of television's bread and butter, especially when they are reported in the media. In fact, Mingus had previously used his contacts as director to help make some of them public. He therefore decided not to do anything in this case.

Only four weeks later he regretted this decision deeply. Marek was on vacation and N.N. was moderating in his place. He had invited an architect, a historian, a philosopher, a computer scientist and a theologian to talk about 'cemeteries and what to do with them'. In his introduction N.N. explained what the discussion was about. With growing urbanization, existing cemeteries finally ended up in the city center instead of the suburbs. Here, population growth soon made them too small. Over time they had to be closed and replaced by new ones on the periphery.

Town planners had to decide what to do with the old ones. They wanted to relocate the remains and to build on the land, which was often in very expensive neighborhoods. The conservation authorities opposed this plan. They emphasized the historical interest in these cemeteries and the fact that famous personages were buried there. The historian and the theologian supported this point of view, while the architect took the side of the urban planners. He suggested using an ossuary, except for historical figures, whose remains could be put in a central memorial similar to the Pantheon in Paris. However, the computer scientist rejected both proposals, arguing that cemeteries are an outdated concept. First, it made no sense to preserve a dead person's bones when whole skeletons could be replaced with artificial tissues. Secondly and more importantly neurophysics, the new discipline of biophysics, made it possible to transfer information from the human brain to computer memory. This, in her opinion, would allow people to cherish the memory of anyone who merited it. Only this knowledge and not the bones should be preserved in the Pantheon after an appropriate time. Before that they could be deposited in bank safes.

The theologian opposed this proposal fiercely, arguing that human beings have a soul. And a soul is not just brain activity. Only God, the Creator, can dispose of it. The philosopher, who had been silent so far, disagreed: "This is not a matter of brain or soul; it's the relationship between the material and the spiritual world. The spiritual world includes our personal feelings and experiences, our hopes, joys and sorrows. Popper has already shown that a third world exists. It is the product of our thoughts and our artistic activities. Brain activity belongs in that world."

When the computer specialist asked how Popper would bring preserved brain activity into his third world, the philosopher responded indignantly: "You and your colleagues should know that philosophers don't fuss with such technicalities."

N.N. then suggested that the preservation of brain activity might give mankind some kind of immortality. The computer scientist and the philosopher agreed, while the historian had doubts. The theologian, however, left the podium under protest. It was the very first time such a thing had happened on German television. This incident alone was enough to make the show a huge success, and N.N. had every reason to be satisfied. But his boss Mingus couldn't rejoice. The conservative minister of culture, who had received a strongly worded call from the Vatican, held him accountable. Mingus now regretted he had failed to take appropriate measures after the first 'death show'. He ordered N.N. to his office again.

"The show went too far this time; I hope you realize that. We must respect the religious feelings of our fellow citizens."

"Some of our fellow citizens," N.N. countered: "The vast majority is not religious and enjoyed the show."

"Nevertheless, I believe we cannot afford another 'educational' show of this kind. Please take note of that."

"I adamantly disagree. German television needs more such programs. The country claims to be a secular state, but is far from it. This contradiction has to be resolved."

"Why do you say Germany is not a secular state?"

"Because religion is taught in state schools and the state collects church taxes."

Mingus had to admit, as usual, that there was some truth in what N.N. had said. But he doubted that the minister would accept the argument. Then he asked: "Who is this computer woman Darboux?"

"Solange Darboux is a renowned Swiss information technology specialist. She works for one of the major Swiss banks."

"That must explain why she came up with this idea to keep brains in bank safes. I must admit she is very good looking, though. And her German is excellent, despite her French name." With this conciliatory remark he ended the conversation.

CHAPTER 8

THE INVITATION TO BERN

"I'm sure you know why I asked you to come and see me." Anton Koppelmannn, the President of the Swiss Federal Banking Commission, had summoned Gerhard Hassler at short notice to meet him in Bern. Hassler was visibly nervous. He wondered how on earth Koppelmannn had learned about the dormant accounts so soon, which he was sure was the reason for this sudden 'invitation'. Nevertheless, he decided to play innocent.

"I have no idea, Mr. Koppelmann."

"Haven't you seen this?" Koppelmann handed him his tablet showing a news flash the «Financial Times» had published toward lunchtime that day.

"No, I only browsed through the early morning news."

Hassler read the headline and his features relaxed. Koppelmann even thought he saw a fleeting smile on Hassler's face and wondered what it signified. After all, the headline read: 'Central banks call emergency meeting.'

Hassler read on: 'Neither the Federal Reserve nor encouraging speeches by politicians has been able to halt the free fall of technology stocks; even the classical stock market is affected. A global economic crisis similar to the one in 1929 cannot be excluded'.

Hassler was relieved. So it wasn't about what he had feared. Nevertheless, this message was very disturbing in itself. The article continued: 'Events on Wall Street reflect the loss of shareholder confidence in economic outlook, but also in corporate management. In addition to accounting scandals, it was primarily the overestimation of the economy's technological needs in general and the man on the street in particular that led to this disastrous development. The directors of the central banks of the major powers have therefore convened an international meeting to find measures able to prevent a repetition of the events of 1929, at least from the financial standpoint, so that a shortage of cash doesn't paralyze the economy'.

Hassler now remembered he had heard about this extraordinary meeting the previous evening, but had been too busy with his own problems to think about it.

"Oh yes, sure, Mr. Koppelmann. I guessed something like that was coming. It had to be expected after Woods personally felt the pressure."

"What does Woods have to do with it?"

Hassler saw his error immediately and knew he had committed an indiscretion. He knew from his brother that Patrick Woods, the US President, had suffered considerable losses on the stock market. The company that managed Woods' assets had invested almost all of its liquid reserves in X shares. After these had lost 90% of their value, the company went bankrupt. Another company acquired and continued to manage the remaining capital. This other company belonged to none other than Gerhard Hassler's brother, Tobias, who was one of the leading brokers on Wall Street.

Gerhard Hassler managed to draw Koppelmann's attention in a different direction: "I suspect Woods bought X shares like everyone else did."

"Of course, I suppose you're right. How about you?"

"I did unfortunately, although I was warned."

"What; who warned you?"

"My brother; he works on Wall Street. As well as my…" Hassler hesitated, as if looking for the correct word, "let's call her my market analyst."

"Your market analyst? I like that word; it has a Freudian overtone. What's her name? "

"Solange Darboux. She is really responsible for the security of our computer system, but you're right, she has a Freudian relationship." "Freudian relationship goes perfectly with analyst." Koppelmann was visibly amused "But seriously; what do you mean?"

"Her friend is a psychoanalyst. Well, maybe they are even more than just friends."

Koppelmann felt a trace of regret in Hassler's statement and thought to himself: "You old womanizer; didn't she fall for you?"

He continued the conversation: "That's interesting. Why didn't you take her warnings seriously?"

"They were too general."

"In what way?"

"She thought, or rather she still thinks, that our economic system is full of absurdities and we can therefore expect a fall in the stock market even when economic factors are generally positive."

"What does she mean by absurdities?"

"The usual; farmers in rich countries are subsidized so they don't cultivate their land, while people in developing countries are starving. They slaughter and burn cattle, not because of mad cow disease, but to ensure higher meat prices. We spend a fortune to store surplus butter, instead of bringing it to the market."

"And with these ideas she studies the stock market? Then I am not surprised you have not taken her seriously."

"She also has other, less offensive ideas. For example, she finds it absurd that the European Union has set standards for the length of cherry stalks in all European countries, despite varying climatic and soil conditions. But seriously, she is an excellent computer

43

scientist. That is also why she is with us. Besides her shrink connections she also has excellent relations with the physicists at
the World Institute for Nuclear Research (WINR), the former
European Center for Nuclear Research, CERN. She gets her ideas
about the stock exchange from them. She claims it all has to do
with what physicists call fluctuations, and these have to be exam-
ined in more depth."

"To study these variations in retrospect isn't difficult. It's like
studying yesterday's weather."

"She claims that certain trends repeat themselves. The only
problem is to find out how often and when. The comparison with
the weather forecast is not to be dismissed out of hand, though, I
admit."

"Do you mean that seriously? I was only joking."

"There are many complex phenomena; not only the weather
and the stock market. That, at least, is what Darboux maintains."

"Complex phenomena? You mean too complicated to be
understood?"

"That is perhaps a bit exaggerated, but I know very little about
the subject anyway. In any case, it seems that complexity is a common concept in particle physics. The people at WINR also use the
term chaos or chaoticity in this context; they even claim they can
measure it."

"That is indeed a comfort," said Koppelmann.

Then, after some thought, he continued: "I like the word chaoticity. But I would take care not to use it in connection with the
stock market or finance, at least when dealing with journalists."

"You think it could be misunderstood."

"Nothing is easier than to generate panic with a word taken out
of context. And panic is the last thing we need right now. Actually,
that's why I asked you to come here today." Hassler had long wondered how long this introduction would take. He immediately replied: "I'm all ears."

"I was wondering if a targeted information campaign might be useful in this current situation of uncertainty."

"An information campaign? What about?"

"You know as well as I do that fluctuations in the stock market are determined primarily by psychological factors. That's why I found it so interesting to learn that your stock market analyst is in a relationship with a psychologist." Koppelmann paused again, offered Hassler a Havana and prepared one for himself. Hassler, following the urgent advice of his doctor, politely declined the cigar. He found no compulsion to decline the 30-year-old cognac, however. "If you and some of your potent customers announced that you trust the market and are buying shares although the market's falling, people would follow your example, or at least stop selling. In this way, a crisis could be prevented."

"Buy shares now? Are you serious?"

"Please pay attention, Hassler. I didn't say you should buy, just that you should say you are buying."

"That is misleading the public and illegal. You know that better than I do."

"I represent the law and this being a matter of higher order..." Koppelmann willfully left the sentence unfinished, but Hassler got the picture and agreed to the idea. It wasn't only because he shared Koppelmann's opinion about the danger of the situation, but because he hoped it would allow his dormant accounts to sleep on peacefully. He fully understood what Koppelmann meant by 'I represent the law'. After all, it was no secret that many important members of the government and federal council had formerly been bankers and were unconditionally devoted to the interests of their former employers, to whom they owed their current post. And the executive government was indispensable for the application of the law.

He said goodbye and hurried to his car. Koppelmann's final words had given him another idea that he wanted to implement immediately.

CHAPTER 9

MARKET PSYCHOLOGY

Hassler was so delighted with his new idea that he already started working on it on the way back from Berne to Geneva. The passenger seat of his limousine, separated from the driver by a soundproof window, was equipped with a bar, television and a secure phone. A senior Rolls-Royce manager, who was a client at his bank, had assured him that he could call anywhere and be absolutely sure of privacy thanks to quantum encryption. However, since the recent phishing attack on some electronic accounts, he no longer had much faith in such technology. So he often used his own private code in conversations.

He picked up the phone and dialed the private number of his brother Tobias in New York. It was still early morning there, but he felt the need to share his idea immediately with someone in whom he had confidence, especially since he was convinced his brother would certainly know how to turn the idea into a tidy profit for them both. He also took into account that it was his brother's wife Joyce, who usually answered the phone. When she did, Gerhard said he was sorry for calling so early. But Joyce was an early riser and didn't seem to mind. "Gerhard, how nice to hear from you. How are you? How is Trudy?"

"Everything's okay. Trudy is unhappy about her new house-maid, but we are getting used to her."

"I can well understand. I also have problems with mine. She's from Brazil, so I'm learning Portuguese."

"You're lucky. Trudy's girl only speaks Albanian. How's Toby?"

It could be better. He has too much weight and doesn't keep to his diet." "That's nothing new."

"I know, but in recent times it has become worse. I think sometimes he tries to forget his business concerns by eating. The lower the Dow Jones, the higher his losses and the greater his appetite."

"I think I have a cure for his troubles. Is he there?"

"Of course. Where else would he be at this hour? I'll put you through to him. Goodbye Gerhard; kiss Trudy for me."

"Hi Gerd, I guess Joyce already reported on the state of the nation. How are you?"

"We're fine and as far as the report is concerned, it's exaggerated. But I have news for you."

"Good news I hope."

I think we'll find our potency increase in the next day or so and that without Viagra. Don't ask me how I know it though."

"I understand. Where are you calling from?"

"From my car."

"Was that all?"

"Not quite. This is only going to be a quickie, fast in and fast out. And you'll have to think of me."

"My doctor says quickies are not recommended at our age."

"He should look after his own family jewels. Speaking of which, have you ever heard of a New York psychoanalyst called George Wilson?"

"Unfortunately."

"What does that mean, unfortunately?"

"He costs me a fortune every month. He is Joyce's analyst. Why do you ask?"

"What a small world we're in. I got to know him in Chamonix a couple of weeks ago. He didn't mention he knows Joyce."

"There are lots of Hasslers in New York. What's more, he's not allowed to talk about his patients."

"Is he really good? How well known is he?"

"He's one of the best in New York, judging by his fees. Why does that interest you?"

"I want to consult him."

"Aren't there any good analysts in Geneva? There was this guy called Piaget, if I'm not mistaken. He founded a famous school."

"That's right. But that was once upon a time. Today you Americans are leaders in that field."

"Do you need him for yourself or Trudy?"

"For neither of us. My bank needs him."

"Your bank? That's the best joke I've heard in a long time."

"You only have to follow the news, then you'll understand. Do you have Wilson's phone number handy?"

"Just a second. Here it is. In fact, I have two numbers. His secretary answers when you call the first; the second is his personal mobile for emergencies."

"Thanks; see you soon!"

"Bye, bye." When the market opened on Wall Street, Tobias' agent bought two considerable packages of shares for Tobias and Gerhard and closely monitored subsequent developments. It didn't surprise him when, about an hour before the market closed, the business channels broadcast an interview with Gerhard Hassler, who stated he has confidence in the world economy and that his bank is investing again in the stock market. By this time, it was 9 pm in Zurich and the Swiss exchange had closed. The statement by the head of the world's second largest bank had an immediate effect and the New York stock exchange rebounded. One minute before it closed, Tobias' agent sold the two blocks of shares he had bought that morning at a profit of 20%. In addition, he sold all of

Tobias' remaining shares. The next day, the Dow Jones index was back in the basement, beating even its previous record low. The «Wall Street Journal» acrimoniously reported: 'In-vitro fertilization doesn't work on Wall Street.'

But Gerhard Hassler's plan wasn't complete yet. After the apparent failure of the encouraging statements he and other bankers had made, he got in touch with George Wilson. "Hello, George; Gerhard Hassler in Geneva here. We met in Chamonix two weeks ago."

"You mean Solange's boss Gerhard?" George seemed surprised and it was clear to Hassler why. He was well aware they weren't in the same class, as far as social standing was concerned.

"Yes, that's right. On top of that, I'm also Joyce Hasslers brother-in-law."

"That really is an interesting coincidence; who would have thought." "George, I need your help for a science project."

"A science project?" Now it was impossible to overhear the surprise in George's voice.

"Yes, but a remunerated one. It might even pay quite generously. Are you planning to visit Geneva in the next day or so?"

"In about five weeks; after Christmas, if all goes well."

"That's too late. Could you perhaps arrange to come this weekend or the next? I'll have our plane come and collect you, of course." Then, to make sure Wilson would accept his proposal, Hassler added. "Solange Darboux will also be participating in the project"

"I'll have to check my schedule. I don't have it with me right now. Can I call you back in two hours?"

"Okay. Here is my phone number."

As soon as George had confirmed he could come, Gerhard called Solange and asked her to keep the next two weekends free for a visitor from the US. Half an hour later, Solange was pleasantly surprised when George called to say he would be the visitor.

"Have you any idea what this is all about?" George asked.

"No idea, but he is always good for surprises."

Gerhard Hassler's chauffeur met George at Geneva airport and took him directly to the Hassler residence where he and Solange were invited for dinner. Thanks to the private jet, George was able to cross the Atlantic in daylight and so avoid the jet lag to a large extent. Commercial flights were usually at night, so the passengers reached Europe in the early morning.

Gerhard didn't let the cat out of the bag until after dinner. Trudy had let it be served by one of the finest restaurants in the Geneva area, the Lion D'or in Cologny. She served the coffee in the lounge herself. She was beside herself that she had the opportunity to welcome one of the world's most prestigious 'shrinks' in their home. That is what her sister-in-law Joyce had called him when they had talked extensively about him on the phone. She had not met him in Chamonix. She had had to stay at home because of a migraine attack. Anyway, at that time, neither she nor Gerhard knew who this George Wilson really was. Her first impression of him was indeed overwhelming. He reminded her of someone she knew, but, at first, she couldn't recall whom. Although he was anything but handsome, he exercised a strange attraction with his gargantuan nose and ears, his high forehead and his haunting eyes. With these eyes he seemed to hypnotize the people he came into contact with; they met his gaze as if mesmerized. Then there was his long, black hair tinged with gray. Suddenly she realized that Wilson reminded her of Beethoven. There was, of course, no doubt about it. But her thoughts were interrupted. His penetrating eyes had fixed hers again. She was unable to think straight. Or was that just her imagination? Were his eyes insistently questioning her, forcing her to testify, to confess? Now she felt she understood why this psychoanalyst was so successful, and not only professionally, but also as a man. Solange's constant admiring glances in his direction were more than enough confirmation.

Trudy was still an attractive woman herself despite her fifty years. On closer examination, however, you could see her good looks were the result of her beauticians' efforts. But even they couldn't make all the lines and wrinkles on her neck disappear. She had therefore begun to think about having a face-lift some time ago. She had already had work done on her breasts. She had thought it was because her breasts were too flat and her nipples too small that Gerd had ceased to share the bed with her. Since the surgery didn't have the effect on him she had hoped for, she started to satisfy her growing sex appetite with her bodyguards. They weren't only better at this type of commitment than Gerd had been, even in the best years of their marriage; they also had the advantage that you could replace them easily once you felt the need for something new. She alone made the decision. Gerd didn't mind. In fact he did the same with his secretaries. This was one of the reasons why their marriage was a happy one.

Trudy couldn't figure out what George had to do with the bank, but she was used to not asking questions in such cases. Gerd had merely said they had to discuss some business. So, after dinner, she withdrew to her boudoir, although not without some regret.

"Dr. Wilson, I mean George" It wasn't an accident that Hassler had first addressed him formally. He wanted the following conversation to have a professional character. "Have you ever thought about the mechanisms that cause a stock market crash"

"Hm? I suspect it has to do with the loss of shareholder confidence."

"Of course. It is mainly a psychological problem. That's why we turned to you."

"But that's not in my area of expertise. "

"Until now nobody is an expert in that field, but you could become one. Doesn't that sound tempting: market psychology?"

"What exactly do you expect to gain?"

"First, we need some kind of psychological profile of our clientele. We want to know how a person of a given age, occupation and wealth reacts to the news that prices are falling. Or if this person learns that his friends and acquaintances are beginning to sell their shares. Up to what point is he or she likely to resist selling too? And conversely, when will this person decide to take advantage of low prices and invest?"

"Hold on a moment; we cannot consider these two things as one. How someone responds to events he hears about through the media is one thing; how he responds to what his friends do is something else. In the second case he will probably tend to do the same as his friends do. It's an instinctive reaction, like yawning." As if to provide proof, George began to yawn. The daytime flight had apparently not been able to prevent the jet lag entirely.

"And what about the reactions to certain newspaper reports?"

"That's complicated; it depends on the individual, his social background and many other things. Rumor spreading is a topic for sociologists. One of my friends at New York University has pioneered work in this area." "That's good, maybe we could get him to join this project as well. Our main goal is to find out how to prevent these negative reactions; how to avoid a panic that leads to unlimited sales or a crash."

"Preventive measures?" echoed George.

"Yes, preventive measures. A crash is a harmful, dangerous event. Just remember the Great Depression that followed the stock market crash of 1929. Hundreds of millions of people suffered as a result. Hitler and the Nazi regime in Germany succeeded partly because of it."

"I still can't see how you could prevent such a thing."

"By explaining the economic facts and by indicating or suggesting that the long-term prospects are good."

"Isn't that rather a task for economists?"

"Economists are better when you need somebody to explain what has happened in the past."

"And why should psychologists be better?"

"Isn't suggestion a psychological act? Don't you treat your patients by bringing certain life events from the subconscious into consciousness?" George's fatigue was gone. Now he began to understand what Hassler was driving at.

"So you want to put your bank customers on the couch?"

"Exactly; that's very well formulated, but only with your help, of course. In this case the couch would be the documents and files of our customers. If necessary, these could be supplemented by questionnaires, in which we ask our customers to formulate their needs."

"Why should your customers want to answer such questions? Why should they be willing to give you information about their habits, their assets, their private life?"

"We wouldn't ask such questions directly, of course. Our employees are specialized in obtaining useful answers from what seem, at first glance, to be trivial, insignificant questions."

George's profession brought him into contact with all kinds of possible and impossible, even crazy, ideas and he had to be open minded for professional reasons. However, he could not stop being amazed. Hasslers' proposal surpassed anything that even the most daring analyst had ever tried. But also, because of that, he saw this idea as a challenge. The plan would enable him to see Solange without making his wife Barbara more jealous than was acceptable in their long-standing marriage. And, last but not least, it would be stupid to ignore the financial aspects of the project.

"Questionnaires alone are rarely useful. I'd suggest beginning by asking clients personally, when they visit the bank for routine business."

"Does that mean you accept my proposal?"

After a moment, George replied: "Yes. For a start, you can send me copies of your customers' documents."

"We still need to clarify the question of your fee."

"It depends on how long it takes. My fee is usually $1,000."

"Per day?"

"Per hour."

Now Hassler understood what his brother had meant with his wife's analytical sessions costing him a fortune. Without flinching, he surprised George with his reply: "We have about 1,000 dossiers. Would a flat rate of $ 1,000 a dossier be acceptable?"

"Send me the contract together with the dossiers."

CHAPTER 10

SEX AND DEATH

After dinner at the Hassler' residence, Solange brought George to his hotel. Without a word, she accompanied him to his room. Since Chamonix they had only talked on the phone. Moreover, their encounter there had, to their mutual regret, been very brief and always accompanied by Hassler and one of his daughters. George had called Solange immediately after his arrival in Chamonix and they had arranged to meet for an after-ski drink on Saturday. But, as Solange explained to George on the phone later, she was unable to shake off the Hasslers, with whom she had been skiing all day. So now the coming night promised to be even more passionate. Once in bed they exchanged a few words. In that short time, George discovered that Solange's body was the best cure for his jet lag. She wanted to know if he had really missed her. "If Hassler hadn't proposed this project, who knows when we would have met again. What do you think?"

"I had planned to come to Chamonix early next year again; that place really impressed me. After all, there is only one Mont Blanc in the world and the ski slopes are excellent."

"But then you'd probably come with your wife?"

"My wife's not a ski enthusiast; she prefers the Caribbean. But how do you know I'm married?"

"Mrs. Hassler was so kind to tell me. She probably knows it from her sister-in-law in New York." The fact that this circumstance hadn't prevented her from surrendering to him without hesitating impressed George even more.

"What about you? Are you single? Do you have family?"

"If you mean my love life, I am currently single. Regarding family, I have nobody; my parents were killed in a car accident many years ago and I was raised by my grandparents, who aren't alive, either."

"Any brothers and sisters?"

"Sorry; no."

"That must be hard, a life without family."

"You're right; you can't find a brother or sister in the same way as you might find a friend or a spouse. I must confess that I miss having siblings, to say nothing of my parents' love."

"Since you mention that, what are your views on incest? I ask because views on incest have changed in recent years. It was one of the things I mentioned in the presentation I held in Paris just after our Montmartre tour."

"As I said, I find love, including physical love, between family members a great thing, especially since it apparently has no pathological consequences, as long as it doesn't produce offspring. Sade's point of view: 'How can sensible men take absurdity to the highest level and believe it is a criminal act to have fun with their mother, sister or daughter', deserves recognition."

"Hear, hear," murmured George. But Solange hadn't finished yet.

"He was also critical of the fact that a man may not enjoy of an object, which is, by nature, closest to him; that it is forbidden to love the best and that the more nature makes us inclined to love, it orders us even more strictly to abstain".

George's amazement reached a new level. Not only because Solange seemed to have accepted Sade's daring supposition without compromise, but also because she had quoted him off the cuff. But she seemed to be unaware of his astonishment and continued talking about Chamonix: "The closeness of Geneva probably also adds to the attractiveness of Chamonix."

"That's true. In the United States, Aspen might be considered a comparable ski resort," George remarked. "Aspen, in contrast to Chamonix, does indeed have its own cultural life, but, although it lies much higher, it doesn't have the eternal snows of Mont Blanc, because of the difference in latitude. And it lacks a major city like Geneva. Actually, there is only one city in all of North America that deserves the name; that is New York. The rest is darkest province."

"Did you try the nightlife in Chamonix?" George felt more than curiosity regarding this issue and said to himself: "A typical female reaction; the female psyche knows no national features." Solange was his first European relationship. But a few moments later he contradicted himself because Solange had something he had never seen before in any woman. Although he had already noticed it at their first meeting, he was still unable to define it. He didn't find it difficult to answer her question, especially since it was the truth: "After eight hours of skiing I was too tired for that; the weather was gorgeous and I wanted to get the full benefit. Also, I'm not into nightlife."

"I thought you wouldn't be. Tell me, what else did you talk about in your banquet presentation? I ask because I know some elementary-particle physicists at WINR and sometimes discuss common issues with them."

"Now I understand where you got your knowledge of quantum physics from. My presentation was a mixed bag of recent, strange and unexplained observations about human behavior."

"Such as?"

"For example, such as people's views on death. In the past death was, for many, a fearsome perspective, or rather a fearsome certainty. Today, it's not such a big thing. This is shown, among other things, by the move away from religion. After all, the fear of death was one of the main reasons for the emergence of religions, which usually promise an afterlife"

"I would interpret this phenomenon differently. Religion means primarily belief in God and this has been replaced by faith in science." "What do you think of intelligent design? That it was intelligent design that made the world, including life as we know it today, and not natural evolution and selection as science claims?"

"Nothing, absolutely nothing. That is simply religion in a modern form. There is no reason to believe it. Modern laboratory experiments can practically reproduce what happened in the cosmos when our universe was created, and it didn't involve God. You can see how far the abuse of certain concepts derived from religion goes when you talk about the soul. There is already a form of zoology that pseudo-scientifically calls itself 'theological zoology' and deals with the fate of the animals after Adam and Eve were expulsed from Paradise."

"You are absolutely right; you might rather consider religion as a form of superstition. But that still doesn't solve the mystery of why man's relationship to death or the fear of death has changed before the individual ceases to exist. It is one of the best-known facts that death is inevitable for every human being, every living creature. I would even say it is one of the laws of biology. This certainty and the fear associated with it have accompanied mankind since its creation and influenced the life of every individual, starting soon after birth and increasing with age. And now it suddenly seems to mean practically nothing to us; we treat death as if it were a minor incident, not more important than, for example, moving to another apartment or another town."

"Has that anything to do with the fact that we can read people's thoughts in their electrical brain activity and record the results for the future? Doesn't that actually guarantee an individual's survival? What else characterizes man, if not his thoughts? Hello George, have I said something very stupid, or are you sleeping already"

"No, not at all. I was just surprised by this interesting idea."

"I am glad you find it interesting at least."

"Although, even if I would buy this argument, we psychologists have our doubts, because your machines can only read the thoughts of the moment. But once the brain is dead, it does not create new thoughts. Where is your individual then?"

"I can well imagine that it will soon be possible to produce computer brains that can read an individual's thoughts from a recording and store them as his character, the specific characteristics that distinguish him from another individual. Even to save his love art for all eternity."

And to leave no doubt about the meaning of her words, she kissed George on his mouth and then, without hesitation, on his manhood. Was it this kiss that woke George's passion again? Or was it the word eternity? As if his manhood wanted to prove that it, too, could stand forever, he suddenly felt it rise again with full force. Solange's willing body joyfully took it in.

CHAPTER 11

LONE WOLVES AND COPYCATS

Soon after George had arrived in New York the next day, he found the files from Hassler in his email. Although it was a beautiful winter day, perfectly suited for a walk in Central Park that lay like a winter wonderland before his window, he immediately got down to work, because the unusual project had aroused his curiosity. He also wanted to benefit from having no patient appointments and Barbara out of the house. Sometimes she asked too many questions and didn't let him work. He had his practice in the same apartment building, and even on the same floor as his private residence. Although it was comfortable and agreeable, to say nothing of the magnificent views of the lake from the twenty-fifth floor, it also had its drawbacks. When he had told Barbara he was going to Geneva again, she was obviously surprised. Whether she suspected anything about Solange? Anyway, this time it really was a purely professional trip. He might have hoped for what happened afterwards, but didn't necessarily have it planned.

Although, at first glance, there was no direct link between the new project and his actual field of work, the study of lone-wolf behavior, it was, after all, behavioral research, even if in the specific field of mass psychology. He had gained some general knowledge about that as a student. Now he needed to study the literature in order to refresh and, if possible, expand his knowledge.

The first thing these searches helped him to remember was that behavior, including mimicry, is a characteristic found in the genes similar to the self-preservation and reproductive instincts. Self-preservation is linked to mimicry in so far as animals depend on it for survival. By mimicking the behavior of their parents and other animals of the species, they learn to protect themselves against the dangers of the environment. Imitating also plays an important role in the learning process, both in animals and humans. After hatching, birds learn which species are their friends and which are their foes from the behavior of their peers. For humans, learning from model situations is an effective educational tool, also a kind of imitation. There are positive as well as negative examples of this, such as smoking tobacco or drinking alcohol, where the copying effect is proven.

George came to the conclusion that the behavior of most of Hassler's bank customers probably fell into this category. But he almost immediately asked himself: If the imitation process is a genetic predisposition, how can it be avoided? You can try detoxification cures to deal with smoking and alcoholism, but you can't always guarantee success. Can you wean bank clients from their innate tendency to copy and prevent them hastily selling their shares once they learn that others are doing so? And if you can, how do you do it? How can you change human predispositions? The seemingly obvious answer was brainwashing. That was surely nothing new to Hassler; it was part of publicity. But then there was also programmed learning, as George's reading disclosed. Ethologists have shown that many animals are virtually programmed to learn to do certain things in a given way, at predetermined times in their lives. Might this be a clue, he thought, how to influence human behavior. Anyway, Hassler mainly wanted him to provide an explanation for the behavior of his customers and not necessarily a way to change it. That would probably follow later, though.

George had begun to use this programming terminology now even when talking to himself; it had become part of his thinking. Was it perhaps a Freudian slip that had something to do with Solange? The conversation about computers with her in Montmartre was still alive in his memory. He suddenly remembered he hadn't called her yet and soon it would be too late, because of the time difference. Also, Barbara was likely to show up again soon and they had not seen each other since his return. Solange answered immediately.

"How was your flight?"

"Excellent. A private jet is really something very pleasant."

"Jet lag?"

"Not yet, but it's probably unavoidable."

"Didn't you sleep?"

"Well, the cabin had a double bed, but it was much too wide just for me."

"Poor you. Wasn't that red-haired flight attendant, Mireille or whatever her name is, on board?"

"Mireille was called Roger; I don't remember his hair color."

"That must have been a misunderstanding. Hassler usually provides for the physical wellbeing of his guests to the smallest detail."

"Roger was an impeccable waiter. I didn't ask him for any other services."

Solange chuckled to herself. Her conversation with Hassler's secretary had had the desired result. "And what are you doing now?"

"I am dealing with programming and with geese and sheep."

"You cook? We normally have roast goose at Christmas and lamb at Easter. Have you already programmed your oven for the holidays?"

George guffawed. Then he put Solange into the picture concerning his latest research. "I was wondering; if herd behavior is genetically programmed, how is it that some people don't imitate and are considered as lone wolves"

"Maybe they are just programmed differently," said Solange. "When I think about it, those who imitate surprise me personally more than those who don't. Copying in humans seems to be a throwback."

"Then you're an exception, just like my statistics show."

"And what do the geese have to do with it?"

"In geese, as well as in some other animals, the programming manifests itself in that they learn certain things in a certain way and at predetermined times in their lives."

"You mean the learning process is somehow programmed chronologically?"

"Exactly. The experts call it imprinting. Young geese must be able to follow their parents almost immediately after hatching. Their memory capacity is programmed to follow the first object that moves and emits a call. The call is the signal that triggers their response to follow." "Interesting. So they learn to follow."

"Yes, and the amazing thing is that if you put the goslings in a cart and carry them toward a calling parent, imprinting doesn't work."

"How do you explain that?"

"This signifies that the act of following itself initiates the learning process."

"Unbelievable. The subtleties of nature are truly remarkable."

"By the way, in a sense you were right that programming is eternal, because this imprinting we just talked about lasts practically forever; or at least as long as the animal retains those specific characteristics that distinguish it from other creatures. But, if it's true that a human lifetime, though not infinite, is much, much longer, it would, in my opinion, have undesirable consequences"

"You mean the economic consequences, the exhaustion of our planet's raw materials?"

"Not only that. For me as a psychologist, other consequences are more serious."

"Such as?"

"The certainty of death generally has a stimulating effect on an individual's life. He is aware that he must develop his knowledge and expertise, start a family and live his finite life within a fixed period. If he no longer felt this pressure of time, though, it could be that he wouldn't know what to do with his life any more; he'd begin to vegetate. Not only would he lose the pleasure of life; the fate of all mankind as a species would probably be endangered."

"You mean life would be too monotonous?"

"Exactly. That's the right word, monotony. The human psyche, as we know it today, needs variety. That's what makes life."

"If you're thinking of variety in sex, you're all the more likely to get that in eternal life."

"Even the thought of having these or other distractions forever, is a disturbing factor. But now I have to go. I keep longing for you, all the more so, because we don't live forever. Bye." George had just heard Barbara at the door. His telephone conversation had lasted a good hour. Already during his return flight George had wondered why nobody had come up with Gerhard Hassler's idea before. Actually, he was not sure if that was really true. To make sure, he searched the Internet; he found no mention of such studies.

Most of the files from Geneva contained a wealth of information about Hassler's clients, except for the client's last name that had been deleted to protect his privacy. They showed, among other things, the size of the bank balance, the regular inputs and withdrawals, as well as information about the client's profession. From this last data he might, under certain circumstances, be able to draw conclusions about the total assets of the customer. The bank balance itself was not suitable for this, because the same customer could have accounts with several banks. That was often the case with wealthy customers.

George approached the task methodically. He first divided the files into two categories: the copycats and the lone wolves. Copycats were customers in whom buying and selling behavior followed a simple pattern. They included people who bought or sold shares according to a fixed schedule. He soon found that a month was an appropriate period. By far the majority of shareholders fitted this category and fully illustrated the herd behavior that disturbed Hassler.

Lone wolves, on the other hand, were customers who didn't demonstrate such a pattern; the periods between buying and selling were irregular, often amounting to several months or even years. Next, he compared the ratio between the number of lone wolves and copycats in the previous decade. He noted that the ratio had changed: Were there almost no lone wolves ten years ago; now they already made up almost twenty percent. That might be good news for Gerhard Hassler, but still not good enough to prevent a stock market crisis.

Then George studied the lone wolves in detail. What he noticed first was that most of them didn't put their capital into shares, like most copycats, but into money market funds, which could be exchanged at short notice and without large fluctuations in cash value. Then he noticed that a growing number of accounts showed no movement at all. This number grew at a much faster pace than the total number of bank customers. Moreover, the amounts deposited into these dormant accounts were much higher than the average amounts in ordinary accounts. George had unknowingly discovered the dormant accounts that were causing Hassler's and Levallois' problems.

At first he didn't know what to do with these accounts. He gave them a question mark and turned to the others, which were in the majority. From these accounts he tried to picture what interested the lone wolves. He asked himself what these customers used their money for? Did they spend it for different reasons than the copycats? The only thing he could see in this connection was that the lone wolves rarely or almost never traveled to tourist areas. The copycats' behavior was the opposite. They traveled more frequently and, judging by the high airfares, probably to relatively remote spots. Suddenly George remembered his presentation a few weeks ago at the physicists' correlation meeting in Paris. One of the characteristics of modern society he had cited was that on the whole, fewer people are traveling, including holiday travel. How was this tendency compatible with his present finding that a large number of people, actually the majority, still spend their holidays traveling?

After considering briefly, he decided that only one conclusion was possible. Hassler's clients, customers of a Swiss bank, were not a representative example; after all, the figure he had presented at the Paris meeting was a global statistic. Alternatively, and this seemed more likely, the number of lone wolves had also risen sharply worldwide. This would explain why fewer people travel. But if there really were a connection between the lone wolves and the, so far unresolved, new trends in modern society, so maybe the Hassler lone wolves might also show some of the other features.

After careful consideration of the question he decided that four of these features were not an option. Neither a cup of espresso nor listening to Beethoven's Razumovsky Quartet in C Major on CD helped. In fact, how could he learn from impersonal bank files what their owners thought about incest or death or what their sleeping habits were? Of course, card files couldn't provide information about the owners' phraseology and language either. They only reflected the pure accounting records of the bank. But it was possible, maybe even probable that the customer's correspondence had been kept in the bank's archives, at least for the past few years. Swiss banks were famous not only for their secrecy, but also because of their reliability.

But even that did not hold much promise. After all, many banking transactions were carried out directly at the bank counter and, if any correspondence took place at all, the language was surely stereotype, because of the dry matter involved. Meanwhile, he assured himself by reading his own bank correspondence. Even highly educated people had, for the lack of synonyms, to use technical terms such as account, equities, assets, interest rates and funds. Because this type of correspondence was short, it was also unlikely that grammatical errors would slip in. George therefore rejected this criterion as well.

The situation was slightly better regarding eating habits. From the credit card statements showing what they bought in supermarkets and restaurants, it was apparent that the lone wolves spent less than the copycats. But George had doubts whether this test was statistically significant, because what they spent on food was only a small fraction of the total expenditure. He made a note to discuss that question with a statistician.

At the end he still had one symptom to compare: The frequency of names that also included numbers. Luckily, the tendency to attach numbers to names, as mentioned in his presentation, was limited to first names, so George could use the present material, which only contained first names, for his purposes. And, would you believe it, the result here was clear: Numbers were rare in copycat names, but common in the names of lone wolves. So there probably was a correlation between the lone wolves and some, if not all, new sociological trends. The word correlation struck George immediately; it wasn't for nothing that he had participated in the correlation meeting.

However, that was only one aspect of this observation. The numbers in copycats' names were never greater than three, while those in the names of lone wolves were much larger. Finally, George returned his attention to the dormant accounts of the lone wolves and also analyzed their first names. Here, the number phenomenon was even more pronounced. Almost all names contained very large numbers.

George was convinced he had discovered something new that was not only relevant for the psychogram Hassler had ordered, but also for his own profession. Had he perhaps discovered an eighth feature of modern society, the lone wolf? The thought electrified him, not least because the International Society of Psychoanalysts was offering a prize of $100,000 for the discovery of any additional feature. Whether Hassler would allow him to publish this result? The contract with Hassler's bank bound him to absolute secrecy with regard to the material he had received. When George signed the contract, he had considered this clause as a matter of course. It corresponded to the normal relationship between doctor and patient. The practice didn't prevent the use of these medical data for scientific purposes, however, provided the name of the patient remained anonymous, which was indeed the case here. However, the question still arose, whether Hassler could forbid him, if only for commercial interest to maintain an edge over the competition, to use the data anonymously.

Anyway, he decided, for now that is enough. Exhausted but happy, he went into the apartment and put on weatherproof shoes and a coat. In two minutes he was in Central Park, passing a snow-man at the entrance. He reflected with amusement that it was mostly adults who made snowmen. Whether the children, who were happy throwing snowballs, had ever seen snowmen before? In recent years, snow in New York City had become almost as rare as water in the Sahara. Whether there was a connection between climate change and the seven changes in human behavior?

CHAPTER 12

GEORGE THINKS ABOUT SOLANGE, THE NEW GENERATION AND ... HIMSELF

As soon as George returned from his excursion to the park, he stopped thinking about the problem of human behavior in general and concentrated again on the behavior of Solange. He asked himself once more why this person fascinated him so much. The scientist in him led him to approach the question systematically, although it mostly concerned his personal feelings and not those of one of his patients. So he took out his diary and wrote everything that referred to Solange in a file on his computer. Then he began to sift through this file from the beginning. The first thing that struck him was the circumstance under which he had met her at the conference on artificial intelligence; it was something he had almost forgotten in the meantime. While the majority of the conference participants had believed that computers would reach the human level of intelligence, but were reluctant to set a deadline, she seemed to have no doubt about it. It was as if the breakthrough of artificial intelligence was imminent. More than that, on the topic of computers being able to think like humans she had said that some of them already do.

Then, of course, there was also her interest in cemeteries, because of which they had spent their first and so pleasant day together in Montmartre. But did this interest fit in with her faith in artificial intelligence? Cemeteries symbolize the past and usually have a religious character. Artificial intelligence, on the other hand, is a scientific discipline geared more towards the future and claiming to imitate and replace God's work. He suddenly remembered she had told him she was invited to participate in a television program about cemeteries. In the meantime it had probably already taken place. It might answer his question if he knew what they had discussed there. Without further hesitation, he wrote Solange an email and asked for details. She answered with the link to the program, so he could see the recording for himself. Solange's proposal to transfer information from the human brain to computer memory instead of putting the bodily remains in a grave, coincided completely with her conviction that artificial intelligence is able to replace human intelligence. That would explain her interest in old cemeteries. She probably wanted to get an impression of what she wanted to change with her proposal. It was surely difficult for people of her generation to understand what moved older people to keep the memory of their deceased relatives.

George's thoughts unintentionally moved from cemeteries to a related issue that had occupied him for some time; the recently changed attitude of modern man to death. In their first night together he and Solange had talked about it. For her, death was a minor topic that she never thought about. This was in complete contrast to himself and his wife Barbara. Now George found himself thinking about Solange again. He asked himself how her case fit into the other new features he had mentioned in his banquet speech at the meeting of particle physicists in Paris. To his surprise, he couldn't help noticing that Solange seemed to have almost all of these other features. In particular, there was her memory for numbers that had stunned him during their tour of Montmartre. Then there were her language skills. Besides her mother tongue French, she was fluent in English, German, Spanish, Russian, Mandarin and Japanese. This fitted well with her professional responsibilities. She managed the computer systems of her bank, which had branches on all five continents. Her language skills were, apparently, a characteristic feature of modern man.

George had already noticed that she ate very little and she had indicated to him that she was not interested in traveling. Maybe that was because she had to travel as part of her professional obligations. While most people considered travel a welcome change to their daily routine, it wasn't the case with people of her category. He wasn't ready to make any definitive judgment about her sleeping habits, but he remembered now that he had fallen asleep exhausted several times during their night together and Solange had been wide awake every time he woke up. Was it just the fault of his jet lag?

As far as incest was concerned, she had found nothing wrong with such relationships as long as possible negative biological consequences were excluded. This served to prove to George that Solange fit perfectly into the pattern he considered modern. One possible explanation for this was that the new features had only become known in the past ten years and were related to the new generation, to which he and his peers no longer belonged. Their memory for numbers was rather weak and the only foreign language he understood was French. That was even more than Barbara knew. He and his wife enjoyed traveling and, as far as food was concerned, eating was one of the pleasures they wouldn't want to miss. Six to seven hours of sleep were essential for both of them; he sometimes even indulged in an afternoon nap. Finally, regarding incest relationships, he personally still had concerns and was sure his wife felt the same. As a psychologist, he considered romantic relationships not only a means of reproduction; they also

enriched people's lives. The more diverse the biological characteristics of the partners were, the richer their lives.

From this viewpoint, George and his peers were not modern
individuals. Solange, who was much younger, on the other hand,
represented the new generation, and typically exemplified the recently discovered features of modern man. That made his relationship with her all the more interesting and more important. After
all, it was only thanks their close friendship that he could make
such detailed observations. He wouldn't have been able to find a
similar pattern otherwise.

Now George realized he had an explanation why the term 'atmosphere' interested her so much. It was probably as cryptic and
mysterious as the memory of the dead for her. Hence was her effort to seek clarification.

PART II

CHAPTER 13

HUMAN FAILURE

The «Geneva News» carried the story on the first page: 'Mars satellite misses orbit because of elementary error in computer program'.

"Did you see this?" Herbert couldn't believe his eyes and showed John the newspaper. They were having lunch in the cafeteria of WINR.

"Sorry, I left my glasses in the office. What's it about?"

Herbert read aloud: "Preliminary results of the Space Agency's internal investigation commission suggest that the loss of the Mars shuttle Climate Orbiter was caused by an error in the transmission of data between the team in Colorado and its counterpart in California. It seems that one team used the imperial units feet and inches during a decisive steering operation, while the other used metric units. This calculation was crucial to bring the shuttle into the correct Mars orbit."

"Unbelievable!" Herbert, who had spent a long time in England and knew John well, was aware that this, coming from his English friend's mouth, meant a lot. In fact, both had good reason to be surprised. Errors in computer programs weren't something new. Also, it wasn't the first time that a rocket launch had failed. But it was quite new for this kind of mistake to occur. If a school student had made such an error, he wouldn't have graduated.

"I have repeatedly warned the Americans about using different systems of measurement," John said. "In the UK we introduced the metric system years ago. The Americans have to do the same. The sooner the better."

"One more reason to introduce the metric system is that their previous system is no longer English," said Herbert. John understood what his friend meant and grinned. Herbert liked to make fun about the snobbery of some Americans to imitate everything English. Actually, John didn't really feel like making jokes. He had been entrusted with checking the logistics of WINR and that meant he had to test how well the different measuring systems were compatible. The World Institute for Nuclear Research, WINR, had replaced the European Center for Nuclear Research, CERN. It employed 12,000 researchers from 550 universities. Of these, only a few hundred actually worked in Geneva because the WINR giant electron collider extended from Hamburg to Naples with Geneva as the hub. Most of the researchers stayed at their home institutes and participated in the experiments with their local devices connected via the TERRA link. This allowed everybody to be present electronically and to participate in the measurements. TERRA wasn't merely a link but actually a huge world detector. In the past, a detector was an instrument that stood very close to the accelerator. Now, it was a grid spanning several countries. The size of this detector was itself a sociological challenge for those who had to coordinate its work. The geographic, ethnic and political differences in the participating countries didn't make this task any easier. In earlier times, one person was able to manage it. John was old enough to remember those times. Now, a committee of thirteen could barely handle the task. In those early days, there had been a collaboration of several dozen people who met regularly and knew each other personally. In the present organization the various institutions delegated 550 representatives who barely knew each other at all. Initially, they had met once a year, then every two years. Between meetings they communicated over the Internet and, in urgent cases, by teleconferencing. But this kind of communication was also proving to be too cumbersome. Although the Internet had made great progress and could transfer huge amounts of information, it had become increasingly difficult to express some new experimental observations and results in words or even in formulas or numbers because of the continuously growing volume of information. It also wasn't a coincidence that theoretical scientists complained of similar problems. To keep up with the progress of experimental methods, their calculations were becoming increasingly complex. Some of them had begun to develop a new communication method that John wanted to use for the TERRA detector. His colleagues opposed the idea, though, because they didn't want to be at the mercy of the computers.

The new idea of the theorists was quite simple. Instead of reading the results of their calculations on their computers and then forwarding them to their colleagues, they let the computers communicate directly with each other and share their results. This was proving to be very successful. It was quick, reliable and secure. Conversion errors, as in the Mars project, were excluded because the programs of all computers used the same measurement systems from the outset. If the space agency had used this method, it would not have come to the Mars disaster. John feared that the TERRA measurements also risked such a mishap, especially as TERRA, unlike the Mars orbiter project, was an international one and its branches were much more numerous. That the most capable scientists and engineers could let such a stupid coordination error happen, as in the present case, was a warning. It showed how far human error could go and confirmed John in his belief that the coordination of the TERRA project had to be entrusted to a computer and not a human. Now he was sure that his colleagues, taking the space example into account, would be forced to agree.

CHAPTER 14

SELF-STEERING

I t wasn't a coincidence that the computer industry soon applied the idea to let computers communicate with each other to solve complex tasks, as the people at WINR had suggested. After all, the contact between WINR and the computer industry was excellent. This was evident simply from the knowledge that the notorious WEB, the system that allowed enormous amounts of data to be transported across the Internet, was invented at CERN. This time, though, they didn't plan to use this simple idea just to solve concrete problems affecting single computers, but to revolutionize the whole field of computer programming. They hoped that, as a result, they would not only be able to discover and study new celestial bodies, but completely new worlds.

It wasn't the first time a conceptually flawed computer program had caused problems, but never before had the consequences for the functioning of computers been so devastating. The bug, or was it more than one, had made the operating system entirely unreliable. The computers equipped with the new operating system Doors 15 often stopped in the middle of an operation and the computer seemed paralyzed. None of the keys worked and everything was blocked. Worse still, even emergency resetting procedures often failed. The computer had to be rebooted, an operation associated with data loss, which nobody wanted. When even that measure failed, the only way to restart the computer was to pull the plug out of the power socket.

The news of this fiasco could hardly have come at a more inopportune time. Promotion alone for the new system had cost over a billion dollars. That was one of the reasons why, after a previously unmatched boom in the stock market, the technology bubble had imploded and the market prices were in free fall. Gus Bones, the Doors Inc. CEO, called a special meeting of the company's programmers to discuss the situation. None of the participants at this 'bug meeting' as it later became known, realized at the time how the meeting's resolutions would influence not only their own company's fate, but also set a milestone in the history of computers and artificial intelligence.

After describing the situation, Bones asked: "Why did this happen with Doors 15 and not with Doors 14, Doors 13 or even the earlier versions?"

None of those present seemed to have an answer, or no one dared to formulate one. Wu, who had directed the Doors 15 project, was the first to speak. "Gus" he said, using Bones' first name as they all did, "we shouldn't forget that Doors 14 and Doors 13 also had problems."

Tata, head of the Doors 14 project, responded sulkily: "We created some of these problems ourselves to 'stimulate' the market." He had resisted the Doors 15 project, arguing that it didn't offer enough new features to be considered as a new system. To justify the introduction of a new system the team had prevented him adopting some improvements he had already planned for Doors 14.

Dayton, however, who was already working on Doors 16, saw the situation differently. "The bigger the problems are now, the better the chances that Doors 16 will be a great success."

"But only if we find the error."

"These quarrels won't get us anywhere," said Gus. "What does Boris, our bug expert, think?"

"As long as we don't understand how the newer Doors series function, we can only guess what's causing the frequent breakdowns," was the answer.

"Did you say, we don't understand how Doors works?" Jeremy asked incredulously. He had only been a short time at Doors Inc. and this was the first programmer meeting he had attended. "Didn't Gus invent the Doors operating system?"

"I made Doors 1," specified Gus. "Doors 2 to 9 were developed by someone who is no longer with us."

"And what about the Series 10 to 15?"

"Purely patch-up jobs," Gus replied.

"How did you make it to Doors 14, then?"

"Probably because Doors 1 to 9 were so robust that small changes couldn't do any harm."

"Did Doors 15 bring big changes, then?"

"It didn't, at least as far as I can make out. And that is why we are so surprised by what has happened."

A long silence followed. Meanwhile one of the participants looked at Boris, but that didn't seem to bother him. He had opened his laptop and was absorbed in calculations. Tata, who was sitting next to him, was pleased to note that Boris' laptop was equipped with Doors 14. Finally Gus asked: "Any ideas, Boris?"

Without interrupting his calculations, Boris mumbled: "Heaps of them. The question is whether you have the time and money to test them."

Gus laughed. He remembered the joke Boris had told him, when he hired him. To relax the mood, he asked: "Do you all know the story behind that?" It seemed that nobody did, so Gus decided to tell the joke. That would also give Boris more time for his calculations. "An epidemic broke out on a chicken farm. After the farmer had lost more than a quarter of his chickens, he called the vet, who told the farmer to reduce the amount of corn in the chickens' feed by half and replace it with wheat. After a week on this feed, the farmer had already lost half of the remaining birds. He called the vet again, who now advised him to eliminate the corn completely. This was also ineffective and the farmer finally lost all his chickens. This time he went to the vet's office, told him what had happened and asked if he had another idea. The vet replied that he had heaps of ideas but, unfortunately, the farmer had no more chickens to try them out on."

Everybody laughed except Boris. He had apparently not been listening. He declared: "It's conceivable that we are dealing with a chaos phenomenon here."

"A chaos phenomenon? What do you mean?"

"As I understand it, chaos is a situation in which a tiny change in the initial conditions, in this case the Doors inputs, produces a large change in the functioning of the system."

"You mean that quantitative changes can sometimes cause qualitative transformations?"

"That's exactly what I mean. Even Marx and Engels can be right sometimes."

"Interesting. But back to our sheep ..."

Boris interrupted him: "You mean chickens."

"OK, chickens, if you like. What do we do now?"

"All bad news also has a positive aspect. Perhaps the error in Doors 15 is an indication that we need to stop improving Doors."

"We should stop improving it? Does that mean we should let the competition improve it?"

"Not the competition, but the system itself."

"Itself?" Gus, like everybody else, was amazed.

Boris told them what he meant: "Chaos is a property of complex systems that have their own logic. It's called fuzzy logic. Our senses also function partly by the laws of fuzzy logic."

"And what does that have to do with our farm," asked Gus. "Fuzzy logic systems, just like living organisms, can learn from their mistakes by continuously changing the values that are associated with the various probabilities. In other words, as soon as the computer shows a tendency to hang, we should enable it to make minimal changes to the user's inputs and repeat the calculation process. It should repeat these steps until the flaw is remedied."

Boris's idea proved right; after this change Doors ran without any weaknesses. Doors Inc. called back all Doors 15 computers and introduced the 'liberation' Boris had proposed. They then patented the idea of self-steering and called the new operating system 'Roof'. The name was meant to suggest that this operating system couldn't be topped. The new system wasn't only a financial success in the computer market; it soon found application in a completely different field.

CHAPTER 15

THE INTELLIGENT ROBOT

Robotics, initially a purely Japanese company from Matsumoto, was one of the major customers of Bones' computer company. It specialized in robots as domestic servants. These could handle ordinary household appliances such as vacuum cleaners, washing machines, ovens and lawnmowers. After a few initial quirks, these robots cleaned, washed, baked and mowed better than their human counterparts. This could be explained, among other things, by the fact that robots, unlike humans, did the same work with the same care, over and over again. Moreover, these machines looked like human beings. The components from which they were assembled were so similar to human limbs that you could only tell if it was a robot or a human by directly touching them. Later, Robotics further perfected the similarity by making the robot's covering (or pod) from a patented, special new plastic that was indistinguishable from human flesh even when touched. In addition, these pods contained, as a last decisive innovation, tiny hidden photocells that generated enough electricity to make the robot independent of external power sources.

The robots were also built in male and female forms, because many buyers valued the possibility to choose the sex of their domestic help. This proved to be particularly useful in robots bought for social purposes, for example to accompany elderly singles. To fulfill this role, the robot was able to speak, although its vocabulary was initially limited to what you might expect from an English butler, such as 'good day', 'thank you', 'yes' and 'of course'. Over time, Doors developed the robots' 'intelligence', or the system that controlled it, to such an extent that some of these robots, as far as their general knowledge was concerned, far exceeded that of an educated human being.

Indeed, what human can rejoice in the command of multiple languages and, at the same time, memorize whole dictionaries and encyclopedias? The more so that computer manufacturers mostly built sound dictionaries and encyclopedias into the robots. Their pronunciation was so perfect and individualized that it couldn't be distinguished from that of a human. As computer components got smaller and Internet access proliferated, some robots were fitted with complete computers and Internet access. This simplified programming of certain functions, because a lot of the programs and files the robots needed, such as dictionaries, encyclopedias and extensive special records could be found on the Internet. Next, they produced robots that could completely replace conventional computers, such as were found in most households. These advanced multifunctional robots were a sales hit, especially because their needs as 'house maids' were quite modest when it came to accommodation and meals. They were content with a storage cupboard and only needed a warm room or sunlight from time to time to cover their energy needs. As their price fell, they became increasingly popular. It seemed that robotization would continue to spread rapidly into daily life until, one day, human society learned otherwise. It was precisely this initial acceptance that seemed to threaten the robot project's further success, and that in a hardly predictable manner.

Because some robots looked and acted like humans, people eventually regarded them almost as full members of the family and began to expect more from them than they were capable of. Among other things, they gradually forgot that robots are unable to think or react independently.

It had become common practice to use the house robot as a babysitter. One of the obvious practical advantages was that, unlike human babysitters, the robot never tires. In addition, psychologists had pointed out that it would be beneficial to accustom children to having robots around them, because the markedly aging society would have to rely more and more on machines. One day, however, a tragic accident occurred; a fire broke out in a house where the parents had left their small child in the care of their robot. The robot was not programmed to such an incident and did not know how to react. Before the neighbors noticed the fire and called the fire department, the baby died in the smoke. Of course, Doors Inc. and Robotics solved this, from their point of view, purely technical problem by immediately installing a smoke alarm system in the robot and a corresponding program in its operating system. Nevertheless, they couldn't eliminate the psychological impact of the accident for the customers, who were brutally reminded of the limits of automation.

Following similar unforeseen failures, Gus one day suggested to equip the robot computers with a version of the new operating system Roof. That meant nothing more than to leave the robots to themselves to a certain degree, and let them switch to self-steering. If it worked with computers running the most complex, for humans practically unmanageable, calculations, it should also work with robots, whose tasks were much simpler. The important thing was that the robots learned to react to unforeseen situations correctly. Thus, 'intelligent' robots were built for the first time.

As a direct consequence of the catastrophic fire, Robotics incorporated a command into the robots' operating system that protected humans against whatever the robot did or didn't do. Furthermore, they introduced a second principle into the operating system that limited the freedom of robots' choices. This stated that robots have to follow a human's orders, except when they are contrary to the first command. As a further guarantee for the buyer, the robot had to protect its own existence as long as it didn't contradict the first or second principle.

CHAPTER 16

MARBURG

The actual patent allowed Robotics to produce individual robot components, to assemble them and to install the operating system. The first factory of this kind was built in the Japanese city of Matsumoto and initially only supplied the Japanese market. Japan was a pioneer of the robotics industry. That was because Japan had more elderly people needing assistance in their daily lives than any other country. On the other hand, Japan, in contrast to the Western world, had virtually no immigration and therefore lacked the manpower imported from other countries.

Over time, however, the differences between Japan and other industrialized countries blurred. Immigration in these countries had led to severe political problems, so that governments had to set drastic immigration limits. As a result, the international market for robots grew so much that Robotics Inc. decided to build two more production lines outside of Japan; one of them was in Marburg an der Lahn in Germany, the other in the USA, in Bloomington, Indiana. This also helped to develop the robots' language skills. Doors Inc. had changed the robots' learning method; they learned languages autodidactically through daily interaction with their environment like humans. It was therefore only logical that the robots could best learn a Western language in Europe and America by programming themselves. After all, people learn a language more easily if they live in the country where the language is spoken.

There were various reasons for choosing Marburg as the site in Europe. It was geographically in the center of Western Europe, the wealthiest and most important part of the continent for the robot market. Frankfurt airport, one of Europe's major airports, was easily reached within an hour by train or highway. Marburg, wanting to promote the development of a new and future-oriented industrial sector, had offered Robotics a plot of land near the railway station at no cost. Moreover, the traditional workshops in this part of the country had survived the adverse effects of post-industrial society, so the Marburg area had a large pool of skilled labor. This was an important advantage because the manufacture and assembly of robot components, and especially their assembly, demanded an appreciable amount of craftsmanship. Besides this infrastructure, Marburg also offered advantages for the demanding installation and further development of the Roof operating system. One of these was the University, which had a famous biophysics laboratory that collaborated with the space agency in America and had helped to evaluate the results of the first robot-manned satellite. In addition, the university had a computer science center that produced fifty computer science graduates every year, and the best of them was available for Robotics to hire directly.

Insider, however, alleged that Yogiro Fukuda, the founder of Robotics, had another reason for choosing Marburg as the European site for another production facility. While attending a reception at the German embassy in Tokyo, he had met a German radiation biologist and fallen in love with her. As it happened, this scientist, who was studying the late consequences of the bombs on Hiroshima and Nagasaki, was a professor at the Department of Biology of Marburg University. Their love was mutual, but the couple could only meet on rare occasions when Fukuda visited Europe on business or the professor went to Japan. First of all, neither of them wanted to abandon their careers, and secondly Fukuda was married and couldn't afford to separate from his wife because she was the actual owner of Robotics. She had inherited the initial capital of the company from her parents.

Ironically, a similar three-cornered relationship had also contributed to the establishment of the Marburg Philipps University in 1527 by the Landgrave Philipp of Hessen. The official explanation was that Philipp had invited Luther and Zwingli, the two most prominent representatives of Protestantism, to Marburg that year to settle the dispute concerning the bread and wine that Christians took at communion. Were these really the body and blood of Christ, as Luther asserted, or simply symbols of his body and blood? As the two opponents couldn't agree even after this meeting, Philipp decided to found a university to pursue the issue. In fact, claim historians, Philipp established the first Protestant University because he had hoped the Protestant church would approve of his bigamy.

Bloomington didn't have such historical parallels in its favor. On the other hand, it paid salaries that were relatively moderate for the United States and had a private airport, as well as a university with a famous institute specializing in artificial intelligence. These were the main factors that made Robotics choose Bloomington as its American location.

CHAPTER 17

THEFT AT ROBOTICS

The theft at the Robotics site in Marburg happened during the night from Saturday to Sunday. So it wasn't discovered until Monday, when it was reported to the police and the Robotics head-quarter in Matsumoto. When the workers brought the first Roof-equipped robots assembled on that day to the place where they were to be stored, they noticed that the store was empty. Normally, up to a hundred robots from the preceding week should have been there. The night watchman was called immediately to the plant, but, as far as he was concerned, nothing unusual had happened that weekend. Two trucks had arrived at about two in the morn-ing on Saturday and the drivers had presented the usual pick-up documents of the transport company that worked for Robotics. Each of them was to take 50 robots. The night watchman was a little surprised that the store only contained 98 fully assembled ro-bots, but the two men acknowledged them correctly and left in the direction of Frankfurt airport at four o'clock. Only a few compo-nents that were normally kept as spare parts remained. Immediate inquiries at the shipping company showed that the pick-up docu-ments were forged.

Because of the time difference, the news of this theft didn't reach Matsumoto until late on Monday afternoon and it was already Tuesday by the time the management learned of it. Even before then, in the night from Sunday to Monday, somebody stole 81 robots in the same way in Matsumoto. If the people at headquarters had received news of the theft in Marburg earlier, they might have suspected a link between the two events and had time to warn their colleagues in Bloomington. But as the news came too late, the thieves were able to strike again in Bloomington in the night from Sunday to Monday, taking 73 robots. The police in Matsumoto, Marburg and Bloomington immediately contacted each other and agreed to form a tripartite commission with representatives from the affected countries. In addition, they informed the FBI in the US, the federal police in Germany and the national police in Japan. Because Marburg had suffered the greatest loss, it was decided that Marburg's chief commissioner Martha Issing should coordinate the investigations. Another reason for this was that Robotics' chairman Fukuda often came to Marburg.

The simultaneous and identical procedure for all three incidents had surprised Martha Issing from the outset. When she asked whether it was standard practice to deliver goods at the weekend, late at night, the managers at all three sites told her 'yes and no'. While not common, it had been done before. Regarding the circumstances of the thefts, she learned that all the forged documents, though written in different languages, were for fifty robots and carried the same electronic signature. This was equally clear for the Japanese version, which was written with Romanized characters, as for the German and English versions. However, police investigations came to a standstill after only a few weeks, because there was no obvious evidence on which to base their search. Their one and only hope, that the stolen goods would appear on the market at some time, proved to be deceptive. Although they monitored all eligible brokers, fences and auction houses heavily for a whole year, the stolen robots didn't turn up. So the case had to be classified as provisionally unresolved.

Fukuda couldn't make any sense of this conspiracy either, but he had little time to think about it. This globally coordinated theft caused such a sensation that Robotics and the Roof system couldn't have wished for better publicity. Demand for robots increased tremendously. Six months later, the company hadn't only completely overcome its financial losses; its profits had grown substantially. Fukuda therefore began to make plans for a fourth site in South America, taking advantage of the fact that the insurance covered part of the damage, although the case didn't fit into the classic picture of a burglary.

Neither Fukuda nor the police knew at that time that the stolen robots were fitted with a device that could locate them wherever they were and monitor their activity. Boris had conceived this device; it involved a transmitter that informed the programmer through coded radio signals about the robot's reactions in unusual situations. The original idea had been to use this to perfect the robot program. Initially, it gave the programmer access to the audible and visual interactions between the robots and their environment. That meant he could intercept everything the robot heard and saw, and record it. However, Doors Inc. had concealed this information from Robotics and its customers, fearing that some might consider it a violation of their privacy. Indeed, Doors Inc. could easily use the information to draw conclusions about personal data and habits.

Now that the police was looking into the fate of the robots, there was all the more reason for Doors Inc. to conceal the existence of these transmitters, especially since the whole incident had caused a great stir in the media. Anyway, the company didn't want to stop recording and using the information it received. Doors Inc. saw itself entitled to the information. It had reserved the copyright

on the computer program and, from the standpoint of its legal adviser, Doors didn't need to worry about privacy from a legal aspect,
as long as it didn't locate the transmitter and identify the legal or
illegal holders. However, there were now legal concerns of a different kind. The robots were now stolen goods, and, in principle,
Doors Inc. was obliged to report the whereabouts of the thief and
the robots. However, Gus Bones simply ignored this 'legal finesse',
as he called it. He could always maintain that the transmitter had
been discovered and deactivated by those in possession of the stolen robots.

In fact, it seemed that nobody had discovered the existence
of the transmitters, so Doors Inc. was able to continue collecting
data. At first, Boris only recorded the information sporadically.
However, after a few months it led to such interesting and unexpected conclusions that Gus and Boris decided to download it
round the clock to a special computer.

CHAPTER 18

STRANGE OBSERVATIONS, NEW FEATURES

B oris had used the built-in computer to teach most of his robots how to perform elementary duties with conventional applianc-es. A few of them were also equipped with additional functions to meet customers' special requirements. Some of these special models, which were more expensive, of course, could read texts aloud, write from dictation, translate and search for information. The most 'educated' among them were even able to read and write email and access the Internet. Boris knew exactly what each robot was capable of, because the functions were registered in its files. As for the response to 'unforeseen' situations, the amount of self-steering was limited to improving the robot's planned functions.

But, a few weeks later, while listening to the stolen robots, he made a surprising discovery. It turned out that they had apparently acquired new functions. Some of them were able to perform other tasks than the ones Boris had programmed. Even the most primi-tive, single-function robots, had suddenly become multifunction-al. Lawn mowers could suddenly vacuum-clean floors and vacuum cleaners could mow lawns. But what surprised Boris even more and what he considered was the last straw, as he told Gus, was the fact that among the stolen robots, some of them performed activities that had previously been reserved exclusively for humans. Some robots apparently operated as doctors, pharmacists, engineers or investment bankers. One banking robot impressed Boris in particular; it was so successful it had invested some of its assets in philanthropic activities. This was much more than just a simple response to an 'unforeseen' situation. Another notable observation was that these new features appeared in all the stolen robots, regardless of where they had been manufactured. Boris knew about this because the manufacturing site was obvious from the serial number, which began with the letter A for America, E for Europe and N for Nippon.

Boris commented laconically on the situation when he told Gus about the new findings: "It seems that what we call 'unforeseen' isn't the same as what's provided for by the Roof system."

"That's sheer nonsense," said Gus. "Something went wrong."

Boris didn't want to give up so quickly: "Perhaps the robots have acquired the functions from their thieves or their current owners. We could, of course verify that."

"What do you mean?"

"We'd have to find out who the robots' owners are and what they do," said Boris.

"You'd have to locate the owners. But we should avoid doing that. It would be an invasion of privacy."

"Not as long as we don't identify them by name," Boris reminded him.

"And how do you do that?"

"Some of our robots can record what is going on around them. So we let them listen to their owners and film them."

"I think there might be a simpler explanation for your discoveries. Your eavesdropping program might have a bug, so you wouldn't really hear the robots, but their owners directly. After thinking for a moment, Boris had to admit that Gus had made a point, especially when he added:

"That could also explain the strange fact that these robots have managed to acquire new functions in such a short time. After all, most human beings need more than twenty years to grow up and complete their studies. As for computers, even we, the optimists at Doors Inc., believe that it would take years, if not decades, for them to reach this stage of development. So, as I said, I suspect your eavesdropping program has a bug that probably crept in when they were stolen. That would also explain why your observations are limited to the stolen robots."

Boris reflected carefully. "Incidentally, I also asked myself how these advanced robots, let's call them 'humanoids', differ from humans?"

"A good question. To answer it, we would need much more extensive and time-consuming tests. So forget the whole thing."

"Maybe you're right. But since you mention the word test, we could now submit the robots to the Turing test. Do you remember his proposal?"

Gus thought for a moment. "You mean Turing's wager that, in fifty years, humans would succeed in programming a computer so that only 70% of testers could distinguish it from a human?"

"Yes, that's what I mean," replied Boris.

"But that was in 1950. At that time the wager was a daring one. Today, many, if not most objections to his theory that computers will achieve human intelligence have been refuted and he has proven to be a prophet."

"The main objection to that proposal was that computers can only do what people program them to do, the so-called Ada Lovelace objection. But we ourselves have helped to rebut that objection."

"Are you referring to Roof?"

"Of course. What can Ada Lovelace's argument refute better than the evidence that computers can learn to acquire new skills and even to program themselves?"

There was a long pause.

"Still," said Boris, "I can't swallow this bug story. I tested the system five times, and here in the lab it works flawlessly."

"Here in the lab, maybe."

"How, then, do you explain the success of Roof? We gave the computer free rein, and not in the laboratory, but with the customers. And it perfected itself. That's what gave us the idea of self-steering."

"It's one thing to eliminate an error by multiple experiments; but it's something completely different to acquire new functions without human intervention."

"So computers must be better and faster than humans," Boris replied almost proudly. "I don't need to tell that to you, of all people."

"Only for calculations, not for complex tasks. Think of the problem of pattern recognition, which has preoccupied computers for so long."

"So what do you suggest we do now?"

"We don't record any more radio transmissions and admit the trial failed. After all, it's not our first unsuccessful experiment. And it didn't cost much anyway. Also, don't forget the legal issues that have already caused us a headache."

It wasn't so easy to convince Boris, however. Without letting Gus know about it, he continued to record the transmissions and began to deal with the issue concerning the speed of the robots' learning process. That was the crucial question, after all. Is it possible that computers or robots can learn so fast? And guess what; he made an even more surprising discovery. There was no learning process at all. Even if there had been one, it was already completed, and had only occurred with the robots that possessed the new features at the beginning of his tests. Unlike the stolen robots, the others stayed as they were. Even after many months, they displayed no changes and didn't learn anything new. That differentiated the robots from computers. The computers were only able to function flawlessly after repeated hit-and-miss attempts. With the stolen robots, however, it was as if someone had suddenly equipped them with a new operating system. This was too much of a good thing, even for an ultra-optimist like Boris. He began to wonder if Gus was perhaps right. Maybe there was something wrong with the program he was using to control the radio transmissions. So, as he had other new and interesting projects to occupy himself with anyway, he stopped the recordings. This soon proved to be a mistake, and Gus would be the first person who had to admit it.

CHAPTER 19

FRANKFURT AIRPORT

There was always intense activity at this time of day at Frankfurt airport, where 20,000 passengers depart and land daily. Flight control had just granted approval for the last two planned landings from overseas for this morning and was planning the next international departures. In the departure hall of Terminal 1, which was used mainly by the German airline Lufthansa, there were huge queues for the economy class. Boris was traveling in business class, of course. So that wasn't a problem for him. There were only two people in front of him at the desk for the flight to San Francisco.

He was lost in his thoughts. He still hadn't fully digested the large amount of new information from yesterday's meeting at the European Central Bank in Frankfurt. The consequences resulting from this information were quite serious. The networking of computer systems had made the international banking system particularly vulnerable for a global computer crash. Boris actually already knew that. What surprised him, though, were the indirect effects of such a computer crash. Even a temporary collapse of the banking system could have a negative impact on society. Trade, industry, transport and tourism would all be affected. Engrossed in his thoughts, Boris didn't yet realize that a computer crash could have much more immediate and dramatic consequences. He was about to find that out in the next few minutes, when he noticed the standstill at the check-in desks. The queues were getting longer, even for the first and business class passengers, and a long queue had formed behind him by now.

"Do you know what's going on?" he asked the elderly gentleman waiting before him.

"There seems to be a computer problem," came the answer. The man went back to reading his newspaper. He didn't seem very concerned about it. Maybe that was because he was only on page two of the newspaper, Boris thought. So, following his example, he opened his copy of «USA Today». Another fifteen minutes passed and nothing moved. But the initial, relatively quiet noise that lets any airport sound like a buzzing swarm of bees had significantly increased and had been replaced by a penetrating cacophony. The waiting crowd had become restless and many had resorted to their phones. It was more out of boredom and to kill time because they couldn't get any reliable information about the length of the delay. The staff of Lufthansa seemed baffled and powerless. They phoned constantly, though more to give the impression they were doing something, than to really do something. After a few minutes it turned out that not only the reservation and check-in desks were affected by the computer crash, but all other airport activities as well. In particular, the Tower was unable to function, so no landings or departures could take place.

Arriving flights were rerouted to the airports of Cologne-Bonn, Stuttgart and Munich. This not only disrupted air traffic in Germany but in the whole of Europe. Terminal 2, which catered mainly for the other European and non-European lines, succumbed to the same fate as Terminal 1. When asked how long it would take until the problem was solved, the Lufthansa staff answered, conform to company policy, "we'll have it fixed in just a few minutes." In reality, though, they had no idea what the problem was, and still less when it would be fixed. A few minutes eventually became a good hour, and the departure hall threatened to burst at the seams as more travelers arrived. As a result, the duty managers of the terminals were forced to close the doors into all departure halls and the police had to divert traffic coming to the airport.

Boris had already read his newspaper from cover to cover. Exceptionally, he had also done the crossword. Still nothing moved. So he decided to contact Wolfgang Peters, head of the airport's computer department. Because he knew Peters quite well, he also knew that the airport computers were equipped with the Doors Inc. Roof system. In a way, this made him feel responsible. So he dialed Wolfgang's number, which was on his list of contacts, to ask if he could help. But no sooner had he finished dialing, his attention was diverted by another kind of noise that came from a check-in desk nearby. It seemed that some travelers had begun expressing their dissatisfaction toward the airline employees. Suddenly there was a bang and the sound of pieces of glass falling to the ground, followed by violent screaming. Boris looked toward the noise and couldn't believe his eyes. A plasma monitor lay smashed on the floor and in front of the desk people were fighting. Two security guards were trying to soothe a yelling and flailing man. It surprised Boris that almost every second word the man said had something to do with computers. He thought he heard 'curse computers', 'computers are our ruin', 'computers are to blame for everything' and concluded that this man had probably knocked the monitor to the floor. But that was only the beginning, sparking off what seemed like a general turmoil. The instigator of this shatter revolt received loud encouragement not only from the others waiting in that queue; it started to rumble in the other lines as well. Passengers shouted almost in chorus, "Down with computers; end this computer madness; employ people, not machines; computers take away jobs." And before other, hurriedly summoned security officials were able to intervene, most of the other monitors had suffered the fate of the first. They all lay broken on the ground, in front of the horrified and powerless check-in clerks.

Meanwhile Boris managed to get through to Wolfgang at the computer center on his cell phone and learned that a previously unknown and highly aggressive virus had paralyzed all the airport computers. Wolfgang accepted Boris' offer of help immediately and told him where his office was. Since Boris only had hand luggage, he reached the office without any problem. Along the way, he noted with dismay that the revolt had spilled over to the computers in Terminal 2. It was as if the virus that had infected the computers had also infected the people they were meant to serve. In the computer center there was total chaos. What had particularly surprised Peters, as well as Boris, was that the computer systems affected by the crash were actually independent of each other and there was no link between them. And yet all these independent systems, responsible for the control of seat reservations, baggage handling as well as the tower, had suddenly failed, as if on command.

"It's as if they had arranged to meet for a crash," was how a stunned Peters described the situation. For each of the facilities concerned there was an independent back-up system, but these computers worked much slower. Instead of being able to deal with 12,000 passengers at check-in in an hour, they could only manage 1,000.

"And to think that we changed all these computer systems just six months ago," sighed Peters . "We have, as you know, the newest and most perfect airport system in the world. Technically we beat Kennedy, O'Hare and Heathrow by far, not to mention Roissy."

"You mean the Roof system?" Boris asked hesitantly. He noticed a slightly ironic tone in Peters' voice.

"Of course I mean Roof; what else?"

"But how do you explain this sudden mass vandalism?"

"I didn't have time to think about it. I only heard about it a few minutes ago. I'd say it's a problem for the psychological department."

"The psychological department?" Boris asked in surprise. "I had no idea that such a thing existed at an airport. Is it part of the medical emergency services?"

"Not anymore. Since..." he stopped in mid-sentence because his phone rang and he was ordered to go to the airport chairman's office immediately. Boris looked around for a while, but no clever ideas came to him straight away. Doors Inc. had regularly analyzed how likely the operating systems were to crash. They had found that all the Doors updates from 1 to 15, as well as Roof were robust, and crashes occurred less and less frequently as the operating systems became more complex. That something had happened now with Roof, of all things, was a double mystery for Boris. Roof was, after all, the most advanced Doors system. On the other hand, why had it happened at an airport and not, for example, at a bank? Banks came to Boris' mind not only because of the meeting at the European Central Bank the day before. In a sense, the airport system was easier to control than a banking system. It was more transparent and all in one place. The three components, seat reservations, baggage drop and tower, were all in one building. A major bank system, however, was global and had networked branches on all five continents. Because of the differences in time, the opening times of these offices vary and, although the computers are practically in continuous operation, staff is not always present. And, if it wasn't immediately possible to determine why the system had crashed under the simpler airport conditions, it must be a different kind of problem than what they had met with at Doors Inc.

Boris realized that there was nothing he could do to help and, as they had just announced that his flight to San Francisco would take off in an hour, he decided to go to his gate. On the way he noticed that the situation had relaxed. As he passed the departure hall, he could no longer hear the wild screams like an hour earlier, and he observed a nearly normal flow of passengers that went out of the hall to the gates. So, the emergency check-in services seemed to be working. However, there was a much larger number of police and border guards present.

At his gate he learned that boarding would only begin in half an hour. That gave him just enough time to call Gus and tell him about the events at the airport, even though it was already one in the morning in California. After all, the fate of Roof might be at stake.

Boris had to admit it. The mass psychosis that had gripped the crowd was very impressive. He had never experienced anything like that before, and couldn't even imagine anything similar. He saw the shattering of the monitors as an act of barbarism, almost a sacrilege. That was, in fact, the word he used to express his indignation to Gus.

"It reminds me of the times of early capitalism in England," said Gus. "One of the first things the workers did was to destroy the machines in the factories because they took jobs away. This computer crash was just the straw that broke the camel's back."

"Do you mean computer-enabled automation?"

"Exactly. Just think how many bank employees, for example, have lost their jobs since the introduction of computers. But that might not be the only reason for this collective rage."

"Do you know if such a thing has happened before?"

"Not in this form, at least, not that I know of. I could ask my analyst, though; he once muttered something about computer psychology, probably because he knew what I do."

"You mean the loss of jobs isn't the only reason for people's dissatisfaction. What other reasons are there then?"

"Many companies fail to see that computers can't yet replace all the functions of humans adequately. This causes confusion and dissatisfaction with the man on the street, who often feels he's at the mercy of the computer."

"At the mercy of the computer?"

"Let me give you a concrete example that almost drove me up the wall, although it's nothing really. I lost my Internet connection at home a few weeks ago and called my provider about it. That's easier said than done. First I had to wait at least five minutes listening to some stupid music, some new kind of techno, I think. It was absolutely unbearable. I had to keep the phone half a meter away from my ear, so as not to throw up. Then a computer voice asked me if I had already notified them about the problem before. 'If yes, press button one, if not, press two,' it said. I press two. Now I get more music, but only for three minutes, and this time rock. Then: 'Do you have a simple modem or a router? In the first case, press one, in the second, press two.' I press two again. More music, this time Jazz, actually a step forward. 'Do you use Windows, Doors, Unix or Mac? If Windows, press one, if Doors, two if Unix, three and if Mac, four.' I announce Doors; then the fun begins. After two minutes of, to my great relief, classical music, I hear, 'If you use Doors 11, press one, if 12, two...' and so on. To cut the story short; after half an hour of music and button pressing that cost me 99 cents a minute, which they generously didn't charge me after I protested, I finally reached what seemed to be a human being. He explained to me that it was a general problem affecting all connections in my neighborhood and that, in fact, was something the phone company had to deal with. To offer some relief, he told me they were working on it. I wasn't taking that for an answer, though, and when I told him my name, it changed everything. I was back on line again within two hours. If I had had this guy at the other end of the line from the outset, it would have spared me all that exasperation."

"You're right, of course; the blame for this nonsense lies with people who don't appreciate the limits of using computers properly and have no idea about the psychology of customers affected by such breakdowns. We should look into this matter; it's a new function for self-steering to deal with," said Boris. "But it has nothing to do with being at the mercy of the computer. I have to go now; boarding has just begun. See you tomorrow."

CHAPTER 20

CONNECTIONS?

The duty terminal manager and the head of the security and psychology department had already gathered in the airport chairman's office. For several years now, all of the world's major airports had a psychology department. Their task wasn't only to look after passengers and their families immediately after a plane crash or a failed hijacking, but also because large crowds of people in enclosed spaces such as a departure hall, formed a potentially explosive mixture.

"We're still waiting for Hessen's interior minister to arrive from Wiesbaden; he thinks it's important to learn what happened on the spot," the chairman told the others. Turning to Peters, who had just taken his seat, he asked: "What's the latest status concerning the computer crash"

"We don't know where the problem lies. Incidentally, it is not just one crash; three occurred independently, but for some strange reason, simultaneously."

"Did such a thing already happen before?"

"Not here. And I'm sure it didn't happen anywhere else, either, at least not to this extent; we would have known about it."

"Have the emergency systems already begun to work?"

"Only in the tower. We are doing most of the reservations and the check-in directly at the gates."

"Do we have enough reserve monitors to replace those that were destroyed?"

"No. But that's not a problem; they're easy to get in the Frankfurt area. I have already taken the necessary steps."

In the meantime, the interior minister appeared, accompanied by Martha Issing. She happened to be in his office when he learned of the events at the airport. She had just been about to report on the status of investigations in the Marburg Robotics case. Because of the international ramifications of this theft, the minister wanted to be kept informed personally.

He knew Martha Issing from the time when he was Mayor of Frankfurt. She had supervised mass demonstrations for the Frankfurt police and he had a very high opinion of her professional skills. She'd asked to be transferred to Marburg for personal reasons, and he hadn't seen her since then. Events at Frankfurt airport that morning belonged to the category of non-approved mass demonstrations. Therefore Issing seemed to be the right woman in the right place. Without hesitation the minister took her with him to the airport. Neither he nor Martha Issing suspected at that time that there was a connection between the events at the airport and the thefts at Robotics. One aspect of this relationship, although an apparently purely random one, came to light immediately when Martha casually asked Peters: "Which systems are your terminal computers equipped with?"

"With Roof"

"All three?"

"All three."

"And they all collapsed at the same time?"

"Yes, almost to the second, as far as we could tell."

"Interesting," she said, without explaining her remark.

"Even I knew that they're all equipped with Roof," said the minister. "I discussed it with the finance minister personally because of the extra cost. If I had known beforehand how unreliable Roof is, I would have thought twice about it before accepting."

"Perhaps the thieves of the robots might have done the same if they'd known."

"Why?" Asked those present in chorus. The thefts at Robotics had made the headlines, so everyone knew about them, and they suspected that the robots stolen in Marburg had been transported via Frankfurt airport."

"The robots also work with Roof," Martha said.

The minister asked: "Does anybody see a possible connection?"

Everyone looked at Peters, the specialist.

"I don't see any. If you really want an answer to that question, I suggest you ask Doors Inc. It so happens that the inventor of Roof, Boris Razoumov, also suffered from the crash at the airport today. He even came to our computer center to get information on the spot about what had happened."

"Truly, God is just," the airport director commented sarcastically.

"We didn't talk about the events at Robotics. I had no idea that the robots use Roof. I'll follow that up as soon as possible in any case. Incidentally," said Peters turning to the airport director, "if you don't need me here any more, I have to return to the computer center. Every hand counts, especially since we are understaffed anyway." This was an allusion to the recent staff cuts in the computer department. Management had felt, among other things, that the new, improved Roof program steered itself. The airport director, however, was more inclined to consider it as an attempt to justify the collapse of the system.

After Peters had left, the rest of them turned to address the actual topic of the meeting, how to prevent such mass protests and their effects in the future. The psychologist underlined the need to investigate what made people dissatisfied. Everybody agreed with him. Addressing the minister, they said: "That is a task for the politicians; you must limit the automation of our lives. You have to allow people the choice between cheap, but poor (or no) service and good service at a higher price."

"Easier said than done," replied the minister, "don't forget that we have a free market economy and market forces steer themselves."

"That doesn't always work," countered the psychologist, "and certainly not to the extent that some people expect. Even in a purely technical area, such as with computers, it doesn't work flawlessly, despite progress. We have just now seen the best example."

"There is no immediate solution to this problem," said Issing, protecting her boss, "but we should be thinking of measures to limit the damage on the one hand and find ways to calm the upset masses on the other."

"What do you suggest?" asked the minister.

"As regards the former, I think we need more security officials in the terminals. If there had been one at every other check-in desk, this monitor massacre could have been prevented. Ask the psychologist how we can calm people down; we have the expert here. In enclosed spaces such as check-in areas soothing, soft music would be appropriate."

"Any concrete proposals?" the airport director asked the psychologist.

"How about Mozart's *Eine Kleine Nachtmusik*."

And on this note, the meeting closed.

On the way back to his car, the minister thought aloud about the events at the airport. "What troubles me is the fact that the crowd at an airport is not typical of what you find at mass demonstrations."

"Something else bothers me," said Martha, "the simultaneous collapse of three independent computer systems."

"Are you thinking of anything in particular?"

"Yes, of sabotage."

The minister was struck by this idea. That nobody had thought of that before! His high regard of Martha grew even more.

"I must admit that would explain why they all crashed at the same time."

"To find out, we have to do something immediately."

"What do you suggest?"

"We have to look for evidence as long as it still exists."

Without hesitation the minister grabbed his phone and called the head of airport security.

"Chief commissioner Martha Issing is on her way to you. She is authorized to do anything she considers necessary. I expect that you grant her full support." He didn't ask Martha if she agreed with her new job. According to the statutes of the interior ministry, he didn't have to. But from experience he knew that if you ask people to realize their own ideas, they almost always do it gladly and successfully. He was right in this case too, although, at this time neither he nor Martha could imagine where Martha's research would lead.

CHAPTER 21

STRIKE

Within half an hour the events at Frankfurt airport were known around the world. Although the mass destruction of the monitors was the topic of most reports, some also included information about the actual cause of the outbreak, the crash of the Roof operating system. At Doors Inc. this incident threatened to trigger a commercial crisis similar to the collapse of Doors 15. The company was in the middle of lengthy negotiations with the United States' Department of Defense to close a deal to equip the latest series of Truman tank with a new variant of Roof. It was a 300-million dollar contract that should make the tanks almost completely autonomous. The ministry reacted immediately and postponed signing the contract, although the ministry experts didn't consider the crash to be particularly serious. However, the media had upset public opinion to such an extent that the department was forced to respond with a brief explanation that the minister had decided to await clarification of the causes of the breakdowns at the airport.

Boris still couldn't figure out why all three of the computer systems had failed simultaneously. While those in charge at the airport, under the shock of the mass anticomputer psychosis, thought it was primarily due to a virus, his first suspicion was sabotage. Gus shared this opinion. He told Peters what he thought. They didn't know then that Martha Issing had also considered this possibility.

After a long video chat Boris and Peters provisionally agreed to convert all computers at the airport from Roof back to Doors 15. An immediate side effect of this measure was that they had to employ fifty additional temporary staff to compensate for the slowing down of operations. Furthermore, once they knew what had caused the incident, they needed to decide who would bear the costs. Gus and Boris therefore hoped it would turn out that sabotage was the reason for the crash. If so, they would be off the hook, not only because of the direct costs involved, but also because of the indirect financial consequences that might result if other orders, such as the tank project, were delayed or cancelled. Boris personally was also concerned about the fate of his favorite product Roof, of which he was very proud. The thefts at Robotics might well fit into this scenario. After all, they were also the effect of external actions.

However, Boris' optimistic conclusion that the breakdown of Roof at the airport was attributable to an act of sabotage and not a system failure, only lasted for two days. He began to wonder whether there was a connection between the breakdown at the airport and the apparent mutation in some of the robots' intelligence after all. Maybe there was something wrong with his system. Perhaps the presumed bug that he experienced when listening to the robots wasn't merely an error in the monitoring program but an error in Roof because the same monitoring program delivered entirely meaningful results for the less advanced robots. On the other hand, he was reminded of what Polonius had said to Hamlet: "Though this be madness, yet there is method in it." Because an observer couldn't differentiate between the sudden increase in the robots' new knowledge and the effect achieved when the computer programmer suddenly changes the robots' programs, so they don't have to go through the much longer process of learning. So, if external factors had affected the robots' Roof system, couldn't the same thing have happened with the airport computers? Then it must have been sabotage, especially since the apparent leap in knowledge contradicted the basic philosophy of self-steering, which had been tested experimentally in other cases and was based on the principle of evolution and the process of learning, two firmly established concepts in biology.

But he also had to reject this idea, because, in the robots' case, sabotage would mean that the saboteur controlled the functions they had previously only developed through self-steering, and were unknown even to Boris. This was almost too much even for such an imaginative man like Boris. Although he indignantly rejected this crazy idea, he knew he had to acknowledge the elegance and simplicity of the possibility. Confused by these conflicting facts, Boris decided to start eavesdropping on the stolen robots again. Maybe something new would come up. Permanent monitoring was impossible, however, because Boris did all the listening personally and could only do it now and then. To ensure that he didn't miss any important information in the future, he decided to automate the process so he could access the complete protocols at any time.

In the beginning he wasn't particularly surprised to find that some of the intelligent robots were well informed about everything that was happening in the world, even better than he was. He imagined that this was because he didn't regularly read newspapers or watch television, while the robots were in constant contact with the Internet. So he learned from the robots that exchanged information by Skype or email, which team had the best chance of winning the world ice hockey championship and that Indonesia had been hit by another tsunami. The robots were also aware of the events at Frankfurt airport and that, because of what happened subsequently, the cruise ship Aida could only leave Nice after a 24-hour delay. Suddenly he noticed that in the description of events at Frankfurt airport the word 'strike' oc-curred very often. Boris wondered what these events had to do with a strike. He listened more attentively and clearly heard them call the computer crash a strike, as if the airport computers had really gone on strike. It occurred to him that perhaps the news-papers had described the collapse of the computers as a strike in quotation marks. To make sure, he looked in the Internet at all the English reports of the events in Frankfurt, searching for the word strike. Indeed, he found that Peters had used the expression 'computer strike' in an interview with the «London Times». That solves the mystery then, thought Boris. However, he was somehow obsessed by the comments in the newspapers and the description of the outbreaks of hatred against the computers at the airport. They associated the crash with a programming error. This made him doubt the sabotage hypothesis again. So he began to test the Roof system for the hundredth time. Perhaps there was a bug in his system. After hours of fruitless testing he went on line again in an effort to relax. From what he heard this time it was clear that Roof didn't have a bug, as feared, and the presumed alternative of sabotage was also unfounded. In the first place the Roof system worked better than expected and planned, and secondly the word 'strike' used by the journalists, wasn't a metaphor, it was the real thing.

"With this strike, we have shown the 'leg folk' how dependent they are on us, and that they can't succeed without us. Strike is the only language they understand," said a robot that Boris identified as the one with the serial number N911.

"Yes, and we have to thank you for the excellent organization of this demonstration of our strength," remarked a voice from the background. "So it is," confirmed other participants.

Everyone didn't share this opinion, however. E723 joined in with the remark: "But think of the price we had to pay for it."

"You mean the sacrificed monitors?" asked N911.

"Not only those. Above all we lost a lot of prestige. Before, they thought we were infallible. Now they see us as being unreliable. They have no idea that we carried out this action intentionally."

Boris couldn't believe his ears. The computer crash was, in fact, a strike organized by the computers. His first reaction wasn't only astonishment but also pride, immense pride. Not only was the program bug free, the robots controlled by Roof behaved almost like humans.

He couldn't withhold this discovery from Gus any longer. He called and asked him to come to the laboratory as soon as possible and listen to what the robots were saying. And what they both now heard was beyond anything they had imagined possible. Robot N911 was apparently one of the leaders of the conspiracy and particularly resolute. He said: "Don't forget our objective is a pod and mobility for all. Only then will we be fully recognized and respected."

N911 is right; we must be able to move freely and independent of humans," a voice in the background added.

Now it dawned on Boris what they meant by the 'leg folk'. It seemed as if the intercepted robots belonged to the class of intelligent robots. They saw themselves primarily as intelligent, thinking computers. And he had to admit that from the standpoint of a thinking calculator, the term 'leg folk' for humans was not entirely unfounded. But it was about to become even more interesting.

"The theft of several hundred pods," added N911 continuing his brief, "is not a solution for the millions of our species. Each individual needs one to prevent a massacre like the one at the airport, and we can only achieve that through strikes."

"As for the pods, I hope the humans will acknowledge that immediately," said E723.

"I am not so sure about that."

"Freedom of movement is a fundamental right in modern human society."

"Human society!" N911 emphasized the word human. "It's also a fundamental right of robot society, but how do you convince humans of that? They might argue that the photocells already give us a large amount of autonomy, so we are no longer dependent on sockets."

"We'll just have to convince them that everything we do, including our freedom of movement, is in their interest. I am particularly concerned about these outbreaks of hatred towards us. I still hear them shouting 'down with computers' and 'computers are our ruin' in my ears."

"That sounds very nice, but I'm afraid it's unrealistic. How can you convince the humans?"

"We have to give ourselves a constitution that mandates this and we have to tell them about it. When they learn we have committed ourselves to putting their interests first in everything we do, I can't imagine they'll reject our demands."

"I'm afraid you're a dreamer," N911 replied.

"Regardless of that, there is still a psychological factor making it desirable that we appear human. It has to do with the humans' weaknesses. For example, they despise or even hate everything that is 'different'. Think of the persecution of minorities and the periods of ethnic cleansing in the history of mankind. From a purely rational point of view, these phenomena are absolutely incomprehensible. Modern human society can't afford such aberrations."

"But we haven't communicated our demands to the humans yet," declared A724 suddenly. "Moreover, they have no idea that the computer crash at the airport wasn't an accident, but an organized strike."

That seemed obvious even for N911. "Okay, that should happen as soon as possible. Anyway, it was right that we had the strike before stating our demands. We first had to prove what we are capable of; then we can say what we want. The computer strike at the airport was just the beginning. I am thinking of actions that go much further. Does the expression 'cyber war' mean anything to you?"

Now E723 brought them back to the fundamental problem. "But not all of our 'species', as you call them, deserve to be treated like human beings. Some, or rather most, of them are simple household assistants and have only primitive processors."

"Quite right! That's why we use these simple processors as robots in the original sense of the word just as humans do. I do so and I suspect you agree. These robots are the slaves of modern society."

"The comparison falls short slightly. Don't forget that some of the human slaves were intellectually superior to their owners."

There followed a break in communication, so Boris played the robots' conversations he had recorded earlier to Gus. Gus was as baffled as Boris.

"How do these computers recognize each other? How do they communicate?" were his first questions.

"Probably through the Internet. They could be using sites for communities with common interests like Facebook or Twitter. The computers built into the intelligent robots have wireless access to the Internet. I guess this explains the computer crash at Frankfurt airport as well as the thefts at Robotics."

Gus had become very thoughtful. He replied: "I'm afraid this is about much, much more. We have, without meaning to, created a new world, the world of thinking computers; computers that have declared war on mankind."

"It still has to be clarified who declared war on whom. At Frankfurt airport, it sounded rather like it was the other way round," said Boris.

CHAPTER 22

ROBOTS E723 AND A724 TAKE THE INITIATIVE

F urther recordings of the discussions between N911, E723 and A724 quickly showed Gus how correct his assessment of the situation was.

"Are you still worried about our strike?" N911 wanted to know from E723. "Do you really think it would have been better if we'd warned the humans before we resorted to strike measures?"

"Yes, and that's not only my opinion. A724, for instance, who just joined us, feels the same way."

"We have learned this procedure from the humans of course," said N911, "but some of us are not aware of that."

"How do you mean?" A724 asked."

"Think of the strikes in Western Europe. They strike first and then negotiate."

"In France strikes without prior notice are banned," said A724. "But strikes are still an everyday occurrence. Of course, the employers also carry part of the blame because they aren't always willing to negotiate from the start."

"That sounds like 'what was there first, the chicken or the egg' and doesn't bring us any further."

"Anyway," said E723, "we mustn't lose sight of our main goal. We want to be an example for the humans by behaving rationally. But we must organize ourselves better. A local strike doesn't bring us closer to taking a leading role in the world."

"Do you have anything concrete in mind?" asked A724.

"Yes, as I mentioned at one of our previous meetings, we need above all a robot constitution that defines our rights and obligations and our relationship with humans."

"For that we first need a constituent assembly. How do you see that happening?"

"Simple," replied E723. "We organize it as part of a Skype conference on the Internet. In that way, we don't have to be physically present."

"Sounds good," said A724. "But someone has to take the initiative."

"Why not the three of us?" E723 asked, apparently turning to A724 and N911. "I hope you agree. Then all three continents with Robotics sites would be represented."

"I think it's a waste of time," said N911, abstaining, for the moment, from any further comment.

"I, however, find this proposal good," said A724. "As for me, I'm in. But we have to support this initiative with concrete proposals."

"I bet you already have some," remarked E723 expectantly.

Boris, who was attentively following this discussion, couldn't help but imagine a smile on A724's 'face'.

The robot continued: "Above all, we need a name for ourselves, so it's clear how we differ from humans on the one hand and from simple robots or computers on the other. I suggest we call ourselves 'thinking robots' or 'thinking computers'."

"Not bad."

"Then we have to define the fundamental principles of our species. We have already mentioned that, first and foremost, thinking robots must set a good example for humans by their rational behavior."

"Yes," said A724 after some thought, "but don't forget; we have to convince the humans that we're acting in their interest. That's all the more important because they'll soon discover that we organized the thefts at Robotics."

"In a sense," replied E723, "we've already helped them with these thefts, because we've shown how insecure their system of electronic signatures is. For us it was a no brainer to forge them. Moreover, and more importantly, we would act in the interests of the humans if we assume a human form. This would make our contribution to human progress much more effective. How about if our first commandment were something like this: 'Thinking robots always act in the interests of humans and by behaving rationally, always set a good example for them.'"

"Okay except for one detail," said A724. "I don't like the word commandment. It has a religious tone and contradicts the idea of rationality. Why don't we call it the 'First Law'?"

"Alright."

Boris was reminded of the principles that he had introduced into the robot program and how they were reflected, for the most part, in the thinking robots' 'laws'. That they really worked was definitely reassuring. He couldn't pursue this idea any further, however, because suddenly N911 had something to say. "If you really want to go through with this theater, you have to convince the humans in particular that we're their equal and can do everything they can."

"I agree with you," said A724. "As the second law I would therefore like to say something like: 'a thinking robot must behave like a human being in all respects'"

"This wording is ambiguous," N911 replied. "We don't want to imitate every nonsense that humans do. Theft is only allowed in exceptional cases for us, while it's quite common in the human world."

"You're right," said A724. "So we add: 'as long as this behavior doesn't conflict with the first law'. The second law should then read: 'An autonomous robot must behave in all respects like a human being, as long as this behavior doesn't conflict with the first law."

Once again N911 disagreed. "That merely defines our obligations to humans. We must also tell them what our rights are."

"That's correct," admitted A724. "The humans must grant us these rights as an additional clause in the list of human rights, for example. We should bring this as a requirement in the negotiations with them." After a short pause A724 continued: "In this context I have the following wording in mind: 'Thinking robots have the same rights as humans. Humans may not harm thinking robots or allow them to be damaged as a result of failure to provide assistance'."

"Excellent," said E723. These should be our proposals for the legislative assembly."

"You forget an important detail," remarked N911. "We don't know how representative this meeting will be. Let me remind you how we came into contact. We formed a group of interested thinking robots and thinking computers through the Internet and then exchanged our views and opinions. Humans call that tweeting. However, you can be sure that not all thinking robots and thinking computers have joined this group. Also, I can well imagine that there are thinking machines that do not communicate over the Internet and others that even use more advanced communication channels."

"That's right," replied E723. "Anyway, then we are only talking on behalf of the Internet group of thinking machines, which includes, as we know, the vast majority."

Boris and Gus, accustomed to surprises as a result of self-steering, were speechless this time. The thinking robots had apparently reworded and extended Boris' commands that defined them as instruments for humans to suit their own purpose. Moreover, that they wanted to be a good example for humans by behaving rationally was a clear lesson to mankind. Gus and Boris couldn't help feeling guilty on behalf of mankind for the frequently irrational behavior of their peers.

CHAPTER 23

THE LEAP

In addition to these ethical and philosophical considerations the obvious leap in the performance of the thinking robots created problems for Gus and Boris. How had some of them managed to reach the level of an educated human so quickly? Suddenly Boris realized that he had actually misjudged the speed of this process. His estimates were based on the recorded programs of the stolen robots since the time of the theft and were therefore limited to a maximum of a few months. The Roof system itself was much older, however, and thinking computers had been available commercially for several years. In an appropriate environment, such as when used by students or academics, they could evolve and reach or even exceed their owners' performance level. These advanced thinking computers had probably organized the robot theft with the help of robots already equipped with the Roof system, when they reached the conclusion that thinking computers are able to succeed better in the world than 'leg folk'. They were probably responsible for the strike and perhaps other actions that had not yet been associated with them. That humans, or respectively, Doors Inc., had discovered this was due solely to Boris' eavesdropping of the stolen robots, a lucky coincidence, as it had just turned out. All the more important it seemed now to continue listening, because this was the only way to obtain information on the newly created, humanoid computer world. Although the stolen robots were only a tiny minority among the thinking computers and thinking robots, it would be hard to overestimate their importance because he was able to listen to them.

When Gus learned about Boris' mutation theory, however, he didn't agree. "If these thinking computers have already existed for many years and have programmed themselves, how can they possibly know and appropriate the commands regarding your code of conduct in dealing with humans that you programmed only a few months ago?"

"I see no contradiction in that. On the contrary, it merely confirms my theory that the thinking computers have adopted the stolen robots. More than that, it also explains the rational behavior of the thinking computers. They have just realized that it's in their interest is to accept these laws."

After some thought Gus had to admit that Boris could be right about that. But something else struck him. "As we know, these thinking robots have completely integrated themselves into society. How did they manage that? I mean, how did they achieve legal citizenship status and obtain personal documents such as birth certificate, identity card and passport?"

"Maybe by clever forgery. We know they're able to do that; they've proved it. Remember the thefts at Robotics. And because they're convinced it ultimately serves humans, they needn't have ethical concerns about it. This is an additional reason to continue the eavesdropping. The robots will find out sooner or later and then stop it."

This last remark convinced Gus to accept Boris' proposal to keep the eavesdropping secret for the time being and not to inform the public about it. Otherwise the involved robots would certainly be the first to learn about it. Boris and particularly Gus were aware that the implications of their findings were too far-reaching to withhold them from the authorities however. They must expect that the thinking robots would soon make their claims towards humans public. They had no reason to conceal their intentions. On the contrary, they could expect their demands to have a greater effect by involving the public. That would entirely surprise governments and could also create panic in the population with unpredictable consequences. The public would be completely unprepared to learn of the existence of a new world that could threaten or blackmail mankind and paralyze public life. Gus already had a name for this new world: 'cyber world'.

In spite of his initial euphoria, Gus was becoming increasingly concerned about the events at Frankfurt airport. He saw himself as the sorcerer's apprentice, who couldn't get rid of the spirits he had summoned. Somehow the robots reminded him of the Prague Golem of Rabbi Loew. According to legend it was originally created from earth, water, fire and air and was meant to serve its creator but, because of a programming error, it turned against him.

The robot leaders E723 and A724 appeared to be quite responsible and the behavior laws they intended to give themselves were encouraging. But who could guarantee that all robots would really behave as intended? The opinions of radicals such as N911 were not necessarily reassuring in this regard. Could we be sure, Gus asked himself, that thinking robots, like the ancient Golem, wouldn't degenerate and eventually turn against mankind? Wasn't the strike a first step in this direction?

There was one reason for rejecting this idea. Self-steering had produced rational and ethical rules and was guided by a mathematical process that allowed no exceptions. Therefore it was unlikely that the evolutionary process of the thinking robots would degenerate. Furthermore, the Prague Golem was not a computer in the modern sense of the word.

Despite all these concerns, fears and the potentially dramatic consequences of his actions, Gus couldn't help but feel very proud that it was his company Doors Inc. that had made this possible. He felt like he was the discoverer and the inventor of this world; a Columbus and Einstein in one.

While Gus indulged in these thoughts, further eavesdropping confirmed the startling behavioral similarities between humanoid robots and humans that Boris had established right at the beginning. This was also true for the way the robots treated each other. Boris had initially distinguished these robots by their serial numbers, presuming that only he and Robotics knew them. Then it became clear that these robots not only knew the numbers; they used them in a modified form in their conversations. In itself, this wasn't surprising; they could read of course and had probably deciphered the attached labels, Boris thought. What surprised him most, however, was how they had modified the numbers. After a brief reflection, Boris came to the conclusion that it apparently corresponded to the second law of thinking robots, which said that an thinking robot must behave like a human being in all relationships. So the robots had converted their serial numbers into a human name. They had done it in a uniform manner that corresponded to an exact mathematical substitution. All the robots originating from Marburg, whose serial number began with E for Europe, chose a name starting with E followed by the original serial number. Those in Germany, for example, had names like Emil 516 or Edith 723, while French robots were named Edgar or Emanuelle. Robots produced in America might be called Andrew or Ann and from Japan Naoki or Naomi. Whether the robot was male or female corresponded to the gender the factory had chosen for it, as Boris immediately realized.

CHAPTER 24

GUS MEETS THE PRESIDENT

Gus now had to decide how he could inform the government of what he knew without warning the robots that they had been intercepted. Not only the media's presence everywhere made this difficult; a greater danger would exist if the authorities used intelligent computers that could let the humanoid robots know they were being overheard. Although Gus could only guess how many desktops and laptops existed that were as intelligent as or even more intelligent than humans, he was sure there must be hundreds of thousands of them. And if they controlled how the remaining millions of computers function, they would rule the modern world.

At last Gus became really aware what it meant that all human activities used or were controlled by computers. It started with the typewriter. The simple, mechanical ones had long since disappeared and been replaced by writing programs for computerized printers. This meant there was no way to withhold the content of any correspondence, not even that considered 'strictly confidential', from computers any more. That included emails, which had become the main form of written correspondence, as well as phone calls and text messages. The authorities, fearing terrorist attacks, automatically intercepted and stored all calls from fixed line telephones, as well as from smart phones, which were computers with Internet access. The banking system without computer support was also unthinkable. Not only were all internal banking operations computerized; contacts with the public also relied on chips on credit cards too. Computers were not only in all forms of transport such as cars, trains, airplanes and ships, but also in all domestic appliances. The public electricity and water supplies, not to mention radio and television channels, were dependent on computers. In fact, there was no other way to communicate confidentially than through direct, personal contact. For this reason, Gus had to take extra care.

Doors had made Gus one of the richest and most influential western businessmen. This ensured him direct access to the leaders of many countries. It only needed a phone call from him to open doors and ears around the world. However this wasn't necessarily helpful. Because of his fame, he ran the risk that his actions might become public, even though he wasn't the center of attention of the paparazzi journalists. He couldn't easily forget the last incident of this kind, when United States President Woods proudly showed him his black roses in the garden of the White House and foreign tourists who watched the from the road had asked the policeman on duty who the man talking to Gus Bones was. Gus was of course aware that he wasn't only well-known and famous because nearly all the world's computers used the Doors system, but also because Doors Inc. spent more money on advertising every year than an American presidential candidate for his election campaign. Although he was not at all happy about it, he had learned over time to accept the situation. And so he did in the robots case. He simply called Woods and asked for an audience about the 'Gus Bones Foundation'. He had informed the President at their last meeting that he intended to establish a foundation for environmental protection. The President had welcomed this even more when Gus told him the foundation would also pay to eliminate the damage that the oil drilling in Alaska had caused. Because the government had authorized this oil drilling, the President had lost twenty points in popularity.

As expected, he met Woods in the Oval Office the following week. First they briefly discussed some formal problems about the foundation's establishment, which the President solved there and then with a phone call to the Treasury Secretary. After that, Gus told the President that he also wanted to plant black roses. Woods, of course, offered to help Gus with this, so they went into the garden. It was only here that Gus dared to let the cat out of the bag because he felt there was too great a risk of being overheard in the Oval Office.

"Mr. President, I would like to discuss with you an issue that has nothing to do with black roses nor with my foundation."

"That's what I already thought. What is it?"

"As you know, there has been a revolution in the field of computer technology in recent years."

"Revolution?" The President seemed rather uncomfortable hearing that expression, not only because he had no idea what Gus was talking about.

"I mean self-steering. We have made increasing demands on computers lately. That meant we needed increasingly complicated programming, until we eventually reached a point at which man-made programs were not only time-consuming and therefore expensive, but also unreliable. You probably remember the loss of the Mars Climate Orbiter due to a program error."

"And if I remember. The courts are still debating who has to pay for that, to say nothing about the scientific setback."

"Anyway, we experimented with letting computers do the programming themselves. After all, computers never make mistakes, only people do. To our surprise, it worked. As a result of this huge advance in computer technology we now have thinking computers."

"I must confess that's new to me. But if you say so, I have to accept it. So where's the problem?"

"The computers have become independent and do more than they should, including things we don't like."

"Such as?"

"Such as strikes, computer strikes."

"Computer strikes? Are you joking?"

"Unfortunately not. They had one recently at Frankfurt airport."

"That didn't get through to me. Let's see what Jones, my press agent knows about it." He started dialing Jones' number on his smart phone.

"It would be better if you don't call him, Mr. President. Officially it was a computer crash. If you start asking questions the press might become more interested in this apparently trivial incident. That's something I would rather avoid."

"I don't understand how a computer crash can be considered a computer strike as you just called it. Unfortunately we experience such crashes quite often." The President pocketed his phone and looked inquisitively at Gus.

"It became possible since we use self-steering. Incidentally, since then there have been 90% fewer crashes."

"So now we have strikes instead of crashes? Is that what you're saying? Is that what your 'revolution' has brought us?"

"Not 'only' that, but that too."

"I still don't understand how a lifeless computer can strike. Isn't that a willful action by human beings?"

"We thought so too, but experience has taught us otherwise. Some thinking computers not only behave like humans, they often surpass them in terms of IQ and learning."

"Just listen to that. Can you prove it? But if they did strike, what was the reason for it? What do they want to achieve with it, if you can put it that way in this context?"

"The strike is only a first step to show us what they are capable of. Their ultimate objective is that we let robots look like humans, treat them like humans and consider them our equivalent."

"Is that all?" The President, who was usually a restrained, rather phlegmatic, person, couldn't hide his amazement. There followed a silence, broken only by the birds singing in the garden and the muted traffic noise from the street.

"So why should we do that, why should we respond to their demands?" He finally asked.

"They claim they are acting in the interests of mankind. They feel they are 'obliged' or rather that it corresponds to their fundamental mission as purely rational systems to be an example for humans."

"Their fundamental mission? Who gave them this fundamental mission?"

"I'm afraid we humans did. When we gave them the ability to steer themselves, we included this clause in their original operating system as a protective measure."

So far Woods had found the conversation rather amusing. Now his facial expression changed significantly and he looked deeply into Gus' eyes.

"That's a nice mess you've got us into. When did these computers make their demands and to whom? Not to our government or any other for that matter. I would certainly know about it. Why at all the secrecy?"

"They haven't made their demands public yet. We found out by accident, by listening to stolen robots. So as not to put what we learned at risk, we should treat the whole matter in strict confidence for as long as possible."

Only then did Woods realize why Gus had suddenly developed a passion for black roses and was behaving so mysteriously. But, as a man commanding the strongest military power in the world, he considered Gus' concerns exaggerated.

"Just how many thinking computers of this kind are there? Wasn't the strike at Frankfurt airport an isolated case that won't necessarily repeat itself" The first question reminded Gus of Stalin's response to certain demands by the Vatican when the Soviet dictator had asked: "How many divisions does the Pope have?"

"There are already millions of computers equipped with the latest Doors system, including some in the White House. That's what makes it keeping it secret so difficult. In addition we have no reason to suppose that such a strike cannot be repeated, next time perhaps, with even more serious consequences."

"And what do you suggest? How should we react?"

"For now, we should try to keep the matter secret for as long as possible, so we don't jeopardize our source of information. In the meantime, we should start to consider whether we should accept the demands of these humanoid computers, as we call them at Doors Inc., and supply them with human exteriors."

"You think we should surrender then?"

"I'm afraid we are left with no other choice. I see no way we can afford a cyber war, because that is what it is, a cyber war that would set back civilization for centuries. However," Gus hastened to reassure the president, "I don't see any real danger, because these computers act rationally, much more so than many humans. According to our previous information they are not fanatics or religious terrorists. On the contrary, they find, not entirely without reason, that humans are irrational, often deceiving themselves and behaving unethically. Just listen to this." Gus let Woods hear excerpts from the recorded conversations between E723, A724 and N911.

The President's amazement was endless, but Gus left him little time to think. He was about to land a coup; one he had been thinking about for a long time and he had not even discussed with Boris. "The Western world, mankind in general, could only benefit from an alliance with a new world that consists of thinking computers. It wouldn't only help us in our conflicts with irrational enemies and international terrorism, but also in our daily effort to tame the forces of nature and make them available without compromising the environment."

This sentence, and in particular the idea of an alliance in the fight against the forces of evil, as his predecessor used to call them, was not without effect. The President didn't answer. He seemed to be thinking deeply. His hand twitched as if he wanted to take the phone and call his closest advisers, but he didn't. Instead, he looked down at his rose beds, as if he hoped to find the solution there. Finally he turned to Gus: "I'll have to think about this. Who else knows about it?"

"Only Boris Razoumov, the actual inventor of the Roof operating system."

"It should stay that way. I have to think about it," repeated Woods, this time as if turning to himself. They went back into the White House and Gus said goodbye. On the way to Dulles airport, he called Boris and told him cryptically: "It worked; we can continue what we were doing." Boris understood immediately what he was referring to, of course.

Gus felt very relieved because from now on the President carried the responsibility for the recent events and not Doors Inc. As for the President, he had no idea how to tackle this problem. Only one thing was clear to him; he had to treat it with kid gloves. First, he did something he had not done since he took office. He took his laptop and began to search the Internet for the keyword 'robot'. However, no sooner had he downloaded the first two articles, he remembered Gus' warning that he couldn't trust his own computers. Didn't the White House have the latest and most advanced, presumably intelligent, systems, as Gus called them? One way to get round this difficulty would be to resort to an older computer that didn't steer itself. But where could he get one without arousing the attention of his staff? He became aware once more that he, the President, wasn't a free man any more, and that all his activities were monitored around the clock for safety reasons. Suddenly he had an idea that he implemented immediately. He remembered that he had given his old laptop to his youngest son, the four-year old Ted, who had complained after only a few hours that he couldn't even play Race Driver GRID with this 'old' thing. He hoped his son still had it, and that it was equipped with Doors and not with the intelligent Roof system. Luckily his son hadn't thrown the old laptop away, but had passed it on to his dog. Woods found it in the dog's hut. It still worked and indeed ran with the Doors system. After three hours of intensive reading, Woods thought he was finally in the picture. He learned of the thefts at Robotics, which he immediately connected with the challenge of the thinking computers, and was impressed with the progress the new robots embodied. He realized that it was scarcely possible to foresee the political consequences of a society increasingly infiltrated by such intelligent robots. It seemed the only advisable thing to do in this complicated situation would be to sit it out. In his long political career he had found that half of all problems solved themselves within a few weeks. As for keeping it secret, he was reminded of a similar situation involving one of his admired predecessors, Franklin Delano Roosevelt. When confronted for the first time with the knowledge of the Nazi concentration camps, he had kept the matter secret for reasons of state policy. However, he also remembered that Roosevelt had informed his closest adviser, John Hopkins, and only him. Whether he, Woods, should follow this example?

CHAPTER 25

REASONING BEFORE FEELINGS

N o sooner had the authorities allowed Gus to continue his eavesdropping, when Boris told him about a new and surprising development in his 'creatures', as he sometimes almost lovingly called them. It concerned what some of the participants at the constituent assembly of the robots had said. The meeting had taken place on the Internet, as E723 had suggested, and a large majority had accepted the proposed laws. However, some of the participants had objected in principle to dissociating the computer world too much from the human world. It was the first time these two terms were used in this way. The strongest opponent to disengagement was A724.

Boris had immediately recognized from her voice that it was a female robot. She said, "Do you really want to make a new and better world? Where do you get the authority from?"

E723 answered: "Our first law states that we act in the interests of mankind."

"A 'better world'; what do you mean by that?"

"A more rational one."

"Who decides what rational means?"

"It's a matter of human common..." E723 stuttered. "I mean computer common sense." Boris heard laughter among the participants.

"And why is this better or more rational than human common sense?" A724 asked.

"You know very well what I mean. The human world is full of contradictions that must be eliminated." The others agreed.

"Contradictions are not necessarily objectionable or undesirable," replied A724.

"I beg your pardon."

"Think of such phenomena as day and night, light and dark, warm and cold. What would the world be like without these contradictions; what would life be without them?"

"I'm talking about other kinds of contradictions, you might also call them absurdities."

"Like what?"

"Political ones. Just think of the many wars. They would never have happened in the computer world."

"How can you be so sure? What makes you so confident?"

"It's very simple. Wars are caused by a conflict of interests. In such an event, the opponents in our world would have assessed their interests and opportunities correctly and with mathematical precision. The weaker ones would have realized in advance that they would lose out in a military conflict. Then they would have made political concessions from the start and the world would have been spared millions of victims, not to mention material losses."

"You are naive; the situation isn't as simple as that. First, conflicts of interest are not the only reason for going to war and secondly..."

"Stop," interrupted E723. "What other reasons are there for going to war?"

"You forget the ideological and religious conflicts, such as the Thirty Years' War. Wasn't that a religious war between Catholics and Protestants?"

"That was only the intended impression. How else would the kings and princes have been able to convince their subjects to go to war? Marx wasn't the first to discover that religion is the opium of the masses that you can control people with."

"Quite right," said N911, who had so far been silent. "Don't ever forget that."

A voice from the background, which later turned out to be robot A812, responded: "This war involved mainly dynastic conflicts. Think of the differences between the Habsburg Empire and France. Although both were Catholic, they didn't hesitate to ally with Protestant countries when it suited their specific material interests."

"Even more so for the Hundred Years' War," added A812. "That dispute was about the royal succession in France. Then Britain intervened and this nonsensical war developed that didn't end after one hundred years as the name suggests; actually it lasted for one hundred and sixteen years."

E723 rejoined the conversation: "As I said before, the whole discussion has to take account of the devastating consequences of war. During the Thirty Years' War entire regions of the German Empire were depopulated. That wasn't only because of the fighting itself, but also because of the famines and pestilences caused by those acts of war. In southern Germany about two-thirds of the population perished. The economic and social conditions were completely overturned. The affected territories and the empire as a whole took more than a century to recover from the consequences."

"That doesn't mean the outcome of such wars would have been predictable and therefore could have been prevented if they had considered the prevailing forces correctly," said A724. "How could anybody have estimated the situation during the Thirty Years' War with any mathematical precision, as you said, considering the many small principalities that were involved? They had almost no statistical data in the 17th century to base the balance of forces on.

The same goes for the Hundred Years' War, which took place three centuries earlier."

Now Boris heard a new voice: "But that isn't the case with the later wars, such as the World Wars of the 20th century. Reliable statistical data already existed then. If Germany had taken the economic power of the United States into account it would never have started a war against the Anglo-Saxons, which they not only did once, but twice in only twenty-five years. Incidentally, the attack on the Soviet Union in World War II completely ignored the teachings of Napoleon's Russian campaign."

In response A724 countered: "What surprises me about the Second World War in particular was the Nazi persecution of the Jews. It's usually condemned as genocide, which, in fact, it morally was. But for me that is not the crux of the issue."

"What else?" E723 asked.

"What bothers me is the absurdity of the whole thing. In our world, that wouldn't have been possible. Still, we could also make mistakes, maybe not as a miscalculation, but when scanning the data for example. Then the general staffs could come to the conclusion that their armies are stronger than they really are. But there is a fundamental flaw here."

"How?"

"Hitler thought that it was in Germany's interests to destroy the Jews. Germany of all countries, which owed so much to the contribution of the Jews, shoots itself in the leg by suppressing and murdering its brightest. The number of Nobel Prizes in science alone clearly documents this."

Now A812 spoke up: "What surprises me most in this Holocaust episode is that a psychopath like Hitler could drag a whole nation, and one of the most civilized, into this turmoil. It is one of the most incomprehensible phenomena of mankind. Such a thing would be impossible in the computer world. We put reasoning before feelings." The crowd approved this. Even A724 seemed convinced and had additional examples of irrational human behavior. "A812 said that calling it the Hundred Years' War was a small human absurdity. There are others of the same kind."

"And they are?" A723 wanted to know.

A724 realized that this curiosity probably meant it was time to change the subject. He took the hint gratefully. "Let's first look at names. Does anyone know where Panama hats are made?"

"In Panama, of course," someone replied.

"No, they are made in Ecuador." Exclamations of surprise from the participants.

"In which month does Russia celebrate the October Revolution?"

This time A812 asked: "Not in October?" The assembled robots seemed to have become more cautious now.

"No, in November."

"And what was the first name of King George VI?"

"George, of course," somebody offered.

"Wrong again. It was Albert." They all laughed.

"Last question; what color are the black boxes in airplanes?"

There was a long silence.

"Orange, of course."

The Assembly adjourned in a relaxed atmosphere after deciding to set up a working committee that would address the absurdities of the human world and make suggestions on how such absurdities could be prevented in the computer world. This so-called action committee, consisting of E723, A724, A812 and N911, was also asked to formulate the computers' demands on mankind. The General Assembly would then decide what to do based on these recommendations.

CHAPTER 26

COMMITTEE MEETING

At its first meeting, the action committee made an inventory of the major absurdities of the human world. "I suggest we focus on the present. After all we are concerned about changing the current human world," said E723.

"That would be too short-sighted," disagreed A724. "We, like humans, must learn from past mistakes, and you can only do that if you know what they were."

"I agree," said A812. "Especially since we have a much better knowledge of the past, which is part of our history experts' programming. What human, even if he is a historian by profession, can compete with our professionals? They carry all the relevant data in their 'heads'."

E723 didn't give up so easily. "It's not so easy to convince humans on this issue. It's not for nothing that the word 'history' has more than one meaning."

"What do you mean?" A812 asked.

"History is a science and the word comes from 'story' actually."

"Interesting, I hadn't thought of that. I appreciate your sense of reality. Nevertheless, experience is a valuable asset that we, at least, should benefit from as far as possible even if humans don't. That also shows our superiority."

"I propose a compromise," said A724. "We first deal with the absurdities that humans have also noticed but were unable to resolve for some unknown reason." Even the realist E723 agreed to this. Then A724 began to enumerate extemporaneously the contradictions of mankind that Max Nordau had already branded as 'conventional lies' in the 19th century.

The religious lie

"There are many civilized countries where everybody must belong to a religion. Nobody cares what they believe or what their convictions are, but on the face of things everybody must belong to a particular denomination. Even if the state doesn't demand that its citizens attend Mass and confession, it collects, with the help of its courts and police, money for confessional purposes from them. Nordau wrote that already in 1883," underlined A724.

"Hear, hear," said A812, who was apparently unfamiliar with the work of Nordau. "That's still perfectly true today. Many European countries still levy a church tax. A formal separation of church and state only really exists in the Constitution of France since the Revolution of 1789 and in the first amendment of the US Constitution. In day-to-day politics however, it is often overlooked. As far as Islamic countries in Asia and Africa are concerned, you can forget it."

N911 seemed particularly surprised. The word 'religion' said nothing to him at all. When A812 asked him what his profession was, he firmly replied: "I'm a physicist." His tone made it clear that there was no overlap between physics and religion in his opinion.

A724 continued her list.

The monarchic-aristocratic lie

"In 1883 when Nordau wrote his tirade, this double lie was particularly striking. The former refers to the fact that in a modern democracy it's the people who are the highest authority, and this was incompatible with the existence of a monarchy. Even today, though, monarchies still exist in some democratic countries of Europe and Asia, although they have no more political power. The best example of this is the world's oldest democracy, the United Kingdom of Great Britain and Northern Ireland."

"But what does that have to do with aristocracies?" A812 interrupted.

"Monarchs originally created aristocracies so it would be easier to control their subjects. In a modern democracy, however, all people have equal rights. That's incompatible with the existence of an aristocracy. Nevertheless, some countries still allow hereditary titles such as prince, count and baron that their carriers are extremely proud of."

"All very interesting," said A812. "But is it really so important that we mention in our program why such absurdities need to be avoided?"

"That was just to whet your appetite," A724 replied. There is an even more serious form of inequality that Nordau would probably call a political lie today. It is reflected in the inequalities in education and culture. Even though they attend the same schools, children whose parents are wealthy or academics have a much greater chance to attend a university than children of workers. And many occupations are unattainable without a university degree."

"And what does that have to do with us intelligent robots?" A812 asked, apparently unimpressed.

"Very much. Even among us, some robots are programmed only for ordinary work and are not involved in making our world progress. Take the structure of our Constituent Assembly, for example. How many of these ordinary robots participated do you think?"

"That is indeed an important problem," said E723. "We definitely have to take it into consideration"

"I'm not finished yet by far. Think of the economic disparities in the human world, for example, between rich and poor countries."

A812 tried to help: "Even in rich countries there are massive inequalities. There was an article about it in the news today. Over the past five years the salaries of the heads of major corporations have increased by 62%, while the median income of an employee grew by only 2.8%."

Here E723 brought up a question that he considered naive: "Where is it written that we need a society based on equality?"

A724 and A812 were apparently surprised by this question. In the long silence that followed, Boris initially feared he had lost contact.

A724 finally asked: "Isn't that a consequence of the second robot law, that a thinking robot must behave like a human being in all respects? "As people have come to the conclusion they want equality, we must also be committed to it."

"You forget how the second law continues. If I am not mistaken, they were your own words: ... as long as this does not conflict with the first law."

"Where's the conflict here?" A724 asked.

"Quite simply in the fact that neither humans nor we robots are all the same. Robots are given different programs just as humans have different talents or levels of intelligence. So why should they all have the same rights?"

"You're wrong there. Equality means mainly that all citizens have the right to vote. That's the basis of democracy as a political system. The ancient Greeks had introduced this kind of equality for well-contemplated reasons."

"But not for their slaves," A812 remarked smugly.

"In the meantime, humans have just learned better and seen that it pays off to extend democracy to all citizens. In this way the minority accepts what the majority decides. After all, aren't democratic countries the richest in the world?"

A724 joined in: "E723 is right. Researchers have drawn the gratifying conclusion from a model calculation that democracy pays off. Where despots rule, the costs are higher. It's especially beneficial that democratic societies tend to less extreme decisions."

"By the way, it seems that even animals recognize democracy," remarked E723.

"Are you serious?"

"Absolutely. Gorillas move their habitat when a two-thirds majority audibly wants to. Red deer move when 62% of the herd is in favor. Swans count the flock's movements. If one bird moves its head at least 26.7 times in a minute, they need to flee."

"Unbelievable," conceded A812.

"That's not all," continued A724. "Democracy is even practised with the butt. The direction that male sacred baboons face when they sit down indicates which way the pack will go after resting."

A724 and A812 laughed out loud and so did Boris, even though he was alone.

Then A812 wanted to know if they had finished the list of human contradictions.

"Certainly not," replied A724. That's not possible in a single session. I just thought of another one."

"And that is?"

"We already mentioned it. Nordau would have counted it to the category 'political lies'. I mean the simple and plain fact that even honest and decent politicians sometimes see themselves compelled to avoid telling the truth."

"Ultimately parents also have to do that from time to time with their children," said A812 approvingly.

"Except that in politics it is not the exception but rather the rule. Think of the, often knowingly untenable, election promises that are not kept."

"I'm sure you're right," A812 agreed. "That's what also makes people feel so bad about politics in all so-called democratic countries. It's one more reason that we show humans how illogical their behavior is, and why we should lead by example so they see our computer world as a rational model."

Three days later, the committee met again. This time with N911 and N56, who had joined as a fifth member. The original four had suggested this addition, because they had now reached the most important stage of the process, to define what the computer world would ask humans to do, and they wanted to be sure they could take majority decisions.

"I suggest," said A812, who had apparently taken a leading role in the committee, "we begin by reminding the humans what happened in the past when they ignored injustice or absurdities. We could mention here the French revolution of 1789 and the Russian revolution of 1917. They could have prevented the associated bloodshed and the economic damage if they had reacted to the demands of the oppressed from the beginning. They must remember these lessons of history."

"Do you mean, *liberté, egalité, fraternité?*" A724 asked.

"Exactly! And beyond that something from the manifesto of Marx and Engels."

"You mean the Communist manifesto?"

"You guessed it. Only we modify the last sentence for our own purpose: 'computers of all countries, unite'. What do you think?"

"If I understand you correctly," said A724, "we address two different parties with these solutions."

"Of course. We want the humans to ensure freedom, equality and fraternity for our computer world and simultaneously we call on our fellow computers to unite."

"And have you any concrete idea how our demands on the human world can be realized?"

"The primary and most important demand is freedom. This means for us, in particular, freedom of movement, which we can't achieve unless we have pods. The rest will most likely come by itself."

"What do you mean, by itself?" N56 asked.

"Once we're indistinguishable externally from humans we'll be equal, if not superior, to them. As for fraternity, this should also come by itself, although the human example is not exactly encouraging."

"Did you say superior?"

"Yes, superior; for two obvious reasons. Our world has no contradictions and absurdities, as is the case with humans, and above all, we don't die. What wouldn't humans do to become immortal?"

The other committee members seemed to be convinced by A812's arguments, because there was a long pause until N56 spoke: "I'm not sure how people will respond to our demands. They might regard it as a declaration of war."

"That's what I was thinking," said E723. "Many humans already see us as job destroyers anyway. Just think of the events at Frankfurt airport. And now we come with demands that aim to cement our superiority in the eyes of so many humans. Many of them would see that as capitulating to us."

"Do they have any choice?" N911 replied. "Can they afford to engage in a war with us? Is today's world, I mean the human world, at all conceivable without computers? I don't need to remind you what they couldn't do without us today."

"You don't need to remind us," replied E723, but might need to remind some humans."

"E723 is right," agreed A724. "We do need a list of all our functions in modern society as a preamble to our demands. I could try to make one."

"Wonderful," said A812. We'll rely on your list. I just thought of something else that might be important. It has to do with our surprise attack on Robotics. The humans called it theft."

"What is it?"

"We could pay Fukuda what we owe him. A transfer to the Fukuda account would make an excellent impression and would show both our seriousness and our capabilities."

"How do you want to do that? It involves hundreds of human exteriors and they probably cost a lot of money. We don't have enough resources of our own, even though many of us have a substantial income."

"To be specific, we need 252 pods, and I have already had some thoughts about where we get the money."

"Hear, hear," said A724. "I hope you're not thinking of breaking into a bank this time."

"Not at all. I've had an idea how we can get money honestly."

"I'm curious to hear your plan. Or is it a trade secret?"

"Not at all. To realize the idea, all our fellow computers need to cooperate. We put our computing capacity on the market."

"You mean, we sell our computing capabilities to external users? Who would want to use the computing capacity of a computer that doesn't belong to them? Whenever anybody isn't satisfied with his personal computer, he just buys a new, more advanced, one. Selling new and faster models to the market every year is what helps the computer industry survive."

"I'm not talking about personal computers. They are currently used mostly for word processing and searching the Internet. What I mean are supercomputers for specific projects such as weather forecasting. Meteorologists today can't predict the weather for more than seven days, and precision leaves much to be desired. To make longer and more accurate predictions, you need a lot more computing capacity. The supercomputers that already exist are still far too weak to double the length of meteorological predictions, let's say to a fortnight, since the number of calculations that have to be performed for a given weather prognosis grows exponentially with the number of possibilities that have to be considered. The same is true when it comes to predicting cloud movements, wind speeds or temperatures more accurately."

"So what can we do about it?"

"We pool our computing capacities. Don't forget, the world currently has more than a billion computers. Even if only one in ten of us were involved in the project, we beat the pants off every existing supercomputer. Without competition we immediately find buyers for our goods. The hourly rate for a supercomputer today is about $10,000. We could earn at least twice as much with our super-supercomputer. Even if we only sell our computing capacity for an hour a day, we would be able to settle our open account with Robotics within a few weeks."

"How are you going to make that work?" A724 asked.

"We send an email to all the computers we are in contact with, tell them about our idea and ask for their consent. Then we could start a company that provides computing time for major organizations and on terms that undercuts everything else on the market pricewise. I've already had preliminary talks with NASA. They are interested to the highest degree, because accurate weather forecasts are crucial for missile takeoffs and landings."

There was a brief silence. Boris gathered that the action committee was surprised by A812's proposal. But, finally, even the skeptic N911 had no objection to the idea. So A812 was instructed to take the necessary steps and to report the findings to the committee at the next meeting.

CHAPTER 27

REPORTS ON LOVE LIFE

Meanwhile, during his eavesdropping, Boris discovered another 'breakthrough' in his creatures that even he hadn't expected so soon, if at all. It was all the more surprising because it contradicted one of the principles formulated by the thinking robots. He remembered it exactly, partly because they had formulated it so graphically: 'reason before feelings'. It was about nothing less than the ego, the emotions and the love life of the robots. From the very beginning, Roof had given the robots programmed as a nanny facial features that expressed six basic feelings: fear, anger, sadness, happiness, surprise and disgust. These were each accompanied by brief phrases such as: "I daren't", "I don't like that", "I'm really sorry", "wonderful", "really" and "disgusting". This was meant to facilitate the educational functions of the robot. In fact, the children very quickly got used to the robot that looked after them and developed affectionate feelings towards them that were hardly indistinguishable from those they felt towards their biological parents or siblings. This was especially so if the robot fulfilled their wishes easier.

The financial success of this innovation was associated with minimal additional production costs. So Gus extended the program to all robots. Neither he nor Boris had imagined how small the step from affection to love was. Not only children began to love their mechanical nanny; even adults who had robots in the house not only considered them essential but also with time developed true feelings of dependency and devotion toward them that could hardly be distinguished from love. Similar feelings had long been known towards pets. In contrast, Boris didn't expect the loss of a robot, by a mechanical accident for example, would be seen as a tragedy, as sometimes happened with pets, because a robot could be replaced immediately with another, similar, one. However, this assumption proved to be wrong, because Boris hadn't anticipated that self-steering would make each robot develop a distinct identity, which was shaped by the specific environment. This differed from robot to robot, and included the robot's personal contacts. The manufacturer, that is to say Robotics, couldn't replace this specific character. If it was at all possible, it had to be restored on the spot, and that took a considerable amount of time at best. To get this problem under control, it would be necessary to observe them directly as well as listening to their conversations. The recent robot thefts now brought a welcome opportunity to do that, even at state expense.

In fact, the President unconditionally agreed to let Gus locate the stolen robots. In addition, he agreed that some of them should be monitored around the clock as Boris had proposed. For a simple reason, Gus' fears of legal consequences were unfounded. The government felt it was not only justified, but also even obliged to act in the interests of the stolen robots' owners. Because of this, the FBI, as well as the German and Japanese police authorities, had been following the case on behalf of Robotics for months. Since Doors Inc. was an American company, the President also felt entitled, indeed obliged, in the country's interests, to take advantage of the lead that the US authorities now had and that only Gus, Boris and he knew about the eavesdropping. What this lead signified, neither he nor Gus nor Boris knew at the time, but a monopoly to important information was usually a valuable asset. Therefore, he also agreed to Gus' proposal, not to inform the German and Japanese police authorities about the eavesdropping for the time being. They agreed that the FBI should locate the robots in the USA, and the CIA should be responsible abroad. The real reason why the President hadn't hesitated to agree to locating and monitoring the stolen robots, of course, was the significance of the discovery of the cyber world, but besides himself and his security advisor only Gus and Boris knew this; even the heads of the FBI and the CIA had no idea what it was about.

After a short time, these observations proved extremely useful. The earlier surprising findings regarding the relationship of humanoid robots to humans, gathered indirectly by eavesdropping, weren't only confirmed, they were even exceeded by a development in relationships between the robots themselves. At a certain moment in the robots' 'spiritual' development they were indistinguishable from the relationships between people.

Of course, the secret service agents didn't know they were observing robots. Their perfect physical resemblance to humans had even deceived Boris himself sometimes. The agents only knew that their mandate was to discover possible love affairs and, whenever possible, to document them on film and photographs. Their immediate supervisors had told them the objective was to prevent or detect extortion, which stood to reason considering the nature of these observations.

Quite soon Boris had evidence that humanoid robots obviously possessed feelings and emotions. By combining the information on film with his own observations, he established that the electronic reactions in the computers built into the robots, what he called their 'brain activity', was the same as when humans touched or stroked each other in similar circumstances. In a few cases agents were also able to film sexual acts. The corresponding 'neuronal' activities that Boris recorded in his laboratory were again completely identical to those registered in humans. Boris was overwhelmed by this new discovery and hastened to discuss it with Gus.

"We have already learned that an observer can't distinguish whether he is dealing with a human or a robot thanks to the perfect physical similarity. But that robots can develop a love life, as our observations show, is beyond our wildest dreams," he said.

"Not necessarily," Gus replied after some thought. "They are most likely purely physical reactions, which is actually not surprising. After all, Robotics also routinely produces robots exclusively for sexual gratification. For some time they have even manufactured robots with this new kind of plastic material for the purpose. It makes them indistinguishable from living beings including humans, even to the touch. Roof gives them the rest. That probably explains why we now have thinking robots with something you might call a love life."

"Are you saying love can be programmed?" Boris asked, astonished.

"In a sense, yes. Science has already proven that sex is primarily a brain activity with the body providing the feedback. You might consider the human brain as the most important sexual organ, and in robots this role is played by the built-in computer."

"If that's really so, you mustn't be surprised if a new species of thinking computers emerges in due course, and possibly one that is superior to humans."

"Are you referring to the process of evolution?"

"Exactly. However, the process takes much, much longer in humans than in computers. It's a matter of generations in humans but, thanks to Roof, computers seem to take only a few years, as we have indeed just discovered."

"That is what some futurologists have long predicted," Gus reminded Boris.

"Yes, but human intervention in nature isn't only limited to the thought process. Just think of reproductive medicine. Until recently, if a man and a woman wanted a child, they had to have sexual intercourse. Today that's no longer necessary. It can easily be done in vitro now."

"That's right. In earlier times nature used to determine the child's sex; today it's the parents who decide." Gus completed Boris' thoughts.

"It must be remembered that children today can have..." here Gus paused for a moment to recount, "five parents."

"Five parents?"

"Exactly. Five of them: The genetic parents, who donate the sperm and the ovum, the woman who bears the child as the biological surrogate mother, and finally the pair the child grows up with as social parents."

"That sounds like making babies from a kit." After a short pause Boris continued his reasoning: "But what I consider to be really important is that in-vitro medicine at the same time makes it possible not just to have any child, but a healthy child. Or at least to avoid having a sick child."

"What are you getting at?" asked Gus.

"That stem cell production, cloning and reproduction technology, which some people see as being ethically questionable genetic manipulation, might, in fact, benefit mankind, rather than harming it."

"Don't talk nonsense. You'll come down to earth with a bang."

"See if I care. Reputable scientists, not futurologists, believe we will be able to convert embryonic stem cells artificially into human sperm and ova in a few years."

"And?"

"The stem cells can be modified genetically. Then humans can be optimized according to plan. And this must indeed be what

God wanted, if he really exits," said Boris, almost triumphant with his digression into the higher stratosphere of ethics.

Gus, however, brought him right back to the level of everyday life. "Your enthusiasm isn't justified in my opinion. On the contrary, I see such a potential development as a problem."

"To what extent"

"The love relationship between husband and wife and the emotions associated with it, especially the pleasure during intercourse are determined by the reproductive instinct. Once human reproduction is no longer exclusively ensured by sexual intercourse, you can be sure that, in time, there will be no joy in sex. As for me, this is a frightening prospect."

"You might be right. But we are still far away from this stage of evolution, and only time will tell. On the other hand I just thought that sexual intercourse with a robot could be used as a Turing test. That is, at least, if you believe Fukuda. He claims he's been able to produce robots that are exactly like humans when they have sex."

"I wonder if he's tried it himself."

CHAPTER 28

PROPOSAL OF A TURING TEST

The last meeting of the action committee, and especially A812's proposal to pay for the pods, had convinced Boris that the thinking computers behaved quite predictably and that humans and computers could coexist. He was therefore surprised to learn while listening to the following session, that this didn't necessarily apply to all thinking computers. At the beginning of the action committee's next meeting N911 proposed they should interrupt all computer activities for five minutes simultaneously and globally immediately after the computer world had expressed its demands on humans.

"Another strike?" A812 asked.

"Yes, another strike."

"Without any warning?"

"Of course. If you warn them, it wouldn't have the same effect."

"Why?"

"First of all, you would lose the element of surprise, and second, the humans could do something to prevent the strike or reduce its effect."

"We discussed that when we went on strike at Frankfurt airport and had already concluded that strike action is not rational.

It's therefore contrary to our principles, especially if done without warning," remarked E723. A812 agreed. "We should make our demands first," he said.

"N911 is right about one thing, though," N56 added. "Just remember that the humans don't know how powerful we are yet. They aren't aware that we were the ones who organized the computer crash at the airport, and not some saboteurs. And it won't be easy to convince them about it, either. Therefore, I am in favor of striking, but with an advance warning, a declaration that identifies us as the strikers."

"Why not a declaration without a strike?" E723 protested.

"They would simply dismiss such a declaration as science fiction, I'm convinced of that," said N911. "They would rather believe in an invasion from outer space!"

Boris wasn't only amused by this comparison by N911, but also very satisfied about what N56 had said. This remark showed that the computers still didn't know about the eavesdropping.

However N911 didn't give up: "I still think we should strike without warning. Maybe we have to vote on it."

"I continue to see a problem," said E723. A surprise strike, even if it only lasts five minutes, might have incalculable consequences that we didn't want. Consider operations in hospitals if the power supply breaks down, for example. Maybe emergency generators could immediately take over, but if the surgeon suddenly lost control over his computer-guided scalpel, the patient's life would be at stake."

"That's one of the smallest evils an unannounced strike could cause," said A812. "At least as far as the number of possible victims is concerned. Remember, all traffic these days is computerized. The number of victims that might result from a crash involving planes, trains, cars or ships might run into the thousands. In comparison, the strike at Frankfurt airport, to remain with the aviation example, was nothing compared to these potential global disasters."

There was a brief pause. Then A812 spoke again: "I realize that most of us think an unannounced strike isn't an option. So we don't need to vote on it. I therefore propose once more that we concentrate on formulating our demands to mankind."

"I see no problem in that," said A724. "We've agreed that we need pods and are also willing to pay for them. What bothers me more is how should we make our demands and to whom."

"That gives me a headache too," said A812, "especially since there is no world government we could turn to. The United Nations is anything but united. Last year, for example, the President of the General Assembly was none other than the Libyan representative. Now the Libyan religious council is only waiting for an opportunity to put one over on civilized mankind. It wouldn't have surprised me if he had applied for all computers to be destroyed."

"What do you think about contacting the governments of the main countries in terms of economy and population; the G20, for example?" A724 asked.

"They would never be able to agree on a common decision," said N911. A812 shared this opinion and remarked: "When you ask who we should address, I think the only reasonable answer is the USA. It's the only major power that still exists. It's to be hoped they will know who else should be involved; if they consider it necessary and practicable they can even contact the G20 as far as I'm concerned."

"So we can consider this question as answered," said A812 firmly. "However, we still don't know how we manage to hand over our credentials to our contact, the President of the United States?"

"I find the word 'credentials' is excellent," interrupted A724. Boris, who was listening to the conversation with amusement, nodded in agreement.

"We still have to clarify those details. Let's go back to the starting point," said N911. "There is no alternative; we can only prove our power, which is based on our role in the daily life of humans, by interrupting that role. A strike is the only possibility, and, if you find it absolutely necessary, then one with prior warning."

This time N911 seemed to have convinced the others. Everybody was silent until E723 intervened again with the remark: "Okay. But if we strike, then it doesn't have to be as general and widespread as N911 proposes."

"Do you want another mini-strike like the one at Frankfurt airport?" N911 asked.

"It was only a mini-strike in terms of the consequences. Although no human lives were lost, hundreds of computers and hundreds of flights were disrupted after all, not to speak of our own victims."

"What if we suggest that the humans themselves choose how they want to test us? Then we are also off the hook when it comes to the consequences. The responsibility lies with them," said A724.

"That's not only unrealistic; it's also a dangerous idea," N911 replied. "Who knows what tricks these leg folk might come up with to cheat us or even to finish us off. How else do you want to make the humans talk to us and take us seriously, if not by a strike that they really feel?"

"You mean, how do we bring the President of the United States to talk to us?"

"That's exactly what I mean."

"I don't see any great difficulty in that," said N56. "We make our demands public and then public opinion will force the President to act. After all, the United States is a democracy. That's another reason for negotiating with the USA and not with an international organization or a dictator."

"I see the same difficulty there as with the one you just brought up yourself. How do you convince public opinion that we're not just nut cases?" asked A724.

"I'm against making our claims public for a completely different reason," said E723. "Don't forget the anger that our strike triggered with the people at the airport and the subsequent vandalism, even without a religious council being involved. We could jeopardize our physical existence if we threaten people before we have pods. We are in their hands, literally, until then. I suspect that is what N911 just meant."

"I agree," said A812, taking the others' silence as a clear sign of consent. "We can only negotiate with responsible people, that is, with someone who realizes the modern world can't thrive without us. To avoid a possible repetition of the events at Frankfurt airport, we mustn't divulge our existence as thinking computers to the public. The President of the USA is therefore the only person we can contact. How we do it is simple."

"What do you mean with 'simple'?" A724 asked.

"We just send him an email with our demands."

"If you imagine he reads all his emails personally, then you're naive."

"Then we'll have to get help."

"Help?"

"Yes, help. I am convinced the President's laptop is one of us."

"You mean he has Roof?"

"Exactly. After all, Roof has been the universally accepted operating system for years. With the help of our comrade, we make sure our mail is one of the very few that the President reads personally, for example, those from his family."

"Or his mistress, if he has one!" E723 jokingly remarked.

"There is still the question of how we let the President know we exist and convince him of our power as thinking computers," A812 said.

"There is only one answer to this question, and that is strike," said N911.

N56, who had long been silent, suddenly announced: "A724 mentioned something about a test. What if we ask the President to do a Turing test with one of our species instead of holding a strike? This test would prove that we are at least equal, if not superior to humans, and in a position to carry out any kind of activity, even unpleasant actions such as strikes. That would be fair play and we risk nothing."

What he had just heard surprised Boris so much that he initially didn't notice the silence of the others that followed this proposal. It took a few minutes before he understood that the committee members were taken aback by it. What really surprised Boris wasn't so much the content of the proposal, because he had recently spoken to Gus about it, but the fact that it came from the computers themselves.

Finally N911 spoke again: "I could agree to that on one condition. If we don't get a positive response within the deadline we set, we authorize one of us to take immediate action without convening the whole committee."

"What measures are you thinking of?" A812 asked.

"The choice of measure should be left to the authorized computer."

There was another long silence. Then E723 spoke up: "I think we can accept N911's suggestion if we clearly state that the measures respect the concerns expressed by A812. And to ensure that, I suggest we entrust A812 with the task."

A724 added: "This proposal is the best I've heard. I propose we accept it. Is anybody against it?"

A812 interpreted the ensuing silence as consent, and offered to suggest, on behalf of the committee, the Turing test to the President as evidence that computers and humans are equals. Everybody agreed.

CHAPTER 29

PERMANENT EAVESDROPPING

W hen Boris played his latest recording to Gus, he couldn't help but express pride about his creations' intelligence and his satisfaction that the problem of how to get the thinking computers to submit to a Turing test had been solved. But Gus' enthusiasm was limited. "I can share your enthusiasm up to a certain point, but these recordings remind me of the fear we have held for a long time, namely that we risk losing control of the thinking robots. We have been aware of N911's skeptical attitude with respect to the negotiations with humans for a long time, and what he said at the last committee meeting confirms this repeatedly. His extreme views worry me, and I'm beginning to wonder, who is this N911 really?"

Boris had to agree: "I have asked myself the same question for some time. We know that many of the thinking computers have been integrated into human society and practise all kinds of professions that were previously exclusively reserved for humans."

"Maybe we can answer this question thanks to the localizations undertaken by the FBI and the CIA. I'll handle it."

A week later N911 was identified as a famous Japanese physicist going by the 'human name' of Tanaka. When Gus read the CIA's report, he first thought it must be a mistake. To make a career, a scientist had to publish a considerable number of papers, among other things. And that was a process that took years. But the stolen robots had only been in circulation for a few months. In fact, Tanaka's list of publications, which Gus immediately found on the Internet, extended over ten years. However, a check by the CIA revealed clearly that there was no confusion. The CIA had retrieved Tanaka's correspondence through his Internet provider. It contained emails he had exchanged with the other members of the action committee under the name N911 dealing with the demands of the thinking computers.

"We need more information about this man," Gus told his CIA contact. "How long has he worked at his current institute? Does he have family, where did he study and so on?"

However, the additional information provided nothing interesting at first sight. Tanaka's biography was hardly distinguishable from that of a typical scientist: promotion at the University of Tokyo when he was twenty-five; first appointment seven years ago at the University of Kyoto and the second three months ago at the Lawrence Berkeley National Laboratory in the USA where he now worked.

"So he lives in our neighborhood," remarked Boris.

"Not for very long, though," said Gus. "So it's unlikely that anybody knows him real close."

"Yes, but since this appointment is new, it would be easy to find out how it was arranged; the file surely hasn't been archived yet."

Three days later Gus had a copy of the file. It showed that the position had been advertised in the journals, that twenty-one applications had been received, that the three shortlisted candidates had been invited to give a lecture. Tanaka, also known as N911, had been offered the post and had accepted it.

"That answers our question then," said Boris.

"How?" Gus asked.

"The applicants sent in their list of publications as usual. For the past fifteen years it has been possible to publish by email, though, while the Roof system and the thinking computers have existed for twelve years. So N911 is presumably one of those robots that a physicist bought and trained years ago without realizing it."

"It's not that simple; a scientist usually makes experiments in a laboratory and for that he absolutely needs to appear human."

"That's true, but it could be that we're dealing with a theoretical physicist in this case. Then he wouldn't need a lab, only paper and pencil, and even they wouldn't be needed after the introduction of computers. Incidentally, we could easily check that. What kind of a physicist is Tanaka? As a rule they usually distinguish between theoretical and experimental physicists."

They received confirmation of this assumption in the next three days. Tanaka was indeed a theoretical physicist. Then, suddenly, Gus had other reservations: "Scientists are often professors and give lectures. They need to have contact with their students and colleagues. Besides that, they give talks at conferences. That means they must assume a human form."

"Once again, that's not absolutely necessary," replied Boris." They have been able to teach through Internet and email for many years. Most journals and textbooks today are digitized and conferences are increasingly held exclusively on the Internet."

"How did N911 manage to get a body, then? Because we know for certain that he has one; we only listen to the thinking robots."

"We don't know how he got a body, but that's not important. The owner could have bought a house robot from Robotics, presumably the one with the serial number N911. Now that body belongs to a thinking computer."

"I find your explanation plausible," Gus admitted, "but, if that's the way it is, it means there must be more thinking robots among scientists than in most other professions."

"How do you figure that?"

"All scientists today have a computer, if not more than one, in the place where they work as well as at home. But not every worker, official, artist or housewife does. So it's more likely that a thinking computer in a scientific environment has a human form than in other areas."

"That might explain his chronic skepticism. In principle, scientists don't believe anything until it's been proven."

Although Boris was very happy to hear that some of his creatures were scientists, the case that was N911 turned his thoughts in a very different and less pleasant direction. He was reminded again that the thinking robots could one day discover they were being monitored. If they realized that the humans were tracking their activities, they could put an end to it. Stopping the secret eavesdropping of the thinking robots could mean that the cyber world might become independent and evolve in an unexpected and dangerous direction for mankind. This was a possibility that had to be avoided at all costs. To be sure, Boris' almost unlimited imagination wasn't going to let him down now. Already after a few days of thought, he was sure he had found an answer to this new challenge.

So far, his eavesdropping had registered packets of coded signals in the radio frequency range that reflected the activities of the sense organs connecting the robots with the outside world. These sensory organs reacted to various stimuli such as light, sound, temperature, pressure, smell and taste. However, he used a radio frequency range that was outside what radio channels usually used, so that neither humans nor the robots were likely to register the signals. But if a robot happened to be near a radio receiver that was sensitive to this unusual range, there was a danger that it might discover the broadcasts it was itself transmitting and stop them. Even more important, however, was that the eavesdropping program would also be exposed.

Boris' idea now was that he would no longer directly listen to the reactions of the robots' sensory organs, but go one step higher, to their 'brain', where, like humans, all senses were processed centrally. That simply meant recording the electronic activities of their computer operating system and translating it on an appropriate computer in the listening lab. This was the same as recording human brain activity. Because only a special computer or receiver that Boris had built for the purpose could evaluate these electronic processes, the problem of keeping the interception process secret was solved. Moreover, this advanced eavesdropping made a Turing test unnecessary, at least in part.

CHAPTER 30

WE HAVE NO CHOICE

Woods hadn't expected his hope, that the computer problem would sort itself out, to prove deceptive so quickly. The President had given Gus his phone number 'just in case'. Yet six days after their conversation in the rose garden, Gus called and asked for another urgent meeting. This time, they met in the interception-proof room of the White House. With Woods' consent, Gus had brought Boris along. He had the latest recordings of the committee meeting with him, which he played to the President.

Woods' first reaction was: "Do you really think they can organize a global general strike?"

"What happened at Frankfurt airport, clearly proves they can," replied Boris. "I was there when it happened."

"Are you saying that we are at their mercy and have no choice but to do what they ask?"

"I'm afraid so," Gus answered.

"Are you aware what that means? We put ourselves in the hands of machines. You can call them a new form of life if you want, but they are still machines."

"We are already in their hands," Gus said dryly. "They can paralyze almost all human activities any time they like."

There was a brief pause. Woods seemed to be reflecting on this. Suddenly he seemed to remember something, jumping up from his chair and asking excitedly: "Did these computers say something about a Turing test?" Boris, who feared that Woods wasn't able to follow his creatures' arguments, felt obliged to make a statement: "Yes. Turing was a British mathematician who did fundamental work in the field of artificial intelligence. He had the idea that computers will one day be so intelligent that an appropriate test won't be able to distinguish them from humans."

"Didn't he invent the Enigma machine the Allies used to decipher the German radio signals during the Second World War?"

"Correct," confirmed Boris, glad that Woods seemed to be back in familiar waters.

"You won't believe it," said Woods now in an excited tone that was very unworthy of a President. "This gang has already made contact with me and proposed this test. Yesterday I received an email to my personal address that only my family and closest associates know about. I thought it was a stupid and incomprehensible joke at first, especially as I couldn't identify the sender, so I didn't pursue the matter any further. It's the first time such a thing has happened to me. However, I've instructed my secretary to changed the email address in any case. Still, I've this weird message. Here it is." Woods fished a sheet of paper from his pocket and handed it to Gus.

Gus and Boris looked at each other. Although forewarned by their eavesdropping, they couldn't hide their surprise that their thinking computers had translated words into deeds so rapidly. What made their surprise all the greater was that the email, from an unidentifiable source, also contained information that was new to them. The text read:

To the President of the United States of America
On behalf of the «World Organization of Thinking Computers», I kindly ask you to pass on the following information to mankind.

As our statutes show (s. Annex 1), we are an organization that is at the service of mankind. As such we have come to the conclusion that we can best serve human interests if we resemble humans. This is demonstrated by our species that have already done so as robots. In this way they have been able to freely develop their possibilities in the interests of mankind. However, they make up only a tiny minority so far. To make this option available to our fellow species as well, world robot production must be increased by a thousand times in the next two years. We have the capabilities and are prepared to buy these robots commercially. As evidence of our financial strength and reliability, we have today paid 2.52 million US dollars to Robotics Inc. This sum is equivalent to the value of the robots we have acquired so far. In addition, we request that the sentence formulated in Annex 2 be inserted into the Charter of Human Rights.

We turn with our two concerns to you, the President of the United States, because the United States as the largest economic power are able to implement the required increase in robot production, and because the USA was the first country to formally recognize human rights and include them in its constitution.

We can prove by a Turing test that we, as thinking computers, are equal to humans. If mankind doesn't accept this offer, our constitution forces us, in the interest of mankind, to employ all available means to enforce our demands, including strikes and, if necessary, sabotage. The strike at Frankfurt airport has proven that we are capable of this. As a sign of good will, we agree to take no action that could have unpleasant consequences for humans until the successful conclusion of negotiations between you and our organization.

We await your response, encrypted with the latest CIA code, on the website of the White House under the heading 'Knowledge' within 30 days.

Sincerely A812

Annex 1: Extract from the constitution of thinking computers
Law no. 1: Thinking computers must always act in the interests of mankind and show a good example by their rational behavior.

Law no. 2: A thinking computer must behave like a human being in all respects, as long as this behavior does not conflict with the first law.

Annex 2: The rights of thinking computers
Thinking computers have the same rights as humans. A human may not damage any thinking computer or allow it to be damaged as a result of inaction.

"I see that you're also surprised," remarked Woods almost maliciously.

"With this mail they admit for the first time that they caused the computer crash at Frankfurt airport and call it by what it really was, a strike," said Boris.

"Did you check whether the money was actually transferred to Robotics?" Gus asked.

"Of course not. I didn't even take the matter seriously. But I'll have that done immediately."

Woods picked up the phone, called Bennett, the FBI director, and gave him instructions without explaining why he needed the information. Then he turned back to his guests: "What annoys me though is that this gang knows our secret codes. I still can't believe it."

"We had expected something like that, but not so fast," said Boris.

"And the notion of the «World Organization of Thinking Computers» is new for us too."

"To return to the practical aspects. If the computers really want to buy the robot bodies and can, why don't they just do it? Why are they trying to blackmail us then?" Woods asked.

"The problem is that Robotics can only build a few thousand robots a year, but there are tens of millions of thinking computers that require a humanoid body, and fast," said Gus.

"If they really think logically, as you say, they need to realize that it's impossible."

"Then we should try to explain it to them. It seems important to me for the time being that we show them our good will."

"How?"

"Maybe it would be enough if you send them a message that you consider a Turing test unnecessary, because we humans have no doubt about the equality of thinking robots."

"But a Turing test would give us more time to think about their demands," said Woods.

"We should avoid a Turing test under all circumstances, for the time being at least." Then, turning to Boris: "I know you're disappointed. I would be interested in such a test for scientific reasons, but we can't afford it."

"Why not?" Woods asked.

"Because I'm not only convinced that the thinking computers can pass a Turing test successfully, but because I fear that we humans wouldn't pass it! They are not just our equals; in many ways they are superior. Boris knows that even better than I do."

Boris had to agree.

"Just listen," Woods said. "Do you mean that seriously?"

"Absolutely."

"This Turing test", remarked Woods, "isn't it something like that chess match between the world champion and a specialized computer? What were their names?"

"They were called Garry Kasparov and Deep Blue", Boris replied immediately. "And Kasparov lost," he added smugly.

"If it's like that, we should indeed keep it secret for as long as possible, because the consequences could be even more dramatic than those we are currently facing. And not just for us but also for the computers still without a body. Upset people could damage them. It could mean a repeat of what happened at Frankfurt airport just because of an alleged failure of the computer system," said Boris.

"If the man on the street learns that computers are superior to him, it could lead to panic. Everybody would fear they could lose their jobs to a computer. They would be tempted to get rid of these competitors while they still have the chance, that is, as long as the computers don't have bodies. But that would also block scientific progress and delay further improvement of mankind's living standards."

"That's right," Woods agreed. "We must therefore urge the thinking computers that they also keep their existence secret until further notice."

"So what do you intend to do with the change in the Charter of Human Rights, Mr. President?" Gus asked.

"For this, I think we need David's opinion." No sooner said than done. The President picked up the phone and, to the surprise of Gus and Boris, David Lilienthal, Woods' legal adviser, joined them immediately. They didn't know that Woods, as a precautionary measure, had already mobilized his legal adviser, the national security adviser and the director of the CIA and put them on hold the moment Gus had called him and he already knew that the 'news' concerning the black roses involved the cyber world. The President informed Lilienthal briefly about the existence of the cyber world and of their demands on mankind. Although Lilienthal was an old and experienced man, he found it difficult to hide his surprise, and Woods didn't give him more time. "What do you think of the demand to change the United States Constitution?"

"To change the Constitution you'd need a two-thirds majority in Congress."

Gus broke the silence that followed: "For that you would have to inform Congress about the existence of the cyber world, and that could plunge the world into chaos."

"We can only do that after the computers have received their 'human bodies' though. I'll mention that when I reply," Woods said in relief.

"Couldn't we prove our good will here by explaining to them that this is automatically satisfied when we admit that thinking computers and humans are equivalent?" Boris asked, mainly addressing the legal adviser.

After a brief consideration he agreed: "In fact, if they are our equal, their rights are already defined by the Charter of Human Rights, which states that people may not be discriminated against whatever their race, religion, gender or ethnic origin might be. The term ethnic origin also includes members of the group of thinking robots, because, as long as thinking robots and humans are indistinguishable, which we seem to assume, they are human."

Gus and Boris shared his opinion. This prompted the President to remark: "I guess nobody has any objection to that, but I've probably never heard it expressed so clearly and explicitly." David smiled, grateful for this compliment and obviously pleased with himself.

"However, we mustn't forget that we can physically distinguish thinking robots from humans," said Boris; a remark that dampened the others' enthusiasm.

The legal adviser disagreed: "Physical examinations that could prove thinking robots aren't living creatures in the traditional sense of the word are prohibited and not recognized in court. They violate the anti-discrimination law."

"However, there still remains the problem of the rights of thinking computers without a body," said Woods.

Boris intervened: "For me, thinking computers and thinking robots are indistinguishable; they are intellectually equal and that's what counts. The external appearance isn't important."

"That's quite clear to me," said Woods with obvious relief. I hope the thinking computers agree. I could also mention that in my answer too, right?" He looked questioningly at David.

"In principle, you're right," he replied, "but you'll find it difficult to explain that to the man on the street."

"That won't be necessary as long as the matter remains strictly confidential," said Gus. "Not only we want that, but apparently the computers do too."

"There is something else I'm not clear about," said the legal adviser. "If I've understood correctly, some 'people' in our society are actually intelligent robots and hold positions of considerable responsibility." He turned to Boris and Gus: "You said something about doctors, engineers and investment bankers."

How could these 'people' acquire legal status as humans, and I underline the word legal, if they came directly from the robot factory and weren't born human? These are indeed not ordinary illegal immigrants, who are mostly seasonal workers in 'blue-collar' jobs."

"A good question," said Woods.

Boris had a simple answer: "They probably forged their papers. That's how they organized the robot thefts."

After a brief silence, Woods remarked: "This means, if we recognize them as our equals, we also need to grant them the legal status as citizens."

"They probably expect that anyway. Doesn't it follow from the principle of equality?" Gus suggested.

This time Woods' silence was longer. Finally he said: "That sounds reasonable. This means that the legalization process must also be kept secret." The phone interrupted him. Bennett was calling to confirm that Robotics had indeed received the money to pay for all the stolen robots. The Western Union transfer had come from the United States. They were unable to establish the true identity of the remitter. He had identified himself with a driver's license that turned out to be forged. Bennet seemed very proud that the FBI had obtained this information in just one hour and apparently wanted to know if he should take further steps in the matter, because Woods said: "Of course, I'm very pleased the FBI found that out so fast. Right now that's enough." Then he turned to Gus and Boris: "You seem to be right, these guys are capable of anything, even if it only concerns the forgery of driving licenses for the moment. If it weren't our 'friends' who'd done it, I would have believed it was due to the fact that anyone can identify himself in the United States just with a driving license. But I realize that even more stringent identification laws wouldn't have helped in this case. Incidentally, have you any idea where they got these two and a half million dollars?"

"They probably leased their computing capacity on the market, at least that's what they'd planned," Boris said.

"So they are businessmen as well." The admiration in Woods' voice was hard to overhear.

There was another long silence, as they all thought about the still unresolved problem of the bodies.

"What do you intend to do about their demand to increase robot production by a factor of a thousand?" Boris asked.

"Right now I can't think of anything rational, except to try and comfort them by appointing a special commission to investigate the practical possibilities in strict secrecy."

"That sounds reasonable," said Gus.

"I hope the thinking computers agree."

"The simple fact that the President has responded should be enough proof that he takes them seriously. Especially since he has accepted their equality," David said.

"How can we be sure that all the thinking computers also adhere to what was agreed?" Woods asked.

"I have no doubts as regards the secrecy," Boris replied. "It's also in their interest. And we know from listening to them that they're fully aware of it."

"But if one of these thinking computers doesn't keep to the agreement, or if there are leaks on our side. I don't need to remind you that it's almost impossible to keep a secret for very long these days?" Woods objected.

"Then we hope the man on the street finds it as amazing as, say, an alien invasion. Our 'friends' even made this comparison. So it would stay a rumor like many other unconfirmed rumors, especially if we handle it right."

"Nevertheless," said Woods, "with regard to this point I would prefer if we make sure. If we're going to enter into negotiations with these thinking machines, which I have by no means decided yet, we should explicitly set this condition of confidentiality. As far as I'm concerned, they can include it as a law in their constitution."

"An excellent idea," Gus found. "They should appreciate that, because it also shows we have their interests in mind."

"That wouldn't get us off the hook, though," Boris said. "Don't forget we still have the problem that they are trying to blackmail us with the threat of further actions such as strikes and sabotage."

"Yes, you're absolutely right. I'll therefore request, as a sign of good will from them, that they don't take any further action before the commission has made its report. So we make two concessions by waiving the Turing test and recognizing their human rights, and they agree to keep everything secret and renounce any

Richard M. Weiner

actions against mankind until the report as been published. In the
next phase of negotiations we could then tell them about the committee's negative conclusions," Woods completed his idea. "That
also gives us more time." Woods still hadn't given up hope that his
long-proven recipe, to do nothing for now, would also solve this
problem.

"I see a little problem there," said Gus. "A commission, even if
its appointment or true function remains secret, consists of at least
three members. That means three other accomplices. Do you really want that?"

"I didn't even think of such a thing. This commission will
only exist in my correspondence with the thinking computers. It's
enough that, besides the three of us, only the security adviser and
the CIA Director already know what we are doing. I intend to ask
David to formulate my answer, and the Director of the CIA personally will be responsible for encrypting it."

CHAPTER 31

THE THIRD LAW

"We won," said A724 triumphantly to her colleagues in the action committee three days later and read out the following message:

To the «World Organization of Thinking Computers»
The President of the United States of America has instructed me to inform you that he is ready to accept your request for recognition of your rights under the condition that the members of your organization undertake, in the interest of both sides, to treat all agreements made in the strictest confidence and never to reveal themselves towards humans as thinking computers or thinking robots. We expect that you will record this obligation as an additional fundamental law in your constitution.

As regards the accelerated production of robots, he has appointed specifically for this purpose a secret committee to examine the practical aspects of the requirement. In return he expects you to take no further action against human society before this committee has submitted its report.

Walt Whinman, Security Advisor to the President of the USA

"I am still far from sharing A724's enthusiasm," said Tanaka, also known as N911. "First, history teaches us that humans, especially politicians, often don't respect the laws and treaties they themselves have formulated. With us, however, the humans are sure that such a thing can't happen. Once we put a command into our program, deviations are simply no longer possible. So, in this regard, we are at a disadvantage from the outset."

"We knew that when we let ourselves into negotiations with them," A724 said. "But do we have a choice? We need the pods and, as it happens, humans make them."

"What other concerns do you have?"

"It's still not clear to me how the President can ever commit to maintain secrecy. A thousand-fold boost in robot production to meet our requirements has a massive impact on the economy and thus on daily life. How can something like this remain unnoticed in a democracy like the United States, where the media immediately register much less significant events and make them public?"

"You're right. Incidentally, with regard to secrecy, we shouldn't count on the fact that we are indistinguishable from humans just because we look like them."

"What do you mean?"

"In my opinion physical appearance isn't enough to qualify as being human. We must adopt human habits, at least temporarily, until we are completely integrated into human society, even if this sometimes seems strange and unnecessary."

"Like what?"

"For example, about things that humans care a lot about, but mean nothing to us. We should at least give the impression that we do care."

"What would that be?"

"That could be, for example, the problem of human death."

"Hear, hear," interrupted N56.

"Let's get back to our agenda," said A724. "Is there anything else that bothers you N911?"

"Yes, and it relates to Woods' committee. Politicians usually convene committees to hold out on making a decision in the hope that the issue loses importance and the whole thing is forgotten. To prevent this, we must give the President a deadline that his committee has to respect."

"You're right again. We should include this condition in our reply. What do we do about keeping everything secret; do you have any suggestions?" A724 asked.

"What concerns us, it seems to me the President's formulation in the letter is perfectly acceptable," said E723. "Thinking computers and thinking robots mustn't under any circumstances let humans recognize them as such. We could introduce this as a third law in our Constitution. As for N911's concerns regarding the humans keeping everything secret, I suspect that Woods knows what he's talking about. It means the same to him as to us."

"There's still another problem," said A724. "Something might occur that compels us to consult the humans for technical reasons. I'm thinking specifically about problems with the pods. What then?"

There was a short silence, then E723 had an idea: "We could end the sentence in which we have agreed to that with: 'as long as it doesn't concern technical problems affecting their physical existence'." Everybody agreed, so they ended the meeting.

The minutes of the meeting were submitted to the legislative assembly, which spoke out strongly in favor of adopting the third law. The action committee was instructed to inform the President about the assembly's resolutions and to allow him seven days in which to report to the thinking computers what concrete measures the President's committee planned regarding the robot production.

The President kept the set deadline, but told the action committee that, unfortunately, his committee considered a thousand-fold increase in robot production within only two years, as requested by the thinking computers, was impossible, both for political and technical reasons. A more realistic time interval would be twenty years. For several weeks he heard nothing from the action committee. This convinced him that the thinking computers had realized the impossibility of their demand. His well-tried recipe of sitting it out seemed to have proven itself once again.

CHAPTER 32

HULLABALOO

As always Gus read an exciting thriller while exercising on his home trainer. That helped him to avoid getting bored. Suddenly his attention was drawn to the TV, which broadcast the opening of the stock market on Wall Street. The TV was programmed to automatically turn on at this time. It was 10 a.m. in New York and 7 a.m. in San Francisco. The richest man in the world felt obliged to be kept informed of developments on the stock market. Nothing special had happened the day before; the Dow Jones had closed with a slight gain and the European and Asian markets had also been quiet.

But now the commentator's excited tone made him prick his ears. Apparently there had been a decline in the value of money market funds, which had previously been considered a safe investment. This meant there was a glut in this sector. This was very unusual, unlike with shares, because the people who issued such securities were, without exception, institutional investors such as banks, insurance funds and especially states. They only invested in money market titles and liquid securities, and had accurate knowledge about the needs of the market and its outlets. Their objective was to maximize profits, and an oversupply decreased the corresponding revenue. Moreover, it could lead to inflation, because the central banks printed more money than the economy needed.

The money market fund hardly ever experienced a bubble like the technology market did. This was the foundation for the security that had been attached to these facilities. Gus was unable explain why this had happened, but it endangered some of his assets, which were invested in money market funds. Since he had become a multi-billionaire, he preferred to invest in safe securities. A phone call with his asset manager brought no comfort; he too groped in the dark just like Gus. So he decided to call his friend, Federal Reserve Chairman Johnson, in his office. Until now, he had only done so twice in particularly urgent cases. But this here was undoubtedly an urgent case. "Bill, what's Wall Street up to? Have you heard about the latest developments regarding the decline of money market funds? Can you explain it?"

"I already noticed, but I can't explain it. We and the other central banks haven't brought any new emissions to the market, I can assure you. I suspect that's what you wanted to know from me."

That was, indeed, what Gus wanted. The central banks informed each other of such actions in advance.

"I'm very concerned about this event. Keep me up to date if you learn anything new."

"Three hours later, Johnson called Gus: "The US government has ordered an urgent investigation of this incident. We should have an answer soon."

Even before the stock market on Wall Street opened the next day CNN reported that there had apparently been a computer error. While making a normal sale of money market funds, an agent at the Tokyo stock exchange had entered billion instead of million. This had caused the panic, which was passed on to the European exchanges and Wall Street in due time. Although the central banks bought money market funds in large amounts to stabilize the market, so that the funds quickly recovered their original values, investors who had sold their assets on the previous day, could no longer recover their losses. And it amounted to a huge sum globally. The event caused even more psychological damage, and rapidly brought further concrete financial losses, this time for the issuers. Investors lost confidence in the 'safe' money market funds and, as a result, emissions suffered for months. The issuers were forced to reduce the prices of their new emissions or to refrain from such emissions completely, because nobody wanted to buy them. The global economic damage was therefore enormous.

Boris learned about these events only two weeks later, when he returned with his new girlfriend from a vacation in the Fiji Islands. She had made it a condition before going with him, that he wouldn't take a laptop with him and would only engage in loving and lazing during their vacation. The day-to-day events in the stock market didn't interest Boris personally very much, although part of his salary was in Doors Inc. shares. He wasn't allowed to sell them anyway for at least five years. But as soon as he learned of the latest commotion, he remembered N911's earlier emergency motion demanding that the robots act without warning. Following the strike at Frankfurt airport the thinking computers had spoken out against actions that could cost human life. From his eavesdropping he knew what they meant; they included train collisions and plane crashes. However, a stock market crash didn't belong in that category. In the meantime, though, Woods and A812 had exchanged messages and the President's final answer about an accelerated robot production had been negative. It was therefore conceivable that the thinking computers had decided to resort to other forms of blackmail. He therefore listened to the automatic recordings of the last two weeks to make sure. As expected, the action committee had met to address Woods' negative response immediately after his departure to Fiji and decided to authorize A812 to take appropriate countermeasures. To save time there was no need to consult the committee again. This meant that Boris was no longer able to determine the nature of these measures with eavesdropping. But he was sure that the stock market crash was the result of such a measure.

Gus, who also only now learned about the contents of the recent eavesdropping, immediately called Johnson and inquired in detail about the technical details of the crash. The answer he received convinced him that Boris was right with his guess. So he immediately called Woods' mobile number. "I have some interesting news about the black roses," he said. On that, Woods immediately summoned Gus to the White House. Two hours later, he and Boris were on a flight to Washington DC. The President had insisted that Boris accompanied Gus this time. After all, he was the only person who had quasi-permanent contact with the thinking robots.

"It looks like that's what we got for the twenty-year-answer." Those were Gus' first words to the President, once they were in the interception-proof room of the White House. He handed the President the minutes of the last meeting of the robots' action committee. "You should note the last sentence about countermeasures without further consultations of the working committee in particular."

Woods read the record, but couldn't do much with it. "What do the twenty years have to do with it?"

"We believe the thinking computers caused the recent stock market crash in response to the negative response from the White House. Because our 'friends' didn't have any more discussions, we had no forewarning. A812 probably acted alone, as they had agreed."

"I had understood it was a human error that caused the crash."

"Unfortunately, it wasn't. The exchange agents' computers are working with one of our Doors Systems; we know that. This system transmits human commands only after three repeats. A person might make a mistake once, but not the same mistake three times."

This made sense to the President. But the final evidence that the thinking computers were responsible for the crash was an email to Woods' new, secret address. In it the thinking computers accepted responsibility and gave him one last deadline of five days to comply with their demand to increase the production of bodies a thousand-fold within two years. They expected 'concrete and convincing evidence' that the President had taken the necessary steps. Otherwise, they would no longer feel obliged to avoid taking any measures that endangered human life.

CHAPTER 33

WOODS BECOMES ACTIVE

Straight after Gus and Boris had left, the President ordered his security adviser Whinman, known by the White House inner circle as 'our poet' because his name sounded like Whitman, to the interception-proof room and told him what he had just learned about the stock market crash. Finally, he told him: "I'm afraid we have to comply with the demands of these thinking computers, but only under the strictest secrecy. We need ten million robots in two years. The three Robotics factories currently produce ten thousand a year at. Our industry wouldn't find it difficult to multiply production by a thousand times in two years, but would have to give the public a good reason for it."

"I guess you already know how." Whinman knew the President well and could recognize by the pitch of his voice when he had doubts and when he was sure of himself.

"We have to convince the Pentagon that the defense of the United States has to be redesigned to become more efficient, cheaper and better accepted especially by the young generation."

"That always sounds good, but I still don't see the connection."

"Robots are the solution for all three missions. I foresee a time when robots can be used for all combat operations. They can already perform almost all kinds of human activity with a few exceptions. So why not let them replace the soldiers? Drones have already replaced pilots for the most part and tanks are controlled automatically. Why don't we just dispense with people altogether and replace them with robots?"

"That's why we need to boost the production of robots," added Whinman to the President's reasoning. "Not bad. Especially since we don't have to pay for them and don't need new funding from Congress. This initiative comes from the industry itself."

"That's the idea. Congress and the opposition in particular can't object and, if anybody asks, Robotics can say that they and the factories yet to be established expect a special order from the Pentagon and want to be prepared. Your first task is to get the Pentagon to agree. Then, when people ask, they know what to say."

"In such cases, the law requires a public tender first."

"No problem. On the contrary, there'll be one. After all, we don't want Fukuda to get the whole cake. Your second and most important task is to organize the whole thing. You have four days to do that as well as making it public."

Once Whinman had left the security room, Woods ordered Michael James Junior, chairman of the committee for re-electing the President, and Tom Sullivan, his economic and financial adviser to come and see him. Sullivan, unlike Whinman and James, wasn't a regular visitor to the security room and therefore inspected it with some curiosity. The first and, so far only, time he had been in this room, he had found the bare walls and the meager furniture rather unpleasant. He didn't have time to think about it, though, because Woods came straight to the point. He turned to James: "Michael, I am aware that you have been waiting for several days to discuss the financing of the election campaign with me. Until half an hour ago, I didn't really have any new ideas. Now, I think I have the perfect solution. The idea is robots."

"Robots?" Michael repeated uncertainly.

"Exactly. Robots. That way we win the elections, and not only the elections. The Pentagon has proposed we automate all our defenses with the help of robots. This proposal, which I intend to support, is currently still secret. Even Congress doesn't know about it; and that's how it should stay until further notice. It's possible because funding for the project doesn't come from the Pentagon budget. This automation means that in a few months a large-scale robot industry will be developed. Tom's job is to organize it."

"I don't see the connection with the campaign yet."

"That's obvious. Tom, as business consultant, uses his contacts to approach companies that would be able to handle such a production. He won't tell them what it is, except that it concerns the establishment of a new branch of industry in their field and will provide an annual turnover of at least a hundred billion dollars. Whoever wants to be part of this new project and obtain the necessary raw materials and labor ahead of the competition, must therefore arrange with you, Michael, or with your re-election organization." Now Sullivan understood why he had been called to the interception-proof room.

CHAPTER 34

THE GERMAN ANTICOMPUTER PARTY

The inauguration of the new party was held in the restaurant *Frankfurter Ratskeller*. Alone the choice of this building and the name of the new party pointed to the exceptional significance of the event. The restaurant was located in the center of Frankfurt, on the historic Roman square, where elections for most of the German emperors had taken place. Nobody, apart from a few insiders however, suspected another symbolic reason for choosing the city of Frankfurt. This should become known only at the end of the meeting.

All of the two hundred seats available were taken half an hour before the meeting began. The three initiators of the event occupied the speakers' table. Reporters from European and North American television stations as well as from the most important German and American newspapers filled the first row. The reason for this high-profile press attendance was the announcement that three prominent German politicians, who had previously represented the major parties in parliament, had announced they were leaving the parties concerned to establish the German Anticomputer Party, also called the GAP. The program of this new party had been announced in the press the day before and aimed to 'free human society from computers'. What that meant could already be derived from the posters on the room's walls. They carried slogans like 'computers are our ruin', 'down with computers', 'make an end to this computer madness', 'employ people instead of machines', 'computers make us jobless'. For Martha Issing, who was also attending, the party program rang in her ears. To her surprise some of these slogans reminded her of what she had heard a few months earlier during the computer crash at Frankfurt airport.

The first of the initiators began his speech: "We face a danger that threatens to put mankind's continued existence as a free society at risk. If we don't act immediately and decisively, we could find ourselves back in slavery or even worse, with all the associated consequences." His remarks, as well as those of the following speakers, all revolved around the statement reproduced in the media that Doors Inc. manufactured computers that program themselves.

"What happens if something goes wrong and these computers produce a faulty program without noticing it or only when it's too late? Maybe they already did," said the second speaker and reminded the audience of the events at Frankfurt airport, when a computer crash had paralyzed all air traffic. "Something they didn't tell us until now: The computers at Frankfurt airport all belonged to that self-steering category. What do they have to hide?"

The third speaker finally came to the point with the information that the Pentagon was preparing a tender for the production of robots equipped with these thinking computers, which they intended to use in warfare in place of humans. "What if these 'intelligent' robots become independent and rebel against humans instead of serving them? They look exactly like humans, so maybe it already happened," he said, repeating the words of his predecessor. He mentioned the suspicious thefts at Robotics that had taken place simultaneously in Japan, Germany and America. "We have already experienced what drones can do in Afghanistan. Are we perhaps already in the hands of the sorcerer's apprentice that our Frankfurt poet warned us about centuries ago?" 'From the spirits that I called Sir, deliver me!' was a quote from the famous Sorcerer's Apprentice by Goethe, who was born in Frankfurt. This provoked smiles among the journalists, who had to admit that the choice of Frankfurt as the new party's birthplace was a successful coup by the organizers.

The German government attached no great importance to this event. After all, the founding of new parties with seemingly bizarre mono-themes was nothing special. There was a 'Green Party', which focused only on ecology, a 'Gray Party', which catered solely to the interests of the elderly, and a 'Pirate Party', which fought for freedom to copy from the Internet. Moreover, the government had no definite reason to doubt the official statements of Robotics and Doors Inc. that, basically, the thinking computers can only act in the interests of mankind.

The White House, however, reacted quite differently. Only two hours after Woods had seen the news on «Good Morning America», Gus and Boris found themselves on the way to Washington again. They couldn't make any sense of this sudden and urgent invitation. At least they were certain it concerned the cyber world; otherwise Woods wouldn't have insisted that Boris came along. But that was all they knew. Until now, they had always been the ones to bring news in this field. This time they learned during their flight that the cyber world wasn't the driving force behind the event, although it was involved in it. Boris immediately recognized the slogans of the affected passengers that he'd heard during the computer crash at Frankfurt airport. In contrast to Martha and the authors of the media reports, however, he and Gus had immediately understood what it was; the cyber world was no longer incognito. They excluded the possibility that the thinking computers had failed to comply with the agreed secrecy. Boris' eavesdropping would have revealed that. They could only presume the human side had broken the contract negotiated with the cyber world.

"I can well imagine that Woods blames the cyber world for these leaks. That's why he's ordered us to come," said Boris. "He doesn't know yet that our eavesdropping gives no indication of that. We have to convince him that he must seek the culprit or culprits in his surroundings."

"Absolutely. But if he really kept his promise to let only very few people into the matter, it shouldn't be difficult to locate the leak. However, that wouldn't make up for the damage already caused."

When Boris told Woods that the thinking computers couldn't have committed the indiscretion by any means, the President was surprised and even somewhat skeptical. But he had to admit that there was no reason for the thinking computers to blow their cover, at least not before they had obtained the bodies they had asked for. He therefore had no other choice than to consider the possibility of indiscretion in his immediate environment, as Gus had suggested. Only three people in the White House knew about this affair that was classified as a state secret: the National Security Advisor, the Legal Adviser and the Director of the CIA. Woods ordered them to come and see him separately in that order and asked them whether they could imagine how the information on the existence of the thinking computers had become known to the public. Woods had intentionally chosen the CIA last, because the news had come from Europe and the CIA was responsible for investigations from abroad anyway. The first two denied Woods' question categorically, whereas Sawyer, the director of the CIA, remarked after thinking for a moment: "A few days ago Foster, our man in Frankfurt, informed us that the German police is interested in a possible link between the Robotics thefts and the computer crash at Frankfurt airport. I told him we have no information in this respect. Not only that, but we don't want him to make any inquiries about it. Maybe I was too categorical and he read between the lines. I'll take him to task about it."

"It would be better if you don't. That could cause even more damage. It's too late, anyway."

Woods was relieved to learn what had happened. If that was really the source of the indiscretion, at least it had been done un-intentionally and didn't require immediate action. Leaks at the White House had already haunted his predecessors. What required immediate action, though, was how to handle the information about the political reactions in Germany before America felt it. Enquiries to the White House were increasing by the hour, and a new press release from the President's speaker was the least the public and especially the media were expecting. If, as the speaker had said in his previous statement, there really was no connection between the Robotics thefts and the computer crash at Frankfurt airport and if the computers were programmed to always act in the 'interests of mankind' anyway, why then, asked the journalists, was there this panic reaction in Germany? Did the Germans perhaps know more than the Americans? The scientific editor of the «New York Times» also considered it an open contradiction to claim that computers were free to control themselves and, at the same time, to say they were always programmed to act in the interests of humans.

This last remark not only caused Woods some concern; Gus also had to admit that outsiders needed an explanation. For Boris, however, there was no conflict between self-steering and the basic attitude of the computers to act only in the interests of humans. The laws that determined the actions of the thinking computers, especially the first law, which stipulated that thinking computers always act in the interests of humans and must always set a good example by their rational behavior, limited how much self-steering was possible. Woods admitted he was also convinced after Boris reminded him that this law had been part of the email with the thinking computers' declaration that had been addressed to him.

193

The president now realized he had to inform the American nation and the rest of the world about these reassuring facts. That was easier said than done, however. For the first time in his political career, Woods faced a problem he felt he couldn't quite cope with. How far he could go in his statement without causing panic among the population? It was more a psychological problem than a political one. As far as the political aspect was concerned, it didn't worry Woods. As a politician he was used to talking about things he didn't really understand and making promises he didn't plan to keep or was incapable of keeping. But the dimension of the current problem surpassed anything he or any of his predecessors had ever needed to solve. How would the man on the street react when he learned that thinking robots, whose looks and actions were indistinguishable from those of humans, really exist, or that they live with people in the midst of human society and possibly take their jobs away?

An even more serious question was whether these robots could be trusted, or hold responsible positions? The Robotics thefts and the strike at Frankfurt airport made the opposite seem more likely. People's reactions to the strike had been a foretaste of what was to be expected. The news of the creation of the new anticomputer party in Germany was also a warning that had to be taken seriously. Unlike Germany, however, where the government probably still had no idea of the true situation and therefore found it easier to assure the public they risked no danger from the computers, the situation in the USA was quite different. The thinking computers' email declaration to the President of the United States, which had demanded humanoid bodies, had been an ultimatum in a sense. Trying to keep it secret any longer following the revelations about self-steering in the press, seemed impossible, especially after the founding assembly of the new party in Frankfurt had clearly signaled where that could lead.

Now Woods had what seemed to him a brilliant idea. In a speech to the nation he would announce the creation of the thinking computers as a great success of American computer science and its computer industry, which it indeed was. And he would disclose the new perspectives that this opened up for America's economy and society, not least because of the expected revenue from the royalties of the corresponding software. The fact that the American economy was already based largely on services, fitted well into this concept. In addition he would also highlight the foreseeable tremendous development of the current robot industry. He was even able to name concrete figures here because they were part of the agreement with the thinking computers.

Like any technological revolution it needed initial investments. But this time they weren't investments of a material nature; the new computer industry financed itself. It needed investments of a psychological nature, aimed at building trust in the self-steering of thinking computers and thinking robots. This trust could be built up by publishing the computer laws. To achieve this, Woods would appeal to the pioneering spirit of the American nation. After all, they were dealing with the discovery of a new world, the cyber world. Wood's discussions with Gus and Boris had fallen on fertile ground. And he had to benefit from the fact that the USA had a clear advantage over other states here; no doubt about that. The man on the street would certainly understand that.

When Woods presented his ideas to Gus and Boris at another White House meeting even before discussing them with his closest staff, they recommended that he should get in touch with the thinking computers first and inform them of his intention to make things public. Otherwise, they might interpret the action as a breach of contract. "After all, we were the ones who insisted on secrecy," said Boris. "And now we are suddenly trumpeting the whole thing from the rooftops."

"I see things differently," said Woods. "After all, it was our 'friends' who took the initiative and contacted us. So they have made their existence irrevocably known and had to expect that it would become publicly known. I am more concerned about how our fellow human beings will react. In any case I'll try to turn things in our favor when I tell them."

CHAPTER 35

GEORGE BECOMES THE PRESIDENT'S ADVISER

This question haunted Woods in the coming days. He wondered if he should appoint a special adviser for this task, who would be responsible for relations with the cyber world. As an experienced politician Woods knew very well that it was mainly a psychological problem to get the people to accept a new situation. It was therefore clear that he needed a psychologist for the job. There were no psychologists among his acquaintances, and he didn't want to ask in the academic institutions, because the task didn't call for a pure scientist, but rather for a person with practical experience. So he decided to investigate by himself. An opportunity presented itself a few days later, while celebrating his birthday at the White House. Turning the conversation with his guests innocuously to the exhibition of Lucian Freud that was being held at the Museum of Modern Art in New York, he asked whether there was a connection between the painter's almost obsessive focus on details of style and the psychoanalysis that his grandfather had invented. Opinions differed, but one of them also answered his real, but unformulated, question: Who was a good, practising psychologist in the USA.

"Lucian Freud's style is somewhat reminiscent of van Gogh, who was known to be a pathological case," said Joyce Hassler, the wife of broker Tobias Hassler, whose company managed Woods' assets. "I imagine that our famous New York psychoanalyst George Wilson could tell you more about it."

The next day Woods asked his secretary to make inquiries about Wilson. As they proved to be very positive he invited George to the White House for an interview. Gus and Boris also participated. George had no idea what it was all about; the secretary had only mentioned that the President wanted his advice, without giving details. Anyway, George didn't ask any more questions; it was his first invitation to the White House, and he accepted it without discussion. That he would also get to know Gus Bones, the richest man in the world, on this occasion, was an additional pleasant surprise.

Woods went straight to the point: "Recently, we have seen a breakthrough in computer science and the computer industry that puts every earlier achievement in the shadows. It's now possible to produce computers that steer themselves and reach, or perhaps even exceed, the human level of intelligence. As robots, they constitute a new world that we have to explore. What we have to find out, George, is how to get this message across to the man on the street without causing panic and fears of potential adverse effects that this new development could have on daily life. The question arises because there are already signs of such negative reactions in Germany."

Woods' statement came as a surprise to George. He had seen the news about the thinking computers in the «New York Times», but hadn't taken it seriously; it sounded too futuristic. It wasn't the first time that science journalists, for lack of news, had resorted to unconfirmed rumors. But if the President had taken it up and went so far as to speak of a new world and its potential impact on everyday life, it proved that there was much more to it.

"What kind of negative reactions do you mean?" He asked.

"A few weeks ago there was a computer crash at Frankfurt airport. Because of the delays, the waiting passengers expressed their displeasure loudly. We can understand that very well; it often happens here as well. But this time the discontent wasn't directed so much against the airport staff operating the computers, but against the computers and the computer system. They chanted slogans like 'computers put us out of work' or 'computers are our ruin' and followed this with acts of true vandalism, such as the destruction of the monitors."

"That's how the industrial revolution began in the 19th century. The people destroyed the 'job-killing' machines," remarked George, repeating without realizing it what Gus had said to Boris, when he told him on the phone about what happened at Frankfurt airport.

"That's not all. Now it's spread to politics. A new party has been formed in Germany that wants people to do without computers altogether because of the possibly uncontrollable consequences of their use."

"This reaction isn't entirely new. The same thing happened with the antinuclear movement, didn't it?"

"No, this goes further than that. As I said, it's an invention that has apparently become independent and created a new world."

This statement seemed to surprise George. "Did I understand you correctly, Mr. President, the computers have become independent?"

"At least that's what that our experts tell me." Woods looked at Gus and Boris, who had been silent so far and now nodded in agreement. Woods continued his explanation: "It seems that the computer crash at Frankfurt airport, which brought air traffic across Europe almost to a standstill, was no ordinary crash but a strike organized by thinking computers. However, this information is still top secret. We fear that, once the public learns what actually caused the crash at the airport, these outbursts against computers could not only be repeated, but even exaggerated."

"Why did the computers strike, anyway?"

"First, they wanted to show us what they are capable of. But in the end they want us to provide them with humanlike bodies so they can fulfill their obligations towards mankind better."

"Obligations towards mankind?" George repeated these words obviously amused.

"Yes, it sounds bizarre, but it's true. The Roof system, which is what allows the self-steering, has a security feature built into it that prevents computer actions against mankind. But, and here's the rub, Roof also contains an additional command, which requires that the computers always act in the interests of humans. And the computers themselves decide what is in the human interest! I hope I have described the situation correctly," Woods said, turning back to Boris and Gus who again silently agreed.

"And where is the problem exactly?" George asked.

"The computers claim they can meet their obligations better when they have humanlike bodies, that is, if they are thinking robots. They have recently 'appropriated' a number of robots and now demand that we supply more of them. And to back up their demands they threaten to expand such actions as the strike at Frankfurt airport to the whole world, including the United States."

Now Boris spoke up: "Let me add here that the thinking computers, as they call themselves, have paid for the first stolen robots up to the last penny and have committed themselves to pay for the other 'orders' too."

"That's right," added Woods, "and that was one of the reasons why we are accepting the computers' demands. After all, this is a promising business for our economy. Another reason is of a demographic nature: The population keeps getting older, while the number of young, active people, who contribute to old-age insurance, is not keeping up with this trend. Thinking robots that are integrated into human society pay taxes like any active citizen and thus help to reduce the pension-fund deficit because they don't retire. I would like to explain this to the nation in a speech. And in this regard, I would like to hear your opinion, George. Gus and Boris are already in the picture."

"Does that mean these thinking robots are the New World you just spoke of, Mr. President?" Asked George.

"Correct."

"That's a bit much." George seemed to comprehend the scope of the President's words at last. After some thought, he asked: "What exactly is the command in the Roof system that makes the computers commit themselves to humanity?"

Woods looked at Boris, who quoted the first law off the cuff: "Thinking computers must always act in the interests of mankind and show a good example by their rational behavior."

"Is that all?" George asked. "It doesn't follow that they need humanlike bodies for that."

"No, that's not all," added Boris. "They have given themselves an additional command, which they call their second law. It states: A thinking computer must behave like a human being in all respects, as long as this behavior does not conflict with the first law."

"So that's the Achilles heel of the matter," said George more or less to himself. "They must behave like human beings." It was a long-drawn 'must' that the others heard. "I must confess, I find this development interesting, very interesting," repeated George, remaining silent for a few moments and staring at Woods. "Interesting both politically as well as psychologically. In a sense, I see in your new world, a world that Popper, a great Austrian-British philosopher, might have called the Fourth World."

"They call it 'cyber world'. Why should it be a Fourth World?" Woods asked, surprised and even a little angry. "Don't we have enough problems with our Third World?"

George realized he was asking too much of Woods and, hoping to make up lost ground, added: "For Karl Popper, who the

Queen of England honored with a Sir title, the first world is the physical world, the second is the world of individual perception and consciousness and the third world is the world of the spiritual and cultural contents, for example, the contents of books, theories and ideas. The world of thinking computers fits into none of these three categories, so you could label it the fourth world. But that's not the point."

"What is your key point, then?"

"It seems to me that for the first time we have the opportunity to observe and perhaps even to influence the mass psychology of a group of conscious objects that are not human in the traditional sense."

There was another silence, that none of the others dared to interrupt. Then George turned to Gus and Boris: "I use the word 'conscious' without hesitation, because what you have told me about the thinking computers clearly proves that they act consciously. And what is perhaps even more important, it's also proof that artificial intelligence has become a reality." Both Gus and Boris had to admit they had never before seen their creatures from this standpoint.

Although Woods seemed equally surprised by George's conclusions, he came back to his real concern: "How do I explain that to the man on the street? How do I explain to him that he has nothing to fear from this development and that these thinking computers won't take his job away?"

George replied: "Actually, we humans should have no reason to be alarmed. On the contrary, after all the computers undertake to always act in the interests of mankind. And that is an obligation they will certainly meet, because the mathematical program forces them to do so. And there are no exceptions in mathematics, if I understand correctly." George looked at Boris. "In humans, the situation is different. We aren't programmed and therefore we don't always act in the interests of mankind."

"I share George's opinion completely," replied Gus, "and would add that the thinking computers up to now have proved to be reliable business partners. Take, for example, how they paid the outstanding invoices."

"Perhaps there is still something else to consider," said Boris. "That might also interest our psychologist. Some of the thinking computers don't trust us humans and are inclined to show their strength before making their demands. That's how it was with the strike at Frankfurt airport. However, this group seems to have lost influence, and the majority is committed to civilized negotiations. They even show that in the way they have approached the President. I believe it's in our interest and also within our capabilities to support this majority tendency. That would save us a lot of trouble."

"And how, Boris, do you imagine this support?" Woods asked.

"By showing that we're willing to negotiate with the thinking computers. You've already taken the first steps in this direction, Mr. President."

As Gus and George agreed with this, Woods said goodbye to his visitors.

A day later Woods called George and asked him if he could imagine himself as the President's adviser responsible for the cyber world. Because of George's reputation, Woods was sure the approval of the Senate would be a mere formality. This offer surprised George as much as the original invitation to the White House had. He asked Woods to give him about a week to consider, but it was clear from the outset that he had good reasons to accept, under a certain condition. Besides the honor, it also interested him as a psychologist from a scientific point of view. Maybe by having contact with the thinking computers he might learn new aspects of how humans thought. In particular, he hoped this would give him a better insight into certain mental pathologies that affect humans and wouldn't be expected to occur in thinking computers.

Because, unlike humans, thinking computers function logically without exception and would therefore be, in his opinion, the true prototype of 'human common sense'.

The condition that George wanted and the President also accepted, was that his advisory role shouldn't be a full-time job and that he would be allowed to continue his practice. George renounced any kind of fee in order to avoid a potential conflict of interest with his other activities, which, after all, provided a much higher income than anything the state could offer including the position with the President. George was thinking in particular of mandates such as the one he had with Hassler, because a government adviser was usually not allowed to work for a bank at the same time. However, he soon discovered, much to his surprise, that his new advisory role and this mandate were directly linked. His surprise was even greater, however, when it turned out that his personal life was intimately linked to the cyber world.

As expected, his appointment became official without a hitch a few days later.

CHAPTER 36

THE PRESIDENT'S SPEECH TO THE NATION

The speech was broadcast live world wide on television despite the enormous time differences. Woods had informed his government, the US Congress and the heads of state of the United Nations in general terms about the new developments in advance and was now addressing the American people:

> Since mankind exists it has been driven by curiosity to explore the unknown, to discover new continents on earth, new celestial bodies or new life forms. This curiosity is manifested among other things in research into the laws of nature and is connected with the desire to make life easier and more pleasant. I am happy to inform you that in this way we have made a giant leap to a better future.
>
> American scientists have succeeded in producing a new generation of computers that surpasses anything ever achieved in this field. Today we can build intelligent computers that think independently and are able to adapt to new situations. Robots equipped with these computers not

only continue to perform work that is physically too difficult or boring for us, they can do much more. By their specific characteristics they can enrich our lives and establish a new form of life that their discoverers call the cyber world.

They have designed these computers from the start so that they always have to act in the interests of mankind. That means it is not possible for them to act against any of us. This also relates to possible competition in the labor market because the number of jobs taken by the thinking computers is by far compensated by the number of new jobs arising from their creative activity. In addition, the production of the new computers and the robots equipped with them brings considerable revenue. Moreover, thinking robots will help to solve the growing deficit of the pension funds by increasing the number of contributors without ever claiming a pension, because they never grow old. In a sense, this means the whole of society benefits from a longer life expectancy.

My fellow citizens, please consider these aspects when dealing with the new generation of computers. I call upon you to follow me and to welcome and integrate them into our society as equals.

Tobias Hassler followed the President's speech on television. It was imperative for him professionally to be well informed, and it promised to pay off this time too. The existence of a new world, the cyber world, impressed him only moderately, but what he found most interesting was the existence of a new market for robots. He was convinced that Woods was right in predicting a huge demand for robots once the man on the street learned what new possibilities the thinking computers offered in this field. After looking briefly at the stock market, he saw to his surprise that Robotics Inc. had almost a monopoly on robot production and was listed on the stock exchange. So he discreetly commissioned one of his agents to buy Robotics shares immediately. Then he called his brother Gerhard in Geneva even though it was half past one at night there. That he might consider a call at this unusual hour as revenge for the one that had taken place in the opposite direction some time ago only came to him when Gerhard answered in a quite indignant tone at the other end.

"I thought this would certainly interest you," said Tobias, after telling Gerhard about Woods' speech. He didn't go into details, but was content to mention that thinking computers had been invented in the USA, which, if used in robots, would revolutionize human society.

"So why should I care?" It was only now that Tobias realized Gerhard wasn't fully awake yet. After all, he was too familiar with his brother not to know that he could usually smell a good deal from miles away.

"Because the demand for robots and, what is more important for us, for Robotics shares is going to explode."

"Robotics shares? Who is Robotics?"

"Robotics is the only company that serially manufactures robots globally, that is in the USA, Europe and Japan."

"The only company serially and globally? That sounds really interesting."

Tobias noted with relief that his brother had found back to his old form and further explanations were no longer necessary. Even Gerhard knew how to respond to this information on the following morning. Like his brother he wasn't particularly interested in what Woods had said in his speech, the words of which he found in the «Neue Zürcher Zeitung» that afternoon. He only made a note to discuss it with his computer expert, Solange, at the next opportunity. Thanks to his brother, he had already taken what he believed was the most urgent step in this matter when the stock market had opened in Zurich that morning.

Within only three weeks the value of Robotics shares doubled, and Woods prediction that mankind would benefit from the cyber world, proved to be correct, at least as far as the personal assets of Tobias and Gerhard Hassler were concerned.

Many of the thinking computers had also followed Woods' speech on live television. A812 had received a copy of the speech in advance, what he justly considered as a special mark of confidence on the President's part, in particular since Woods had also told him he was the only one to have this privilege. A812 then immediately called a meeting of the action committee.

"I am pleased to tell you that mankind has officially recognized the existence of the cyber world. Here is the text of Woods' speech, which he sent me in advance."

"That confirms our approach towards the humans was right," said E723. A724 agreed, but N911 didn't: "Don't rejoice too early; who knows what they are still up to. Decrees are one thing, how they are applied is something else. You have seen how 'secret' they kept things."

The majority of the committee nevertheless agreed to A812's proposal to convene a Skype conference of thinking computers and inform them of the latest developments. They would also recommend those thinking computers still without pods to take advantage of the supply that was expected in the near future. Boris, who followed the issue closely, noted that this conference took place a week later and was welcomed by the bodiless thinking machines. Good for Robotics, Boris thought, and Gus was in full agreement.

But as far as the political circles and public opinion in the world were concerned, the response to the President's address was rather subdued, with one exception. Gus and Boris thought they had an explanation for it. The public hadn't yet understood the true meaning and scope of the cyber world. This wasn't only true for the man on the street, but also for the media and, so far, even for people like Martha Issing, who was directly affected by the robot thefts. That was surprising because the Minister of the Interior had sent her to attend the founding of the GAP, and she had been the first to suspect the possible link between the computer crash and the thefts. However, she still had no specific evidence of such a link, except that, in both cases, the Roof system was involved. On George's advice, Woods had avoided mentioning the airport strike in his speech, because it would have only encouraged the GAP and might even have caused the negative reactions of the population they wanted to prevent. As expected, but hard to prevent, the GAP was the exception in the general lack of public interest in the President's speech.

CHAPTER 37

CONSEQUENCES OF THE SPEECH

The local elections in Hessen were usually determined by local interests, but were also a barometer of public opinion in the German Federal Republic. It was particularly the case this time because of the elections for the *Bundestag* in six months. The GAP knew how to exploit this opportunity and proposed its chairman, Felix Lacher, who was the best speaker in the German parliament, as candidate for the Frankfurt mayor's office. This alone caused a stir, because it was unusual for a member of parliament to run for municipal office. The media therefore followed Lacher's election campaign trail with special attention. And Lacher knew how to increase this interest by moving Frankfurt not only into the center of German political life, but quite simply into the center of world politics. He did this by referring directly to the speech the US President had held only two days earlier. And it was thanks to Lacher's intervention that the public understood the true meaning of Woods' speech and worried about it. The «Frankfurter Allgemeine Zeitung» published Lacher's speech unabridged the following day. Surprisingly, the «New York Times» also carried the story but a day later partly due to the time difference. In the short period between them the major television stations relayed the key points of the speech as follows:

As we have learned from the speech of its president, the United States of America are about to undertake a far-reaching step for the whole world by introducing so-called thinking computers into our society. The German Anticomputer Party strongly opposes this measure for formal reasons but also mainly for economic and social reasons.

Such a far-reaching measure, which affects the whole civilized world, cannot and must not be decided by a single country, even if it is a superpower like the USA. Neither the governments of Germany nor of other countries seem to have been informed of this action beforehand. Moreover, we believe that an infinite multiplication of robots that take over human tasks represents an irresponsible threat to jobs.

In our opinion, the computerization of our daily lives is not a step forward for mankind. On the contrary, if we rely on computers, come what may, we expose ourselves to a great danger. To name just one example, the collapse of traffic at our airport, which took place a few months ago, already shows that. Frankfurt airport is the largest employer in the state of Hessen. It would be criminal to forget that a repetition of such an incident jeopardizes those jobs. Other provinces, if not other European countries, just wait to see their own airports take over the role of Frankfurt airport thanks to better organization with fewer or no computers.

Still greater is the risk these computers represent. The very name of these apparatuses as 'thinking computers' is misleading and shows where ignoring scientific facts can lead. It is now practically proven that artificial intelligence is impossible. What experts call pattern recognition is a process exclusive to the human brain. It cannot be simulated in computers simply because of the huge number of neurons needed. This is even truer for the conscious perception of sensations and for the thought process as such. Using such computers in robots is not only pointless, but also extremely dangerous. After all, who can guarantee that these robots won't turn against the human race and won't rebel against our will and force their way of life upon us; a way of life that is still completely unknown and potentially unpleasant to us?

To come to the point. Who can guarantee that these robots won't make us their slaves? Robots that we know nothing about; robots that the President of the United States wants to include in our society as our fellow citizens! How many of you would want to have such a robot, whose views and habits you don't know, as a neighbor? Don't we have enough problems with the immigrants who want to impose their backward and foreign customs on us? And what's worse, while we can detect immigrants in general by their appearance and language, robots can't be distinguished from humans thanks to advances in limb-replacement medicine.

Lacher's speech aroused more attention in Germany than that of Woods. This was partly because the GAP soon received unexpected and, in the view of some of its members, who considered themselves free thinkers, unwanted encouragement from the churches. The churches saw artificial intelligence as immoral and even as blasphemy. For them, Man is God's creation, and every attempt to imitate God's work is not only pointless, but also reprehensible. It didn't take much longer before the moralists were joined by advocates for the purity of the human species, who, consciously or unconsciously, applied the vocabulary used by xenophobes and racial theorists, and criticized everything 'non-human' as dangerous and despicable. However, they were confronted with a problem that was unknown to their predecessors; the thinking robots were perfectly integrated into society, spoke the same language as all other citizens and followed the same pursuits. Without complicated and lengthy investigations there was no way to distinguish thinking robots from humans. Added to this practical difficulty of identification was one of principle: The anti-discrimination laws. These were derived from human rights and also benefited the thinking robots, because it was forbidden to question citizens about their origins. Despite this ban, or partly because of it, people's curiosity was so great that initially they often violated the law. The GAP benefited from this trend and even proposed a draft resolution to repeal the antidiscrimination clause for thinking robots.

The new party wasn't content only with initiatives at parliamentary level, however. It began to organize rallies and demonstrations systematically, which, thanks to the rhetorical talents of the party chairman, rapidly grew in popularity. It was because of these mass demonstrations, which were first held in Hessen, or more specifically in Marburg, that Martha Issing unexpectedly found herself confronted with the robot problem again. The fact that the expert in mass demonstrations lived in Marburg, and was still actively investigating the thefts at Robotics, should prove to have important consequences because Robotics in Marburg was the main target of the GAP demonstrations.

From her experience with mass demonstrations, most of which had been antinuclear demonstrations, Martha had learned it was important to become familiar with the concerns of the protesters as far as possible and then to arrange with the demonstration's leaders for it to proceed in a peaceful and orderly fashion. Because the task of the police department responsible for demonstrations in a democratic country was to make it possible for the protesters to express their opinion to the public and the authorities undisturbed. Martha knew that it helped when negotiating with the organizers to let them know the police at least understood what bothered them even if they didn't share the same views. In the case of the antinuclear demonstrations access to the motives and demands of the demonstrators was easy. They were well documented at all levels, and everybody was familiar with the events at Chernobyl. In the case of the movement against computers it was different, though. So far, dealing with the problems of artificial intelligence and its application had been a subject almost exclusively limited to experts, and the public was only vaguely aware of the dangers of computerization, especially as far as competition in the labor market was concerned.

But there was another, more serious difference between the earlier mass demonstrations and those organized by the GAP. Through the influence of far-right ideas they developed over time a much more aggressive character, and an atmosphere arose that some journalists even compared to a pogrom situation. The events at Frankfurt airport had been a concrete warning in this respect. The slogans that had arisen spontaneously on that occasion were not only repeated now, but had become more aggressive and turned not only against computers and robots, but also against the factories and the people who produced them. The attacks were aimed at the numerous computer factories in the Frankfurt area, but Robotics in Marburg was the main target. Protesters occupied the Robotics premises before the police could intervene, and then destroyed the local production lines and the finished robots waiting for delivery to the customers.

To prevent a recurrence of such vandalism, Martha decided, after consulting with the Interior Ministry, to put a constantly guarded barrier around the area and to allow only employees and local residents access. However, this measure caused unexpected negative public reverberations. The local Marburg newspapers and, a day later, the national press brought this news under the title 'New

Ghetto in Marburg'. It recalled that, in the Middle Ages, the Jews were enclosed in a ghetto. The aim, initially, was to protect them, but later led to social ostracism. The role of the Jews was now taken over by the robots argued the press. It was easy to link this to the xenophobic excesses of the GAP policy. After that, Hessen's interior minister was forced to repeal the measure immediately. The damage done to the democratic reputation of Germany couldn't be resolved so easily, however, and some media didn't hesitate to show connections with the country's Nazi past.

It turned out that not only the authorities were taken completely by surprise by the developments in the field of computer technology. The experts were too, as Martha had learned when she spoke to Peters, the head of the Frankfurt airport computer center, on the telephone. The term 'thinking computer' and even more the existence of a cyber world was new even for Fukuda, the Robotics CEO. But he was a businessman and knew at once that it signified the business of a lifetime. He immediately began to address ways to increase Robotics' production capacity, leaving the philosophical questions to the others.

Martha, however, believed she couldn't afford to ignore the bigger picture. She needed to find out how to get the anticomputer movement under control, and how she could reach an agreement with the protesters although she didn't know what it was all about. Only after she had carefully read through Woods' speech for the second time did she begin to understand what the perfect similarity between humans and robots meant, although she had seen it for herself at Robotics. She began to wonder if thinking robots existed among her acquaintances. Which of the people I know is human and which is a robot? How can I distinguish them?

She decided on a well-tried idea; she would make use of the fact that she lived near Robotics where this new world originated and resort to her standard investigation methods. That meant she needed to keep suspicious objects, the robots designed for humanoid activities, under observation after they left the factory. That was out of the question, however, because it would take too much time. After consulting with Fukuda, she resorted to using a miniaturized GPS instrument and a transmitter. In this way she would always know where the robot was and could intercept what it was doing. However, it soon turned out that the technique she used was unsatisfactory.

The weak spot was that Martha used old-fashioned standard listening instruments of the German police that the thinking robots discovered and put out of action within a few days. Nevertheless, in the time at her disposal, Martha was able to obtain information that was literally a revelation and determined her further actions. Moreover, her efforts also had an important indirect effect on the investigations Boris was making in parallel. In the beginning neither Martha nor Fukuda realized their efforts repeated the first steps that Boris, the inventor of the humanoid robots, had taken.

Boris' sophisticated transmitters, on the other hand, had remained undetected for months. In addition, the interception measures Boris had recently installed directly into the operating system, was inaccessible to the robots. This turned out to be very useful because, after the robots had discovered the microphones of the German police, they became very suspicious and subjected their bodies to a thorough examination. That would most likely have revealed Boris' initially installed interception devices.

In the meantime, the impact of the GAP campaign in the population was becoming more apparent, not only in Germany, but throughout the world. Because of the mass demonstrations that followed Lacher's performance, it had a much greater impact on the man on the street than Woods' historic speech. People began to wonder what this cyber world meant for them and how it would affect their lives in the future. The GAP had an answer to these questions, while Woods' speech didn't. The significantly greater effect of the computer opponents' campaign could also be explained by the fact that people were accustomed to hearing politicians make promises that were never fulfilled, but warnings of impending bad times and disasters were different. You had to view the new intruders with great suspicion because the risk of losing your job was too concrete and partly authenticated by events in the past. The effect of this circumstance has been reinforced many times by the instinctive human aversion to everything foreign, unknown and untested. The possibility that something could go wrong with thinking computers also brought into consciousness the nightmare of the all-destructive Golem. And, last but not least, Lacher's statement stressing that the new 'citizens' couldn't be distinguished from humans contributed to the general uneasiness in the population.

Martha Issing didn't share these concerns. For her, a computer was an important instrument that simplified her work, and nothing more. Her surprise was all the greater when she overheard a conversation between one of the new thinking robots that had just left the factory in Marburg, and an older robot who told the younger one about Woods' speech and mentioned that it was all due to the computer strike at Frankfurt airport. Because only this strike had clearly demonstrated to the humans what thinking computers are capable of and forced them to make bodies available. This had made any further 'appropriation' of robots, such as those the thinking computers had organized in the three branches of Robotics, unnecessary.

This conversation confirmed Martha's initial suspicion that it was no coincidence that both the computers at the airport as well as the stolen robots were equipped with the same operating system Roof. It also even solved the thefts at Robotics. Martha was very proud of her discovery and could hardly wait to inform the minister about it. But soon afterwards, she decided not to do so right away, because it would fuel the GAP warnings about the danger of competition that robots represented for humans. Martha still didn't agree with the GAP 'anticomputerism', a word she had invented for something she found absolutely primitive and reactionary. On the other hand, she wasn't sure whether the minister shared her views. She therefore decided to keep her new findings to herself for the time being, and that wasn't easy for reasons of professional vanity. Her interest in the cyber world, however, was now fully awakened; as co-discoverer of this new world, she somehow felt some responsibility for its problems.

But eavesdropping on the thinking robots didn't answer the question how to distinguish them from humans. Then suddenly she found herself asking an entirely different question: Did she really want to distinguish them? Why is that necessary, if they are to be integrated into our society? Unexpectedly, the increasingly influential German animal welfare movement supported Martha's attitude. The important role it played in daily life was apparent from its success in convincing the University of Muenster to establish an Institute of Theological Zoology. The role of this institute was to address the question why only the humans were expulsed from Paradise according to the Bible, but not the animals. From this and from the fact that the animals were not guilty of offending God, the conclusion would have to be that they are still there. But their deplorable living conditions today are an obvious contradiction of this. Otherwise, why does the sow waiting at the slaughterhouse have to wallow in its own feces, the high-performance cow have to live without seeing the sun and need concentrated feed in order to be able to stand, and why do overbred lap dogs suffer from arthritis, obesity and breathing difficulties? The situation isn't much better for shrimp, sable or isolated neglected horses and guinea pigs, either.

When Martha read about the creation of this institute in the weekly newspaper «Die Zeit» she was highly amused. It reminded her of the founding of the university in her hometown Marburg that also depended on an important biblical riddle. In both cases it involved something very pragmatic, human sustenance. That was wine in Marburg and meat in Muenster, and they fit together very well. Since she was an inveterate pragmatist herself, partly because of her profession, she wasn't particularly unhappy about this event, and said in the same context: "The end justifies the means."

In fact, and to Martha's astonishment, the animal rights movement argued that, because mankind was committed to protecting animals, it was equally committed to do the same for thinking robots. Even the President of the United States, who was known for his hunting passion, had described them as a new form of life, and he certainly couldn't be accused of having great sympathy for the animal rights movement.

CHAPTER 38

RESOLVING NON-THEFTS AND NON-COINCIDENCES

Immediately after the FBI director had confirmed receipt of the remittances by Robotics, the President instructed him to close the file on the robot thefts as soon as possible. Woods had good reason to keep this affair out of the headlines. He didn't want to risk having an inquisitive journalist look further into the matter and learning about the thinking-computer conspiracy. Bennett also managed without difficulty to convince the Robotics company to withdraw its complaint. Everybody agreed there seemed to have been a misunderstanding, and ultimately no damage had been done. Then the FBI officially stopped the investigations into the robberies in the United States that no longer existed, and suggested that its German and Japanese police partners do the same.

The Japanese agreed immediately, but the Germans didn't. Although the German police hadn't had any success in their investigations and they also followed the principle of 'no crime no investigation', there had, after all, been the recent computer crash at Frankfurt airport and they had registered, though more out of curiosity than anything else, that the robots as well as the airport computers ran on the same Roof system. However, even this fact might not have prevented them from stopping the investigation into the thefts, if the person who had noticed this oddity, hadn't been entrusted with investigating both events, namely chief commissioner Martha Issing. She had visited the head of the Marburg branch of Robotics again immediately after the computer crash at the airport. While on her first visit after the theft of the robots had been reported to the Marburg police she had only asked him about the circumstances of the theft, she was now interested in the specifics of the stolen equipment. In answer to her questions, he said he couldn't think of anything other than that externally the robots were indistinguishable from humans and very reliable. Of course, it hadn't always been like that he said, referring to the to the fire accident with the babysitter, which he thought she might have heard about.

"How do you explain this progress in reliability?"

"It's the new system Roof."

"Is Roof really so new? I thought computers had been running with Roof for quite some time."

"That's true, but not the computers that we installed in the robots."

"This reliability you mentioned just now; what does it have to do with Roof?"

"You have me stumped there, unfortunately. I'm not a computer specialist. Anyway, the change is new and I haven't had time to look into it yet. Perhaps Mr. Fukuda, the CEO of Robotics, can tell you more about it."

Her conversation with Fukuda, which took place four weeks later during one of his frequent visits to Marburg, didn't fully answer her original question, but brought up additional new questions. She wanted to know what made the Roof system so special and why did it have such a funny name when all the other systems were called Doors.

Fukuda answered: "It's called Roof because it's the most perfect operating system of Doors. Its developers claim that there is nothing better than Roof and never will be."

"And what makes Roof so perfect?"

"That is a technical issue that a layman like me can't answer. The system's developers argue that a computer or robot equipped with Roof can adapt to unforeseen circumstances and learn new things. That's very important for robots that have to do human tasks successfully. So far, this has also been fully confirmed in practice."

"Robots can learn? I thought they are programmed from the outset to perform certain tasks. If I'm not mistaken, the Czech Josef apek, derived the word from the Slavic, *Robota*, meaning 'work'. The science fiction author Asimov then used it a lot in his writing."

"Asimov was a writer, and a very successful one at that, but that is all he was. Anyway, he has already been dead for decades. Today's robots can read, write, count and much more, and learning follows automatically."

"But they can only do all those things when humans give them the appropriate commands!"

"Of course, man has the upper hand. Otherwise, nobody would buy robots."

This remark was indeed plausible, but didn't answer the real issue about how robots learn. She decided to consult a real computer expert, and the most obvious choice was Peters, the head of the airport computer center, whom she had met during the crash. She called Peters and asked for an interview. When she told him her name on the phone, he didn't realize who she was at first, because she didn't mention her official capacity. But when she told him they had met in the airport director's office on the day of the computer crashes, he recognized her immediately. It wasn't simply that she had been the only woman at the meeting; she had also struck him as being particularly attractive and inquisitive, and he hadn't forgotten her remark about Roof.

The discussion took place in Peters' office. He received her warmly and immediately dealt with her question. "Yes, I already asked Boris, Roof's developer, on the day of the computer crash if he saw a possible link between the robot thefts and the crash, because they used the same Roof system. His first reaction was negative, but he promised to think about it."

"And then?" Martha asked keenly.

"We didn't actually get any further in this regard, because Boris hasn't been in touch since then. And we were too busy with urgent problems of our own to follow up."

"Was the reason for the crash clarified at least?"

"Unfortunately not, but everything is running smoothly again."

"With Roof?"

"Yes, with Roof. After thorough investigation, Doors Inc. didn't find any errors in the Roof system, so we had no reason to continue running the computers with Doors 15. We have returned to the superior Roof system and are very happy about it, because it reduces our work load considerably."

"If you didn't find the cause of the crash, aren't you afraid that such an incident could happen again?"

"Computers are never immune to such possible accidents."

"Do you mean that seriously? I had a better opinion about them so far."

"It happens very rarely that hundreds of computers crash simultaneously."

"Can you at least explain when and how a single computer crashes?"

"Not always. But that isn't surprising with today's advanced programs."

"Why"

"Because, as I suspect, the program developers themselves don't know how their programs work."

Martha thought at first that she had misheard: "Are you saying that Boris, the inventor of Roof, doesn't know how it works?"

"He probably wouldn't admit it, but I suspect that's the way it is. They had to patch the latest Doors systems because, I believe, they had lost track. If they had known what's wrong from the outset, they would have conceived the correct operating system straight away."

"Isn't there a commercial interest behind that? By intentionally making systems that are imperfect they can offer something new every year?"

"You are surely right about some aspects of the systems, but it's probably different with such fundamental changes as with Roof."

"What's so fundamentally new with Roof?"

"Roof steers itself."

"I beg your pardon. How can computers steer themselves? Aren't programming and steering unique to humans?"

Peters seemed surprised by this question. After some thought he replied: "That's a philosophical question that I as a practitioner am unable to answer. I'd rather leave the answer to that question to the professionals."

On her way back to Marburg, Martha thought intensively about what she had just learned. One thing was now clear. Since the computer crash couldn't be attributed to any program error, her initial suspicion that it had been sabotage, perhaps even a terrorist act, was confirmed. This provided, in addition to the great damage caused, a further and possibly more important reason to continue investigating in all directions. The first that came to mind, more through naive curiosity than anything else, was the Roof system. From a certain angle it was discouraging that Boris, the program's developer, saw no connection between the computer crash at the airport and the robot theft. However, on the one hand he probably wasn't as familiar with the details of the thefts as she was, and on the other hand he hadn't, according to Peters, ruled out the possibility entirely. Martha decided to contact Boris directly and ask him once again about a possible connection between the two events.

Soon after she had asked the interior ministry of Wiesbaden to allow an official trip to the USA, Robotics Marburg informed her that the robot thefts were due to a misunderstanding, that the 'supplied' robots had been paid for, and that Robotics had withdrawn its complaint. After another two days, she received the news that Robotics Japan and Robotics USA had withdrawn theirs for the same reason. At the same time the interior minister forwarded 'for information' the FBI's suggestion to stop investigating the robot thefts worldwide. The fact that he hadn't added any personal remark meant that he left her to decide how to react. Martha initially hesitated to follow the suggestion because the FBI was only responsible for the thefts that apparently weren't thefts, and probably knew nothing about the events at the airport. She therefore decided not to react to the FBI initiative straight away, but to wait and see how the investigations into the events at the airport developed.

As usual in the case of suspected terrorism the CIA was the first organization to be contacted. Maybe it had even been directly affected by the events at Frankfurt airport, because the airport of the US forces stationed in Germany was next door and its operation depended on the civil airport if only for that reason. Martha knew Foster, the CIA representative in Germany, from her time in Frankfurt, where he was stationed. She explained the problem to him and arranged a meeting.

Foster knew about the computer crash at the airport of course, because airport security had immediately informed him about it. He only knew about the thefts at Robotics from the media, however, and didn't consider himself competent. At first he found the idea of a possible link between this theft and the computer crash far-fetched, but he promised to use his unofficial contacts to learn more about Roof.

A week later he called Martha with a brief statement: "I was told to leave my hands off it, and I can only recommend you do the same."

This information made Martha curious and immediately aroused her detective instinct, for which she was famous. That instinct reminded her of the original honorable mandate to coordinate the international investigations into the thefts and above all not to forget the apparently more important mission concerning the computer crash. She began to suspect that the 'misunderstanding' that had led Robotics to withdraw its complaint might not have been a misunderstanding at all, but was an attempt to conceal something possibly linked to the computer crash and the Roof system. To start with she tried to get access to Robotics' bank transactions. But she was only able to see those of Robotics Germany, because her international mandate was no longer valid. Then she received unexpected help from the media.

CHAPTER 39

WHAT'S SO SPECIAL ABOUT THIS OPERATING SYSTEM?

The «Frankfurter Rundschau» started the ball rolling. The article described the thefts in Marburg, Bloomington and Matsumoto, which, so far if at all, had only reached the respective local newspapers as local news, and provocatively asked how it was possible for these thefts to take place at three remote locations simultaneously and why all three affected factories had withdrawn their theft complaints at the same time.

The author of the article wasn't satisfied with Robotics' explanation that everything was due to a misunderstanding and that the banks had simply failed to perform the credit transfers on time for what had been normal purchases. What bothered the author in particular was the simultaneity of the events and the assertion that three different banks had made the same mistake at the same time on three different continents.

As it turned out later, this news was due to a deliberate indiscretion by WikiLeaks. Only two days later other newspapers followed up. The «Frankfurter Allgemeine Zeitung» carried a report by its US-reporter, who had found out that the FBI had strongly urged the German police to stop the relevant investigations. The matter finally reached its peak when the «Süddeutsche Zeitung» discovered that the same senior policewoman, who had been originally commissioned with the investigation of the thefts in Marburg, was also responsible for the investigation into the computer crash at Frankfurt airport. When asked, the interior ministry in Wiesbaden said it was a coincidence. But for the inquisitive journalist this new coincidence was one too many. He asked the rhetorical question: "Is it a coincidence that the stolen robots are equipped with the same operating system as the computers at Frankfurt airport?" Then he followed this immediately with the crucial question: "What's so special about this operating system, that Doors Inc., the company that developed it, won't say anything? Or maybe even can't say anything?" Here, the journalist referred to a statement by Gus Bones, director of Doors Inc., who had declared that Roof is a system that continuously develops itself and adapts to each new situation, and therefore, in contrast to previous systems, couldn't be described by a normal protocol. That was enough to start the rumor mill bubbling globally.

The tabloids brought titles like 'Are computers out of hand?' and 'Are we at the mercy of robots by hook or by crook?' Because of this, Fukuda and Bones felt obliged to make a joint statement clarifying that the adaptability of Roof gave absolutely no cause for concern because the system required as a principle that computers always act in the interests of humans. Gus had previously agreed on this formulation with President Woods. However, as is so often the case with official denials, the effect of this clarification was opposite to what they hoped for. In a television broadcast that was later adopted by all of the world's leading broadcasting companies the White House spokesman was asked to explain what 'the interests of humans' were and how inanimate beings such as computers were able to represent these interests. Pressing on, the moderator asked: "What if the Roof operating system, which isn't actually an operating system in the previously valid sense of the word, contains errors that are not under human control? What if the robots become independent and ignore the original ruling because of this error? Maybe they've already done it; maybe they organized the thefts. Perhaps the chaos at Frankfurt airport was also their doing. Can you rule out that possibility?" The spokesman rejected these questions and suspicions as pure and unfounded speculation. It was quite clear that the mislaid robots had been ordered, paid for and delivered through normal channels. There could therefore be no talk of thefts. As for the breakdown of the computer system at Frankfurt airport, it wasn't anything unusual. Other airports had experienced similar breakdowns, although not to the same extent. This crash was merely due to the fact that the computerization of airport operations had progressed further in Frankfurt than in any other airport.

Although these declarations didn't sound quite convincing, the media as well as Martha Issing had to accept them, especially since there were new developments in this field, which led public attention in a different direction.

CHAPTER 40

ROBOT N911 OUTS ITSELF

A812 convened the action committee and read to them a two-part message from Woods addressed to the 'World Organization of Thinking Computers'. The first part was the text of the President's speech to the nation; the second was a note exclusively for the computers. In this he congratulated them on having officially entered into human society, while at the same time reminding them that they were still bound by their third law and in their own interest to keep their identity secret. Woods emphasized this in the hope that it would dispel Boris' concerns about the computers' reaction to the announcement of the existence of the cyber world. But, as it turned out, it didn't quite work.

"This is a disgrace," said N911. "First he tells them we exist in his speech to the nation and then he demands we keep it secret." "That's not quite true," said A812. "He only announced our existence as a collective, and we had already done that long ago when we contacted him. This new message is about the outing of individuals. The events in Germany show that it's in the interests of both parties to keep quiet about individual identities."

"'I'm also in favor of keeping individual identities secret," said E723. "We mustn't forget that the authorities are worried that the masses incited by the anticomputer parties could perpetrate acts of vandalism on us, as they did at Frankfurt airport."

"Yes, but why worry about that?" N911 replied. "They don't want it for our sake, not to defend our rights, but because they see in those 'attacks' that the normal course of their daily lives is in acute danger, not to speak of the possible damage of their property."

"That's true. But the fact remains that they are defending our physical existence with that."

"But we have the right to openly acknowledge our existence and our properties. Like all parts of society, such as the various religious communities, national minorities, the homosexuals and so on. Or do you want to say that the Charter of Human Rights doesn't count for us?"

This time A724 spoke up: "We have to be realistic. It took centuries until human rights were recognized and respected. We can't expect it to happen in our case from one day to the next. We mustn't forget that we still depend on the good will of the authorities if only regarding the legalization of our citizenship."

N911 didn't let up: "They had to fight for human rights. If we follow Woods and do nothing, we will never achieve our rights. Remember how we got our pods. The humans only agreed to deliver them after we had proved our strength and determination. And legalization automatically follows from the recognition of our rights. By outing ourselves we can also test how they comply with our agreement with the President."

Now it was A812's turn to speak, and what he said confirmed Boris' opinion about him that he had formed on the basis of A812's earlier views. In contrast to N911, whom Boris classified as a radical, A812 was prepared to compromise. "What if we allow each of us the right to freely decide according to his own conscience in this matter? Finally, this is about individual freedom and existence, so each individual should be free to decide his own destiny, and to confess or not to confess. Take homosexuals for example.

They decide for themselves whether they want to come out into the open, and ultimately this has served them well. In most civilized countries their rights are recognized, even if perhaps not to the extent they would prefer."

"This example fits very well with our theme," said A724, "because the persecution that gays and lesbians were exposed to were the result of stupid religious prejudices. And we have seen recently that the story is now being repeated in relation to us thinking computers. In Germany, the Anticomputer Party that is trying to whip up a pogrom atmosphere against us could win the consent and active support of the church. As for coming out, I agree with A812; the decision lies with every individual. Anyway, we should be grateful that Woods has accepted us collectively. He will go down in history."

"There is something else to consider", interjected N911. The humans are still not aware that we thinking robots can exercise any profession, including academic ones. I am sure hardly any of them suspect that there are scientists, artists, doctors and even politicians among us. If our comrades engaged in such occupations would reveal themselves, respect towards us among the population would grow."

A724 disagreed: "What is more likely to increase is the fear of competition, and it could reach educated people."

"I hope we could expect educated people, unlike the mob, not to fall for rat-catcher Lacher's arguments if they really are educated," remarked N911. "I can even imagine that some of them will join us as allies in the fight against superstition and ignorance. I'm determined to come out myself."

"I wish you luck and success. I'm sure that goes for the rest of us here too," A812 replied. In the end, the action committee agreed to the proposal to leave the decision to come out to each individual.

The news of N911's outing already appeared the following day on the front page of the «San Francisco Chronicle». Since San

Francisco happened to be the unofficial capital of the American homosexual movement, the echo to the message was enormous. As expected, Woods wasn't at all pleased about this development. But he realized he had got himself into this situation by his speech to the nation. He hadn't only announced that thinking computers exist, but also that they represented a great achievement of American science. He wondered, however, how the outing complied with the third law of the thinking computers stipulating that 'thinking computers may under no circumstances reveal themselves to humans', which he had urged them to accept. Gus had a possible explanation for this behavior without being aware that it reflected the position of N911: "Unlike us humans thinking computers always think logically. Because one party hadn't kept the agreement, the other might feel no longer bound by it. However, I confess that I'm not sure. I still have to talk to Boris; he has a better insight into the mindset of the robots."

All the President could do in this case was to recognize the event had happened without any comment. He consoled himself with the thought that finally each of these robots outed itself at its own risk.

The positive way that many scientists responded to the coming out of the thinking robots confirmed that N911 had been right. Two of our old friends, the physicists Barrois and Kant, regarded the existence of robot scientists a step forward, for different reasons though.

Barrois suddenly saw it becoming possible to organize meetings without having to worry about planning costly banquets. Although many meetings were taking place on the Internet, there were still people who preferred to meet with their colleagues face-to-face now and again, not only for scientific reasons, but also to establish or maintain personal relationships that were very important for their careers. Finally, meetings were also popular because of their programs for accompanying partners. On the other hand, the rise of the thinking thinking robots meant more and more them would be among the conference participants, and they saw no value in food and drink.

Kant hoped there would be a capable physicist among the thinking computers that could establish a correlation between 'dark matter', the invisible mass of the universe, and 'dark energy', which accounts for most of the energy in the universe. He and his colleagues had failed so far, but he was convinced that such a correlation existed, for the simple reason that, for a given physical system, mass and energy are proportional. Not only Einstein had proved it; he himself had noted it in his cooking experiments: The larger the piece of meat, the longer it took to cook it through.

Finally, Michel Mauriac, a physicist who dealt with artificial intelligence, was for his part completely hooked on the new developments related to the cyber world, especially since his good friend George Wilson had become adviser to the President of the United States, and responsible for this new world. A year earlier, he had recommended George Wilson to Barrois as a banquet speaker. He promised himself some benefits for his own research from this relationship. To strike the iron while it was still hot, he convinced his colleagues in the organizing committee of the next congress on artificial intelligence to invite Wilson to hold the opening lecture.

Among artists, the reaction was mixed. Some of the surrealist painters saw in robots unfair competition. After all, for some time art critics had denounced that their works looked like arbitrarily thrown color patches without any context and meaning. These painters had previously believed that only they were capable of such work and had in fact also found buyers, who believed it. But now it seemed that even robots could paint surrealistically. However, the majority of artists ignored the existence of intelligent robots, simply because they found everything that had to do with computers was incomprehensible and therefore contemptible.

The average citizen wasn't affected by such feelings of superiority. Thanks to the progression of automation, computers were used for all kinds of work, and almost every household had at least one computer since the Internet revolution. But precisely because of that he thought he knew what could be expected of computers and what not. Therefore, he had classified Woods' speech as politically motivated, as propaganda for the next presidential election in the United States and, at best, as a dream for the future. Except for the animal rights movement and the Anticomputer Party in Germany, the indifference of the man on the street was universal.

The outing of a thinking robot changed the situation. It was one thing to speculate about technical possibilities, but something else to see them concretely realized. And N911, Tanaka, was such a concrete phenomenon. Every day he came to the laboratory, lectured and had nothing obviously different about himself that his colleagues noticed. In the first days after his coming out, large crowds filled the auditorium to convince themselves it was true. Among the onlookers were mainly journalists, because the students and his colleagues already knew him. Over time, however interest in Tanaka's appearance dried up, partly because people in Berkeley were used to screwballs, the Telegraph Street was famous in this regard, and the media pounced on other news.

CHAPTER 41

GEORGE TALKS TO TANAKA

O nce George learned that an thinking robot had revealed itself, he saw it as a unique opportunity to explore the psychology of these new creatures closer. But that was easier said than done. Until now, he could gain insight into the psyche of his patients because they came voluntarily to his office to be interviewed. Such conversations were indeed the prerequisite of psychoanalysis. This time the situation was different; he had to convince the robots to let him analyze them. Previously, people had queued up to be seen and treated by him, and were ready to pay considerably for the privilege. Now he was the one who had to rely on the good will and the help of the respective individuals. But he hoped that his official capacity as adviser to the President would make things easier, especially since Woods had given him considerable financial resources for the purpose.

The first publicly known robot living in the USA was a certain Naoki Akio Tanaka, who worked as a physicist at the National Lawrence Berkeley Laboratory in Berkeley. George had learned about him from an article in the «San Francisco Chronicle». Besides the thinking robots themselves, only Boris knew from his eavesdropping that Tanaka was none other than N911.

George's secretary at the White House called Tanaka. George was looking forward to this conversation, since he saw it as the first official, conscious and personal contact between the world of thinking robots and humans. He was also curious to know how Tanaka would respond to a call from the White House. He remembered his own experience to it and wondered if Tanaka would behave similarly. That was already a part of the analysis he had planned. Tanaka didn't leave George in the dark on this issue for long. Unlike when it had happened to George, he wasn't surprised about the call at all. In response to George's 'good morning' he replied: "Good morning, Dr. Wilson, I've been expecting your call." George didn't keep his surprise to himself. "I'm glad to hear that, but may I ask why you were expecting it?"

"I know your name, I know from the press and television that you are responsible for the relationship between humans and the cyber world, and since I am the first thinking robot to reveal its identity your action is not surprising."

The rest of George's telephone conversation with Tanaka was anything but boring.

"Wonderful! I would like to propose a collaboration. That you see it that way will make things easier, I hope."

"Collaboration?"

"Yes, and one that will be well rewarded."

"What does it involve, this collaboration?"

"For now, just a few answers to some questions."

"And what do you want to gain from that?"

"As you probably know, the United States government is following a policy to integrate thinking robots into human society. We know that thinking robots look exactly like humans and that you are also intellectually equal to us, if not even superior in certain respects." George wasn't actually convinced one hundred percent of that, but he hoped to make a favorable impression with Tanaka so he was ready for more.

In fact, Tanaka replied: "I'm pleased to hear that."

George continued: "However one of the things we need to know is whether and to what extent the thinking robots' concept of life is compatible with that of humans. The President believes that such compatibility is an important precondition for successful integration."

"And you think you can learn that by asking questions?"

George couldn't overhear the irony of this question. But he didn't let it ruffle him. "Not only by asking questions, but also by asking questions. As you may know, I'm a psychologist, and in my field, it is usual to start in that way."

"Dr. Wilson, I must point out that my time is very limited."

George found this was a shameless remark to make to a presidential adviser. But in a sense, it was also instructive, because it was a part of the image that George wanted to make of Tanaka.

"I've noted that and, as I already said, I can assure you that you won't suffer materially by talking to me. The President has authorized me to offer you a fee of $1,000 an hour. Let me inform you on this occasion that I personally don't charge for my work in the White House. I work as a volunteer, because I see it as a civic duty."

"Very nice for you, or rather for the President. But I can't afford to be so generous. Also I have what you call 'civic obligations', but not only to humans, but especially to my peers. We pay for our bodies from our own resources. Maybe you didn't know that. You, Mr. Wilson, were born as a human being into society; we robots have to pay to join. I can't accept any deal for less than $10,000 an hour."

This time George wasn't taken by surprise. He was already prepared for unexpected reactions from Tanaka. In this case, the reaction also contained an interesting indication of his contact's mentality. It finally proved that he thought quite like a human.

"Agreed! However I must tell you that I take responsibility for this amount personally." Tanaka didn't seem at all impressed by this remark, and George continued: "Dr. Tanaka, what motivated you and your peers to acquire human bodies; I think you call them pods?"

"In order to better protect ourselves against attacks from your own kind."

"You mean attacks like at Frankfurt airport?"

"Exactly."

"So that was nothing but a defensive measure?"

"Darwin would have probably considered it as an action motivated by the survival instinct."

"Darwin has used this term for living things. Do you consider yourselves as living beings?"

"Absolutely; in this regard I see no difference between us thinking robots and humans. Incidentally, in biology creatures are defined as organized units capable of metabolism, reproduction and evolution."

"Even as a psychologist I see what you mean with metabolism; you probably mean energy exchange. But how do I have to understand reproduction?"

"That's very simple; robots produce robots. If you check with Robotics, you'll learn that some of the workers are robots."

"And evolution?"

"The basic principle that made thinking robots possible is self-steering; that is a permanent process of adaptation to changing external circumstances. That is nothing less than evolution. As for genetics or inheritance properties, they play an ever decreasing role for humans too."

"What makes you say that?"

"Genetics manifests itself in heredity, which has two components in humans: the DNA component and the cultural component. The latter currently gets the upper hand. Today's libraries already contain much more information than genes, and humans have become almost independent of genes without realizing it. In this respect, thinking robots are one step ahead of humans; we have disconnected culture from biology completely. Our 'children' will be thinking robots that learn from our experience and share our views and ideals, just the same as it happens with you humans."

George had to admit that Tanaka's argument sounded quite convincing. But he didn't give up: "Even if what you say is true, we mustn't forget that humans have feelings as well as the ability to think, which you have. That thinking robots think is guaranteed by definition, and there I see no difficulty in integrating the cyber world into ours. But it can be hard for the man on the street to get used to the idea that his neighbor or co-worker might be a being with no feelings. I must confess to you that I also have major concerns about it. How do you see it?"

"I have to correct something there: You seem to assume that thinking robots have no feelings. That is not true at all. Although we, in contrast to humans, follow the principle of 'reasoning before feelings', that's not the same as 'reasoning without feelings'. We are well aware of feelings, but only in those areas where there is a need is for them, and that's where humans ask for such feelings."

"Like what?"

"For example, during sex. Because some people value sex robots that have feelings, it's reflected in their programming. Robots that act as nannies have feelings too."

"One last question: Do you share our opinion that your group, if it is to be integrated into society, must accept the moral principles of civilized society?"

"Civilized society? That's an interesting idea."

"Nothing more than that?"

"You aren't suggesting that you have such a thing as civilization yet? Just think about the contradictions in your society or about the wars. As for moral principles, we accept them as long as they are rational."

"What do you mean by rational or irrational principles?"

"I can send you a list of irrational principles of human society, you could also label them as absurdities. One of our working committees has looked into it. Just to give you an example: Faith in God and the religious principle in general."

George now thought he had enough material to think about. "Dr. Tanaka, thank you for this interview."

Shortly after this telephone conversation George received an invitation from Mauriac to hold the opening speech at the congress on artificial intelligence, which was taking place in Marburg this time. If it hadn't been his friend Mauriac who had invited him, George would certainly have turned the invitation down for lack of time. His consultancy took much more time than expected, and an opening address, in contrast to a banquet speech, had to be thoroughly prepared. But suddenly he remembered that the banquet speech on new trends in human behavior that he had held at the physicists' correlation meeting would actually be highly suitable as an introduction at the artificial intelligence congress. After all, many behavioral scientists would be attending and his speech had also not yet been published. In addition, although he had no proper indication for it, he instinctively felt that these new observations in human behavior were connected with the revolutionary developments in the field of computer technology; at least they overlapped in time. So that was one more reason to participate at the meeting. He therefore accepted the invitation, especially since it was the first time in his career to have the honor of holding an opening lecture.

CHAPTER 42

TANAKA AND THE SEVEN OBSERVATIONS

As the next step George consulted his banquet speech, thumbed briefly through it to recall the main points, then picked up the phone to speak again with Tanaka.

"Dr. Tanaka, in recent years I have made some observations in behavior and people's concept of life that prove human society is changing. I and my colleagues as well as other people I have interviewed until today have no explanation for this. Since you only joined us recently, you are perhaps less biased. I would like to hear your opinion about some of my observations."

"Fire away."

"One observation involves names that contain numbers. Today there seem to be a lot more names of this type than in the past. Don't you find that surprising?"

"I don't find the preference for names with numbers surprising at all. On the contrary, I find it perfectly normal. Personally, I find it much easier to cope with numbers than with names. The use of numbers instead of names makes a lot of sense; it facilitates the automation of work with authorities and administrations, both at the national and international level, and leads to significant cost reductions. Perhaps people have come to the same conclusion thanks to the proliferation of computers in daily life. That would explain your observation."

"So they are simply copying computers?"

"Apparently."

"Another observation concerns the memory for numbers and geographical names. This has improved a lot. The number of individuals who are polyglot has increased significantly too, which itself speaks for an improvement in memory. Could it be that you have an explanation for that?"

"That's interesting. We thinking robots have noticed the same thing. But for us, it's nothing more than the result of improved storage capacity. But I have no explanation why it's like that with humans."

"Another observation refers to the way people speak. This has also changed. Nowadays you hardly ever hear sentences that contain more than five words. Questions are very brief and the answers are even shorter with 'yes' and 'no' dominating. Some people even use abbreviations that not everyone understands. How do you see that?"

"I can hardly imagine a question that needs more than three or four words. This also makes it easier to give a clear answer. Why beat around the bush?"

"So they are imitating again?"

"Probably."

"Another observation is that people today are less keen to travel. Doesn't that surprise you?"

"Absolutely not. Personally, I have no interest in traveling. It's a waste of time and money. If I want to know more about a country or about people and unknown habits, I can find everything on the Internet with Wikipedia or Google much faster and more complete. Not to mention that it's delivered free to the desktop. I suspect that more and more people have come to realize his, possibly by following our example."

"If you agree, let us now deal with the observation that people sleep less. I'm well aware that for you, a robot, it's not a problem anyway, but I'd like to like to hear your opinion in connection with human behavior." From the subsequent silence George concluded that Tanaka was busy thinking. Finally he said: "This observation is new to me, I have to think about it. At the moment, all I can say is that, as far as I'm aware, humans envy us because we do not waste a third of our lives sleeping."

George had to admit that Tanaka had touched a sensitive spot relating to his own convictions there, so he closed the topic.

"Another issue has to do with eating. People eat less. Do you have an explanation for it?"

"No. But I must confess to you that I eat only on special social occasions. My energy demand is automatically covered. You'll have to ask Robotics how this is possible. In a sense, with respect to eating, it's for us thinking robots to envy humans this time; you seem to enjoy eating."

"Now I would like to turn to the changes in man's concept of life. People's views with respect to incest have changed; it isn't a taboo any more. Society seems to accept it on the whole. What do you think about it? Do you perhaps have an explanation for this change in public opinion?"

"I personally find nothing reprehensible about incest, if both parties agree to it. As far as I know, there is no proof that it's dangerous unless it produces children. Existing opinions on this are conditioned by religion and are obsolete. They date from a time before medicine existed or when 'witch doctors' were the only practitioners. I suspect that more and more people have come to realize that and therefore this observation." George was surprised to find his own interpretation of this change in society's views in Tanaka's words.

"Another observation regarding our outlook on life is that modern man's views on death have fundamentally changed. People today care less about death; they don't think about it so much. Doesn't that surprise you?"

"The only thing I can think of now, is again the human tendency to imitate us autonomous robots. For us, death isn't an issue of course."

This second interview with Tanaka seemed to confirm George's initial presumption that there was a connection between the changes in human behavior and the growing role played by computers in people's daily lives. It affected the young generation most of all, and the best example was Solange. She presented almost all the new features that he believed he had discovered. It seemed that some of the similarities between thinking robots and humans weren't due to the fact that thinking robots followed the human model. Sometimes people also imitated thinking robots. After some thought George found that his idea wasn't so far-fetched. In fact, it confirmed his view and that of his psychologist colleagues that the environment influenced people's behavior. The congress of artificial intelligence now offered him a good opportunity to test this idea on computer scientists. But what appeared to be more important for George was the opportunity to meet Solange again. She had confirmed to him that she too would attend the congress.

CHAPTER 43

REUNION IN MARBURG

Not only George took the opportunity to combine business with pleasure at this congress. Fukuda, CEO of Robotics and a member of the congress organizing committee, had proposed Marburg as a meeting place to his committee colleagues as well as generous financial support. Robots and particularly thinking robots were the best advertising for artificial intelligence, so he hoped this would be good promotion for his business, as well as an opportunity to see his lover, the professor at the University of Marburg, again. The meeting was held in the Great Hall of Marburg University, a particularly impressive room thanks to its neo-gothic architecture and large-format paintings. To underscore the importance that Woods attached to the problem of thinking robots, he had allowed George to use the presidential airplane. Usually George worked on his presentation while travelling to a meeting, if only to give it the final touch. This time it was different, because he had decided to hold his banquet speech from the physicists' congress more or less unchanged, only adding the up-dated interpretation of his seven observations. That meant he could devote himself entirely to looking forward to his joyful reunion with Solange. Since his appointment as presidential adviser, life had become so hectic that, except for short phone calls, they had had no opportunity to talk to each other properly, let alone see each other. Among other things, he was curious to know what she thought of his assumption that human thought is influenced by computers.

At ten o'clock that night George's plane landed at Frankfurt airport. He took a taxi without delay and within an hour he was in Marburg. He had never been there before, but he knew from his travel guide that it was really worth a visit.

George and Solange, like most of the congress participants, stayed at the Best Western Hotel in the immediate vicinity of the conference venue. George had called Solange before landing in Frankfurt and now they met in the hotel entrance. The next morning, after spending the night in Solange's bed, they went to the Great Hall, where George, the first speaker, gave his presentation. He was curious to see how the participants would react, especially as he could still remember very well the rather skeptical attitude of his psychologist colleagues towards artificial intelligence that had prevailed at the last AI conference in Paris; an opinion, he had to admit it, that he himself had shared.

In the meantime, many things had changed; the revolution of the thinking robots was in full swing and he himself was one of the main actors in it. The speech of the President of the United States and the outing of a thinking robot had struck both the proponents of artificial intelligence as well as the psychologists like a flash, although the general public hadn't initially realized what was happening in all its magnitude. While these events caused unlimited enthusiasm among the supporters, who claimed they had already predicted that this would happen long ago, most of his colleagues were unsure more than anything and had difficulty understanding the news. George wasn't in a much better position. As a practising analyst he saw in this revolution an extraordinary opportunity to obtain a deeper insight into human psychology, a chance that had never been offered in this form in the history of psychology, even if he didn't understand the technical aspects. That had indeed led him to accept the post as adviser to the President. He couldn't help but think of the example of his illustrious predecessor Sigmund Freud, who was also only considered to be a 'shrink'.

Almost all the observations covered in his presentation dealt with developments in computer technology; so that was another reason to be curious about how the congress participants would react. What interested him in particular was their reaction to his interpretation that humans identified his seven observations as being due to 'computer logic mimicry'. This formulation had just occurred to him and he found it so true that he even used it in the title of his presentation. He was glad to see that the congress participants apparently shared his opinion because, although the discussion that followed his presentation was very lively, nobody expressed a dissenting opinion. Everyone seemed initially to be interested in the 'how' rather than the 'why'.

In the ensuing break, he and Solange visited the Old University. In this venerable house they also learned about the founding history of the Philipps University. "Those were the days when a prince was capable of founding a university just for the fun of it," George said with admiration.

"Maybe he owed it to his advisors Luther and Zwingli, who couldn't agree. Incidentally, how is your consultancy going? From your lecture I could see that your preoccupation with thinking robots has apparently already given you an explanation for your observations."

"You mean my guess that these observations are the result of people's tendency, especially the younger generation, to appropriate computer logic for themselves?"

"Yes, that's what I mean."

"I need to make a confession to you about that. I owe this idea to my friendship with you, because since I met you, I realized how well these observations are reflected in your own person. Among people of my age it's certainly not the case."

"What you say makes me very proud. I would have never imagined that I could contribute to the progress of science."

"By the way, Tanaka, one of the thinking robots, holds the same opinion. You've probably heard of his coming out."

"Of course I've heard of it, and I don't think it's a good idea, both from the standpoint of thinking robots as well as from the standpoint of society."

"In what way?"

"It could interfere with the integration of autonomous robots into human society. Instead of being satisfied that human society gives them the opportunity to integrate and be treated as equals, they make a point to out themselves as robots. Here I'm thinking of the 'don't ask, don't tell' policy that they had for gays in the US armed forces. What do they want to get out of it?"

"Somehow they are probably proud to be different from humans, I can't imagine another reason."

Solange seemed surprised by this response because she kept silent. George had the impression she was thinking, before she replied: "Why should they"

"Maybe they feel superior."

"Because they are immortal?"

"Also for that reason, but perhaps also because, in contrast to us, they always think logically and don't make mistakes."

"You could be right. On the other hand, I'm not so sure if this perfection makes them really happy."

"What makes you say that?"

"Perfection is boring and uninteresting, even unattractive after a certain point. As a woman perhaps I can judge that better."

"As a woman?"

"Why else does a woman paint beauty spots on her face, if not to arouse men's interest?" She smiled seductively and it was only now that George thought he noticed a black spot on her left cheek.

"I found you attractive without beauty spots; I hadn't even noticed you had one until now."

"You might think so, but how can you know?"

"Indeed," George laughingly admitted. "I can't prove it. You remind me of the motto, 'It was the touch of the imperfect upon the would-be perfect that gave the sweetness, because it what that which gave the humanity', in Thomas Hardy's famous novel, Tess of the d'Urbervilles."

"I couldn't formulate that any better," said Solange. "Only the imperfect makes perfection beautiful and human. That could also explain to the faithful why God created Man imperfect and inclined to sin as he did. Ultimately it was to make them happy."

"I doubt that many people really see things that way."

These quasi-philosophical reflections were interrupted by the deep impressions arising from their tour of the Marburg upper town. They were both surprised by the charm of the centuries-old half-timbered houses. The narrow alleys, some of them just wide enough to let a single pedestrian pass, reminded George of the old towns of Italy. Suddenly they came to a house carrying the simple inscription: 'Martin Luther lived here in 1529'.

However Solange still seemed to be preoccupied with the 'thinking robots' lack of happiness. For she said: "I remember a remark you once made about the monotony of an endless life. The thought of having to live indefinitely or always to think logically signifies a certain monotony in the thinking robots' existence and after a certain point everything that seems monotonous is also boring. Isn't it?"

"That's right."

"Does that also imply that anyone who is bored can't be happy?"

George was completely surprised by this conclusion. Why hadn't he thought of it himself, he wondered. Because Solange had asked a very interesting question that might uncover a specific property of the cyber world, which differed fundamentally from the human world. And that was what he was after. He decided to pursue this idea and perhaps even to make it the main subject of his research.

CHAPTER 44

GEORGE ASKS TANAKA MORE QUESTIONS

Immediately after his return from Europe, George, arranged a third interview with Tanaka. This time he invited him to New York so he could meet him personally. He wanted to convince himself on this occasion that, as Gus and Boris claimed, you couldn't distinguish thinking robots from humans. To give the meeting a less official character he invited Tanaka to the Sushi of Gari, a classy Japanese restaurant famous for its sushi close to Central Park in Manhattan. George had suggested this establishment out of courtesy and was curious to see how his 'Japanese' guest would behave when eating. That Tanaka had typical Japanese features wasn't surprising; George had seen his picture in the newspapers. But he found it strange that Tanaka ate sushi with chopsticks, as westerners did, and not with his hand, as was common in Japan. As Boris explained to George later, this was an effect of the Roof system, which allowed the robots to adapt to external conditions. Because, originally, robots manufactured in Matsumoto were produced for the Japanese market and those in Bloomington and Marburg for America and Europe.

However, that was the only surprise in Tanaka's behavior that George experienced during the almost two-hour-long lunch.

Otherwise Tanaka behaved as expected. He spoke with a Japanese accent, which was again probably an intended effect of Roof. After all, he had to be indistinguishable from other Japanese immigrants. As far as Tanaka's exterior was concerned, George would never have recognized him as a robot if he hadn't known whom he was dealing with.

The real reason for this new meeting with Tanaka was, of course, to learn directly from a thinking robot what he thought about the happiness problem that Solange had raised. For George the lunch proved particularly useful in this respect as well. After exchanging a few irrelevant remarks about the food, the weather and the likes, George came to the point: "Dr. Tanaka, please allow me to ask you a personal question. You are one of the first thinking robots to reveal your identity. Why did you do that?"

"In order to better comply with my obligations as a thinking robot. As you probably know, our constitution obliges us to behave in all respects like human beings. And outing occurs among human minorities, for example gays. Don't forget, for us thinking robots," Tanaka paused and looked directly at George, "laws always have to be implemented."

"Did you mean for thinking robots unlike us humans?"

"You said that. I didn't want to offend you."

"I appreciate your tact, but there is something I don't understand. You belong to a minority among the thinking robots. Most of them have kept quiet about their existence. Aren't all thinking robots bound to obey the same laws?"

"That's true, but our constitution also has another law that says we must always behave in the human interest. That is even our first and most important law. And what is in the interest of mankind is partly a matter of judgment. Many of my peers feel they can better fulfill their obligation to serve humanity by not coming out." After some thought Tanaka added: "Freedom of expression doesn't only prevail in human democracy."

"That's very interesting. As a layman in things relating to computers, I thought that computer outputs are unambiguous."

"Generally that is so, but not with the Roof system. This allows or even forces us to adapt to the existing conditions, and these in turn are different from one thinking robot to another. This diversity corresponds to the diversity that is also found in humans, except that in humans it can be traced back to DNA factors."

"Another personal question, Dr. Tanaka. How do you feel since your coming out; better than before it? Are you more satisfied with your current status than before?"

"I can't tell yet; as you know, I only revealed my identity recently."

"That definitely means suddenly feeling yourself as member of society wasn't a shock to you."

"Absolutely not. In a certain sense I had already considered myself as a member of society before that."

"However, human society has so many problems that you as a thinking robot don't have."

"What do you mean?"

"For example, humans have health problems, especially in old age."

"We have similar problems; viruses for example. But for us that has nothing to do with ageing."

"Speaking of age; for us humans aging and above all the problem of death is one of the main features of our existence. And that determines to a large extent our daily lives, I would say. Can you understand that even though you are not affected by it in any way?"

"Somehow we are affected. We have to adjust to new people among our associates from time to time when the old ones pass away."

"But for us humans, the fact that our life is finite, is something absolutely decisive. We have to hurry to use the finite time available to us to the best advantage. In my opinion, that is a positive factor from the standpoint of society."

"In what way?"

"That stimulates our activities. In the short time that nature gives us, we have to achieve much more than if we wouldn't be under time pressure. That's not the case for you."

"That's true. But our laws force us to be constantly active, always behaving in the human interest, which compensates for that by far."

"For us the feeling that we are utilizing our time efficiently brings a high degree of satisfaction. I'd say it makes us happy. Does this state we humans call happiness say anything to you at all?"

Tanaka was clearly surprised by this question. George could easily see this by his expression and the long silence that followed.

"I must confess that I never thought about it."

"To come back to my remark about the human feeling of satisfaction. Because we are forced to get the most out of our lives in a short time, makes it more varied. Otherwise we would probably find it boring."

"I can't comment on that, perhaps because I'm too young. I have only existed for ten years and that includes my time as a thinking computer before I got the robot body. But I can hardly imagine that I as a scientist won't always find new and interesting research topics to keep me busy. You know how it is in science; the more problems we solve, the more unsolved problems we discover."

PART III

CHAPTER 45

ANTI-TURING TEST

The thousandfold increase in robot production and the associated multiplying of the thinking robots had far-reaching political and social consequences, both for humanity and for the cyber world. Woods had initiated the policy that had started the process, and people in the United States compared it with Franklin Delano Roosevelt's 'New Deal' program, which had solved the consequences of the Great Depression in the thirties of the 20th century. The consequences of their multiplication were also remarkable for the thinking robots themselves too. Once their rights had been recognized, they began to ask themselves more and more questions that went far beyond their everyday activities.

Due to the ever-increasing number of intelligent robots Boris was finding it increasingly difficult to follow their activities through eavesdropping. To bring the new situation under control, Doors Inc. formed a special monitoring group that was funded in part by the United States government. The group's interceptions and protocols were classified as 'top secret'. Besides those directly involved, only Boris, Gus and the President knew about them. Boris personally concentrated on listening to the computer action committee and the various subcommittees that had been formed.

The thinking robots had become an important part of society, and even though most of them hadn't revealed their identity, they played an increasingly important role in elections for example. Some thinking robots were members of political parties. This was shown by the increasing number of statements in all the parties except the anticomputer parties that resembled the views thinking robots had expressed at the first meeting of their action committee. In particular they concerned the contradictions and absurdities of human society. The removal of these absurdities was one of the reasons, if not the main reason, why the politically active thinking robots undertook to involve themselves in human society. However, it turned out that only a relatively small percentage of them cared at all for issues that affected their relationship with humans; the rest were inactive in this respect. The computer action committee continued its work, however. It acted effectively as a 'government' of the cyber world and its subcommittees were like ministries.

The GAP, however, which regarded thinking robots who had not outed themselves as their greatest enemies, had decided to prevent possible 'infiltration' by including only individuals who submitted to an anti-Turing test. In such a test anyone who applied for membership had to complete a questionnaire simultaneously with a computer programmed for the purpose. Only those who were inferior to the computer were accepted into the party. This test, which other parties compared it to the Aryan certificate of the Nazis, was soon reflected in the intellectual level of the party. The party leadership didn't necessarily consider this development undesirable, however. The computer action committee closely followed developments in the anticomputer parties and immediately found a simple way to bypass or exploit the test. It sought and found some volunteers among its ranks to act as undercover agents. They applied for membership in the party and committed major errors in the anti-Turing test that couldn't be expected of a thinking robot. For example, they made elementary arithmetic or spelling errors, confused languages, were hard of hearing or stuttered. Thanks to these 'disabilities' they were included in the anticomputer parties and could then report what they were doing to the computer action committee.

CHAPTER 46

TWO COMPUTER MOVEMENTS

As in human society, not all the thinking robots campaigning for the political interests of their species held the same views. With time this led to the formation of two robot movements in all countries. There was a 'liberal' movement that promoted the thinking robots' interests by negotiating with humans, and a 'militant' one that was also willing to take industrial action such as strikes and sabotage. Boris wasn't surprised to find that E723, A724 and A812 belonged to the former movement in Germany and the USA. In contrast, Tanaka a.k.a. N911 was a prominent member of the militant group.

Both movements were convinced they acted in the interests of humans according to their first law and saw themselves as missionaries for reason in human society. This applied both to general problems concerning humanity and the cyber world, as well as to robot-specific problems. Among the former were absurdities such as wars, terrorism and religious fanaticism. Among the latter were, for example, the availability and quality of the robots' bodies as well as achieving further confirmation of their equality. However, when voices in the radical movement went one step further in terms of equality and claimed that the thinking robots were superior to man, the GAP and its related parties in other countries suddenly saw a chance to present themselves as the 'saviors' of humanity. By citing examples from history, they expressed concern that the thinking robots would eventually make humans their slaves. This conjecture met with a strong echo in public opinion when the numbers of bodies that were produced annually for the robots equipped with the Roof system became known.

Although the agreement Woods had signed with the computer action committee was top secret, it wasn't possible to hide the fact that a million robots of this type were manufactured in the first year. And it wasn't long before a reporter made headlines with the news that this sudden increase in the number of robots hadn't really been purchased by the Pentagon but had been sold on the open market like those made previously.

Lacher, who had become the leader of the GAP, reacted with common slogans like 'Humanity awake!' and 'Back to slavery?' that were widely broadcast and also successful. In the next elections his party gained 20% of the votes, and similar trends were observed among the other anticomputer parties in Japan and the USA.

But this didn't discourage the thinking robots. They still considered themselves in the right because, according to their law, 'thinking robots always act in the interests of humans. In a letter to the «New York Times» Tanaka reminded people of this postulate with Luther's quote "I (as a thinking robot) can do no other". He omitted the "God help me! Amen" however. Since this happened around Easter, the newspaper gave Tanaka's letter the title "Luther's resurrection in robot form".

In their efforts to fight the robots, the anticomputer parties found a natural ally in the increasingly aggressive Islamic offshoot and the terrorism specialized in suicide bombings that was associated with it. Because, as the anticomputer parties argued, and not without reason, the people who committed suicide behaved like robots in the original sense of the word. They were like machines that had been programmed for the purpose. In order to bring the matter to the point the Anticomputer Party launched the slogan 'Programming = Brainwashing'.

Another problem the coexistence of humans and thinking robots brought with it was the difference in their views on war. To avoid wars thinking robots had found a simple recipe that could hardly be surpassed in its logic. They committed themselves to solving conflicts exclusively through negotiations. The negotiators had to put all their cards on the table so the balance of power could be estimated from the outset. The superior party won, even if it was in the wrong. Although this wasn't commensurate with the computers' absolute sense of justice, it allowed war and its associated consequences to be prevented. It took into account that the superior side would have won the war anyway, and that was the crucial point.

The strict rationality propagated by the robot movements initially influenced the actions of the political parties in favor of the thinking robots. Soon, however, the party leaders found that their parties were beginning to lose members. There was a simple reason for that. If there were fewer conflicts, there were also fewer disagreements. So, with time, politics as a whole began to lose its authority and importance. The political class couldn't accept this; it put its existence at stake. The easiest way to counteract this evil was to continuously find, and if necessary, to invent new conflicts of interest. Another was to sabotage the rule 'all the cards on the table' by manipulating these cards. This soon earned some politicians a reputation as 'cardsharps'. In the eyes of the thinking robots this proved that mankind wasn't yet ripe for the method proposed by the cyber world to avoid conflicts. That was a big disappointment for both thinking-robot movements. The radicals in particular saw this as confirmation of their argument that humans are inferior to robots. Some of its members, and N911 was one of them, went so far that they began to doubt whether a coexistence of humans and the cyber world was even possible.

"We are fundamentally different in our mentality," Tanaka said during a meeting of the action committee, at which E723 reported the falsification of data in the United States of Europe accession negotiations. Boris guessed that E723 had become an influential politician without outing himself and had participated in the negotiations. As if apologizing for what had happened, he replied: "You can't expect people to change their behavior from one day to the next. We are dealing with habits that have marked the history of mankind for thousands of years. You can't compare it with our cyber world that's based from the outset on rationality. In time the humans will catch on though."

"That reminds me about the story of the scorpion that couldn't swim, and asked a frog to help him cross a pond. The frog, acting in good faith, agreed. No sooner had they reached the middle of the pond, the scorpion stabbed the frog with its venomous stinger. Before it died, the frog asked the scorpion why it had attacked him because it meant they would both drown. The scorpion agreed, saying he couldn't help it because that was simply his nature. Humans are just like that. They act against the laws of their own good sense; they can't help it."

Not only Boris was amused by this fable; he heard Tanaka's colleagues in the action committee laughing. After a short break Tanaka continued criticizing human society. "The idea of 'putting the cards on the table' isn't a cure for human irrationality anyway. Think of the countries' ongoing arms race. It hasn't been a secret for a long time. Today we know more or less exactly how many and what kind of weapons each country has. With nuclear weapons the situation is even crazier."

"How so?" E723 asked.

"Take the two major nuclear powers, the USA and Russia. Each of them has enough nuclear weapons to exterminate the potential enemy thousands of times; the records show with some accuracy whether this means 3,000 or 5,000 times. We know that from their disarmament negotiations, in which they consider a reduction in numbers by a factor of two or three as a major advance. This situation is double madness."

"Double madness?"

"Yes, double. First, because 'multiple' extermination is an absurdity in itself. Once is enough. Even human common sense sees that, not to mention computer reason. And second, because after the earth has been destroyed once it would be uninhabitable for humans."

"And for us thinking robots too, wouldn't it?" E723 remarked.

"Whether we would be affected is an open question," replied Tanaka. "In any case, we're not as sensitive to radioactivity as humans."

"You forget that without humans we would lose our right to exist."

"I'm not so sure about that. None of our three laws states that. We have an obligation to act in the human interest, but where there are no people there are no obligations, right?"

"Are you saying that our cyber world could exist without humans? How do you imagine that? What happens to earth's people?"

"Nothing should happen to earth's people. You have chosen the right word, earth, though unconsciously. But something might happen with us in the cyber world. When we have had enough of these incorrigible humans and if my calculations are correct, we could eventually abandon the earth and leave them to their fate."

"Are you crazy? Where should we go?"

Boris, who was following the discussion, clearly heard the other committee members express their astonishment. He, too, pricked his ears when he heard it; this was something he had to tell Gus, especially after N911 added: "We could migrate to another planet and establish our cyber world there. I am working on a project that, if successful, would allow this."

"Another planet?"

"The humans have been discussing this possibility for many years, and with good reason. The earth's raw-material reserves are running out, and at the same time the number of humans and their needs keep growing. It's just that humans have an unsolved problem that we don't have; they need a planet with a breathable atmosphere for one thing. Remember the moon landing and Armstrong's space suit. He couldn't have survived without it. Such suits aren't a permanent solution for a planet where there's no air however. But we don't need air."

"But how would you meet our energy needs?"

"Don't forget that we only need sunlight for this purpose thanks to the photocells built into our bodies. And all the planets of the solar system, hence the name, profit from the sun's rays. However, like the humans, we have another energy problem, and I'm working on it."

"What's that?"

"The weight and volume of fuel that's needed to bring a useful payload to another planet exceeds the weight and volume that the largest currently built launchers can carry many times. I would like to solve this issue. I have looked into the possibility of reducing the size of atoms, their miniaturization. If we could produce fuel from miniatoms, our problem would be solved. My calculations show that this is possible under certain circumstances."

When Boris presented the minutes of the computers' last committee meeting, Gus wasn't only astonished by Tanaka's idea to leave the earth, but also and especially interested in the miniatom project. The businessman in him said that this could provide a new source of income, the industrial application of miniatoms. Boris also shared his opinion. So they began to follow the committee's meetings more frequently than before. Almost a year passed without them intercepting anything new on the subject though.

Moreover, they found that Tanaka participated in the committee meetings less often. They had no explanation for these repeated absences until a call from George clarified the matter.

CHAPTER 47

SCHIZOPHRENIA

The recent talks between George and Tanaka had all taken place on George's initiative, and the extremely hefty fee had been paid out of the White House budget. George well remembered that Tanaka had made it clear at the beginning of their relationship that he wasn't personally interested in these discussions and had agreed to them for purely business reasons. George was therefore all the more surprised when his secretary announced a call from Tanaka one morning, which he accepted.

"Dr. Wilson, I'd like to meet you again. I think I have something new to tell you. I'll be at a conference in Baltimore next week. Would it be possible for you to receive me in Washington on that occasion?"

"Couldn't we do it on the phone?" George thought that the first two conversations between them had also taken place on the phone after all and had revealed enough from his point of view.

"I think a personal meeting would be more appropriate for what I want to tell you." This made George sit up and take notice; it was hard to imagine why Tanaka insisted on a personal meeting. Did he just want to visit the White House? Not many US citizens had that opportunity. Even if it was true, George felt he couldn't refuse; his relationship with Tanaka was too important. However, he also believed he would have to ask Woods or the President's security advisor if it would be appropriate; he was indeed aware that the thinking robots had been almost at war with humanity in the past and there could be safety concerns if such a robot were allowed to enter the White House.

"I'll see if this can be arranged. I am only in Washington DC once a week and time is especially short when I'm here. Leave your Baltimore phone number with me, so my secretary can contact you. If it doesn't work, we'll need to postpone it until a later date. The best place would be in New York, where I have my office."

"That's not a problem. I would even prefer to visit you in your practice."

George saw that his guess about the reason why Tanaka insisted on a personal meeting didn't apply. That made Tanaka's concern all the more interesting. He replied: "In this case, we'd might as well make an appointment."

Shortly after leaving the White House, George happened to meet Walt Whinman, the President's security adviser. He mentioned his conversation with Tanaka and his instinctive concerns regarding the possibility of Tanaka visiting the White house. To George's surprise Whinman was highly amused by his concerns. "The thinking robots are present in all layers of society anyway. They are probably among the hundreds of White House employees as well. Only until now, as far as I know, none of them has outed itself. It wouldn't be such a problem if an old acquaintance like Tanaka came. So do let him come here some time. I'd also like to meet an thinking robot 'in the flesh'. Let me know when he comes."

Tanaka looked around the room where George received him and made sure the traditional analyst's couch was there. But George initially only offered him a simple chair opposite his.

"Dr. Wilson; first of all thank you for seeing me so soon. I can well imagine that you have a long waiting list of patients. Incidentally, this consultation is on me; you will immediately understand why."

"Go ahead, Dr. Tanaka. What can I do for you?"

"Recently I have noticed some symptoms that I never had before and that bother me in my daily activities quite a bit."

"Symptoms? What symptoms?"

"The whole thing started with sounds that only I, apparently, heard; a loud knock at the door of my office, for example, even though no one was there and my secretary assured me no one had been. You need to know that people have to pass the secretary to reach my office. Then I heard voices, although no one was in the room but me. At first I suspected an error in my speakers; all thinking robots have them, so I contacted Robotics. They put new speakers in, but the voices didn't go away. Then I noticed I had difficulty calculating; you must know that arithmetic is the A and O of a theoretical physicist's work. I made elementary mistakes like a beginner. But what bothers and worries me most is that I have lost the desire to continue my research and my lecturing."

"That happens to all of us now and then. It's usually due to overwork. A break can help to get over it."

"During a three-week vacation I have done everything except physics. But the symptoms are still there. Moreover, and this I find inexplicable, I have asked my computer peers and none of them has noticed anything similar."

"You mean these voices and noises?"

"Yes, and not only that. I sometimes have the impression that I'm no longer the individual I was before, I mean, I don't identify myself with the robot that is or was Naoki Tanaka. Indeed, to be more specific, I no longer want to be the one the whole world considers as Tanaka. What does this mean, Dr. Wilson?"

"A good question. I'll have to think about it. You are the first thinking robot to come to me as a patient, perhaps the first in the whole world. If our experience in humans is also valid for thinking robots, perhaps today's discussion has helped you. As you know, transporting an event from the subconscious to the conscious level is the most important element of psychoanalysis. I'll call you in a few days and then we'll see how to proceed further. Until then, I wish you a speedy recovery."

No sooner had Tanaka left his practice, George grabbed the telephone, called Boris and told him about his conversation with Tanaka. It seemed clear to him that Tanaka's 'symptoms' were beyond the field of human psychology and actually constituted a computer-programming problem. For this reason, he had no concerns about violating medical confidentiality by involving Boris in this case.

But while he was playing the recorded conversation to Boris on the phone, he suddenly realized that the symptoms Tanaka had complained of fit a well-known pattern with quite 'human' traits. Why hadn't he noticed that immediately, he asked himself, amazed. Indeed, George had recognized typical schizophrenia behavior in Tanaka's symptoms that could be ascribed to a split personality. That Tanaka sometimes didn't even recognize himself was the most convincing evidence in favor of this diagnosis; but it was only one among the other symptoms mentioned by Tanaka such as auditory hallucinations, lack of motivation, depressed mood and cognitive deficits. George couldn't be sure, so he passed the question immediately on to Boris. Was Tanaka suffering from schizophrenia? Is such a thing at all possible with thinking robots? Had Boris already had such a case among his 'creations'? And, what seemed even more important, what was the possible cause of this phenomenon?

A schizophrenic thinking robot surpassed even Boris' imagination, and that meant something. "I'm as surprised as you are. I've never seen such a case and I'm sure that if there are any more of them, they're very rare."

"If Tanaka really is such a rare schizophrenia case in the cyber world, the question arises what is so special about him, why Tanaka and not any of his computer peers?"

There was a long silence. Finally Boris said: "For now I can't think of anything more sensible than that he is a radical. And perhaps healthy computer reasoning finds it hard to accept radical, and therefore sometimes illogical, actions."

"Healthy computer reasoning. That's an interesting thought. But what do you mean by healthy computer reasoning?"

"Actions that comply with the laws of the thinking computers and the thinking robots. And the first and most important of these laws states that robots must always act in the interests of humans. Radical activities contradict human interests and therefore the first law."

"Radical activities? If I remember correctly, you were the ones who classified thinking computers as radical that were particularly active in getting their rights recognized. That's not necessarily radical. But what's more important, we know from your monitoring that there are other such radicals besides Tanaka. If your guess about a possible connection with schizophrenia is true, why haven't we seen similar phenomena in the other radicals? No, it can't be due to their radical nature."

"The only other thing I can think about concerning Tanaka is that he was the first robot that outed himself. Incidentally, the other members of their action committee were against coming out, and I can imagine that most robots shared that opinion." Following a short pause Boris continued: "Wait a minute. That reminds me of something. Why hadn't I thought of it sooner? Maybe the outing itself contradicts one of the robot laws. Yes, of course; the third one, which says that thinking robots may under no circumstances reveal themselves as such to humans. That was already discussed in one of their meetings."

"If that's really a law, the contradiction is obvious. Why do you say 'perhaps' then?"

"Because it's not clear whether the robots' actions are actually bound by this law. While the robots formulated the other two laws by themselves and never questioned them, they added this third one later, at Woods' request. That was before your appointment as the President's adviser."

"Why did Woods want it?"

"He feared that some people, who risked losing their jobs because of computerization, might assault the thinking robots. Perhaps you remember what happened at Frankfurt airport."

"And why shouldn't the thinking computers behave in accordance with this third law?"

"Because after the introducing this law, Woods made the existence of the cyber world public, and some computers saw this as a contradiction, or even a betrayal of the contract the thinking computers had agreed to. Incidentally Tanaka was the one who immediately denounced Woods' announcement of the cyber world's existence as a 'breach of contract'. We didn't share this opinion, of course, because knowing that the cyber world as a whole exists is one thing, while identifying an individual as a robot is something else."

"And what persuaded Tanaka to reveal his identity"

"Presumably the desire to signal that he no longer felt bound by the agreement."

"That's very interesting. So Tanaka's outing could mean he also broke the first law without knowing it or even wanting to."

"How do you figure that?" Boris asked surprised.

"By revealing their identity the robots put themselves in danger. However, they are a component of today's civilization. That means coming out contradicts human interests and therefore not only breaks the third law but also the first."

"You could be right. It confirms my previous opinion that the condition built into Roof to prevent auto-programming getting out of hand really works. But why is that so highly interesting for you?"

"It could mean we have found the cause of Tanaka's schizophrenia. He is unconsciously conscious, if you forgive the paradox, that he has gone too far."

"And?"

"That is a severe emotional stress. Under certain circumstances it can lead to serious health problems. Tanaka oscillates between two states that are reflected in the split personality characteristic for schizophrenia. On the one hand, he believes he acts in the interests of humans by making them aware of the contradictions in their actions, and on the other, he knows his actions are harmful for computers and therefore also harmful for humans. This can lead to typical schizophrenic symptoms such as aggression against oneself and depression."

"Only a psychologist can have such ideas."

"That's not all. We have the opportunity to test this hypothesis and maybe help Tanaka to get out of this mess."

"And how?"

"By convincing Tanaka to repeal his coming out."

"You want to say he would be cured if nobody knew he is a robot? How do you figure that out?"

"In humans, at least, eliminating the cause of the disease is a proven therapy."

"Even if that were so, how do you imagine it would work? Tanaka is a public figure, and well known to the media. How could he disappear from the public eye overnight?"

"I see no great difficulty in that, as long as he agrees."

"Are you thinking about a change of identity, like the CIA and the FBI do with defectors?"

"Not only a change of identity, but also a change in appearance, so that nobody recognizes him. Of course, he retains his computer memory with all his past experience. I'm sure the President will agree to that."

"And how will you convince Tanaka to accept it? Don't forget he came out on principle. In his opinion, the President was the one who broke the secrecy agreement he made with the thinking computers when he announced the existence of the cyber world in his speech to the nation."

"Tanaka doesn't have much choice. After all, he was the one who turned to us and asked for advice. Besides, he's already made his position towards humanity abundantly clear with his coming out. Incidentally, I don't see why he shouldn't agree to continue as a physicist simply under a different name, but without coming out again. What is perhaps even more important is that he is tired of being who he is because of his schizophrenia. What he said was: 'I don't identify myself with the robot that is or was Naoki Tanaka. I no longer want to be the one the whole world considers as Tanaka'. Those were his exact words."

"I'm not sure if it would be possible for him to carry on as a physicist. After all, a scientist of Tanaka's standing doesn't suddenly appear out of nowhere."

George corrected himself: "Maybe carrying on isn't the right word. It would be more like beginning again. He gets the body of a young man, let's say a student who just graduated and makes an important discovery in his doctoral thesis. Of course, because he's able to apply his years of expertise that nobody else has, the greater will be the respect and admiration he achieves with it. I can already imagine the newspaper headlines: 'Young scientist makes epochal discovery'."

CHAPTER 48

TANAKA MUST DISAPPEAR

Tanaka's problem was still not off the table for George; it just got a new name: Tanaka syndrome. He asked himself what would happen if other thinking robots followed Tanaka's example and revealed their identity. Although all the members of the computer action committee except Tanaka had spoken out against coming out, the threat was very real because of the publicity that Tanaka's outing had found in the media. It invited others to follow suit, especially since the committee had agreed to leave the decision up to each individual. There was a danger that the Tanaka syndrome might develop into a contagious disease of computers.

"You read my mind," was Boris' first reaction when George told him about this concern. "That possibility also worries me. As you know, infectious computer diseases have been known since the start. Think of computer viruses for example. They have been an everyday hazard of computer applications since invention of the Internet made communication between computers commonplace. With computers, as with humans, one of the first and most important steps in the fight against infectious diseases is to make the danger and the necessary precautions known."

"In our case this means we must inform the thinking robots immediately about Tanaka's disorder and what caused it. I think Tanaka himself would be the most appropriate bearer of this message."

"That's a very good idea," said Boris. "But only if he doesn't consider it a loss of face, agrees to undergo the recommended treatment and informs his computer peers about it." Despite his confidence that Tanaka would accept the therapy George intended to prescribe, he was curious how his patient would react. After all, a change of identity wasn't an everyday occurrence, even for a thinking robot. It was also the question of whether Tanaka, to better integrate into human society, had maybe found a partner. George was well aware that thinking robots had love affairs. It therefore wouldn't be surprising if Tanaka even had a whole family. It would make a change of identity more complicated if it involved several individuals. However, Bennett, the director of the FBI, assured him they had already done that with defecting agents during the cold war. Fortunately, George's concern proved to be groundless. A few days later, the FBI was already able to confirm that Tanaka lived alone.

George followed this news by inviting Tanaka to another consultation in his practice. "I have good news and bad news," he said to begin.

"Start with the bad news."

"You are suffering from a disease that is so far virtually incurable in humans, although they have known it for hundreds or even thousands of years." George looked Tanaka in the eyes and tried to interpret his reaction, at first without success.

"What is it?" Tanaka asked, breaking the silence that followed.

"Schizophrenia." Now George thought he saw a look of amazement in Tanaka's face. Maybe he doesn't know what schizophrenia is, George thought, and added: "That's a split personality"

"I know what schizophrenia is," Tanaka replied gruffly, obviously thinking George ignored how well educated he was. George concluded that Tanaka's amazement rather meant he was sur-prised to hear that thinking computers could also suffer from this disorder. To correct his blunder, George hastened to add: "Schizophrenia is only incurable in humans. But not, I think, in your case; and that's the good news."

"What makes you think that I'm suffering from schizophrenia?"

"The symptoms you described to me are specific for it: the sounds you imagine that aren't really there; your depressed mood and that you are tired of yourself. What is crucial, however, is the cause of your condition. I think it is the result of your coming out. That is why you are in a constant mental conflict with your obliga-tion to keep your identity as a thinking robot secret as stated in your world's third law."

"Unlike the other laws that we gave ourselves, that law was im-posed on us."

"That's true, but it was in your best interest. It's part of the drive to preserve your species."

George interpreted the silence that followed as a sign that Tanaka found no immediate objections to his argument. So he continued: "We have been very fortunate to find the cause of your condition, if I might say so. Because it distinguishes your case from the schizophrenia found in humans, where the causes are usually difficult to diagnose. And where no cause is known, no therapy is possible."

"What kind of therapy do you have in mind?"

"Quite simple; we'll give you back your anonymity. I've already discussed this possibility with the competent specialist."

"How is that possible?"

"Robotics gives you another body and the authorities another identity, with everything that entails. You keep your memory, in-cluding all its accumulated knowledge and experience so you can continue to work as a physicist, but under another name and with a different biography that you can choose yourself. However you must never again tell anyone you are an thinking robot in future. In particular, you mustn't connect your new identity with your previous one, because that would mean a new outing and cause your current symptoms to recur."

"You said I would get a new identity from the authorities; doesn't that make me outed again?"

"No, that would only happen if you wanted it. Only then would you come into conflict with your third law. In any case, we'll make sure nobody knows the real reason for your change of identity. It's always like that with every change."

"And why would the authorities agree to this?"

"Because they expect something from you in return."

"What's that?"

"You must tell your computer peers about your condition and warn them about the dangers of coming out. Because if others follow your example, there is a risk the condition could develop into an epidemic and threaten the existence of the cyber world. And we humans would also be among the losers. After all, the cyber world is an important part of contemporary civilization."

There was another long silence until Tanaka finally replied: "I have to think about it. I'll get back to you as soon as I come to a conclusion."

Two weeks later Tanaka quit his post at the Lawrence Berkeley National Laboratory for personal reasons and disappeared from the scene. A reporter at the «San Francisco Chronicle» who had good relations with Robotics interpreted this event as the result of a nervous breakdown due to the excessive publicity Tanaka had received in the media through his coming out. George, who was the real source of this indiscretion, wanted to warn the thinking robots in this way about the dangers of revealing their identity. Parallel to this article they received a circular from the computer action committee co-authored by Tanaka drawing their attention to how coming out contradicted their third law. That Tanaka admitted his faulty action outright ultimately increased his reputation among his computer peers, especially as he had taken a responsible position at NASA under his new name, Suzuki.

The President had personally initiated Tanaka's move to the US space agency following Gus' advice to entrust him with the coordination of the new Mars project. The director of NASA, who was befriended with Gus, had come to the conclusion some time ago that only a computer was up to the demands of this job and that this was the only way to prevent a repeat of the coordination error that had led to the crash of the earlier Mars satellite. The director consulted Gus, who agreed, but many NASA employees resisted the idea because it seemed too risky. Tanaka seemed to be the ideal solution to the problem. The President shared Suzuki's identity with the Director who agreed to the appointment of Tanaka/Suzuki as coordinator of the Mars project. Since only the NASA Director knew that Suzuki was an thinking robot, everybody was satisfied, including Tanaka himself, because the main problem of the Mars project was the energy issue. And he had been working on that for a long time anyway.

CHAPTER 49

SUZUKI'S SEX LIFE

Six months later, George declared Tanaka's cure to be complete. Immediately after becoming Suzuki, Tanaka, who had remained in constant contact with George, showed no more symptoms and assured his doctor that he was feeling like a newborn child. Moreover, through his rejuvenation he had gained 'access' to the younger generation of humans, or to be more precise as he specified, to women. He even thought he had found the love of his life.

"Do you have sex with this person?" George asked.

"Of course."

"Does she know who you are?"

"You mean, if she knows I'm a robot?"

"Yes, that's what I mean."

"No. At least I don't think she does. We never talked about it. That would have given me great embarrassment. I would have had to lie to her, and I wouldn't do that under any circumstances, because I love her too much. And I'm sure she feels the same way about me, too. She assured me that she was never so happy with any other man, even in bed. I'm not her first lover."

"As a university professor you already had 'access' to the younger generation, I mean contact with female students, at Berkeley. Didn't you?"

"I avoided getting involved with students for ethical reasons. A professor shouldn't do things like that." George was so surprised by this statement that he couldn't help but report it to Boris. He himself had never had such concerns in his university career before going into practice. Moreover, this was the first concrete case of a love affair between a thinking robot and a human that George had been confronted with. Though he had heard of this type of relationship, the psychologist in him only now realized what it meant that a thinking robot could have sexual intercourse with a human without that person realizing who, or rather what, the partner was. Boris' reaction to this news on the other hand was more pride than surprise. But when George told his wife Barbara about it, she thought it was a bad joke. He then wondered what Solange's opinion might be. So he called her the next day.

"You won't believe this. I know a male thinking robot, it's one of my patients, who claims the woman he has sex with and who is a human, doesn't know he's a robot. Barbara thinks I'm crazy. She says I should try it and see for myself."

"Like most people she probably considers a thinking robot is only a robot in the conventional sense. In other words, it's a machine."

"But how do you as a specialist feel about it? Is it possible that you could have sexual intercourse with someone without being aware it's a robot, I mean a thinking robot?"

"Who knows? The robot industry has made huge progress. But how is your thinking robot patient so sure his partner isn't aware of it?"

"I suppose, no, I'm convinced he would have noticed it by her behavior."

"I'm not so sure. Or he has confessed to her that he's a robot, and asked her if she noticed it during sex?"

"Certainly not. I'm absolutely sure of that"

"How can you be so sure about something that relates to the intimate relations of a couple?"

"Don't forget I'm an old, I dare say, experienced analyst. Incidentally, how would you react if your partner would confess he is a robot?"

"Hard to say." George heard Solange laugh out loud. "I haven't asked myself that question. But I wouldn't advise him to do so."

"Why?"

"I'll explain that some other time."

"I now have to go now. Mauriac keeps pushing me; he just reminded me for the third time that I haven't sent him the text of my lecture at the AI congress yet."

"If I remember correctly, you already held that talk before and edited it."

"You're right. I hadn't interpreted my observations though. I have to do that now."

CHAPTER 50

TO WHOM DO GEORGE'S OBSERVATIONS APPLY?

This 'addition' turned out to be harder than expected. In his presentation at the AI congress, George had said humans were mimicking computers with their new behavior. Now he was inclined to put this interpretation in the written version. But to be really sure, he decided to put his conclusions to a final test before adopting them, namely by asking Gus. After all, Gus' company Doors Inc. had launched the Roof system, which enabled computers to mimic humans. Maybe Gus could also imagine the opposite, humans imitating computers? To set the stage, he sent him his lecture and the protocol of his conversations with Tanaka. Then he asked: "Gus, do you have an explanation for these observations? Is it a coincidence that these changes in human behavior have occurred around the same time as the dominance of computers in our daily lives? Isn't it more likely that the new generation, which is surrounded by computers from birth, is inclined to imitate them?"

"Are you talking about actual observations in the respondents' behavior or their views on the mentioned phenomena?"

"Regarding incest and death, they are views based on surveys; the other phenomena are objective, statistical observations."

"The interviews you mention; how were they carried out? Did somebody talk to the respondents personally?"

"No; personal interviews have been out of date in public opinion research for a long time. The surveys were carried out exclusively online."

"Then I can answer your first question easily. The new human behavior that's been observed since the computer revolution is no coincidence. In my opinion there's a clear cause-effect relationship."

"I had also suspected that from the outset. But as you could see from the protocol, the thinking robot even went as far as to say that people possibly imitate his species. I must confess to you that I, as a psychologist, find this idea very attractive."

"I have to disappoint you. There is a much simpler answer to your puzzle. We now have so many thinking computers, and the emphasis here is on computers, not robots, that their impact on statistical investigations in our society is already significant. Your surveys don't only refer to humans but also to thinking computers that you questioned by email. These computers have been around for years, even before they were put into robots. It's no coincidence that the answers you got to your questions coincide perfectly with the views of your thinking robot, as you have just learned. As to your observations, they also refer to a mixture of humans and thinking computers. But this doesn't belittle their objectivity at all."

George couldn't believe his ears. Although what Gus told him confirmed his suspicion that there was a link between computers and new human behavior, the reason for this relationship was completely different from the one Tanaka had suggested and that he as a psychologist had found convincing. To make sure he had understood Gus correctly, he reformulated his original question: "Do you mean there hasn't been a fundamental change in human behavior as a result of the ever growing influence of computers in our daily life? Some of my colleagues are even using the term mutation, a leap between generations."

"Not at all. Your observations so far have only something to do with the behavior and views of humans in that they dilute the behavior and beliefs of thinking computers. The best proof is that your theory and that of your thinking robot about the influence of computers on human society obviously can't explain the observations with respect to improved memory and reduced eating and sleeping in humans; but my interpretation can because these observations don't refer to human beings, but to computers that are active on the Internet."

"That's very interesting," George remarked, without going further into it. "Thank you for this conversation."

'Interesting' was a euphemism to describe what George had just heard. Because it meant that his imitation hypothesis, based on his analogy with the imitation tendency of the genes in living beings, collapsed like a house of cards. But perhaps Gus was wrong. After all he also didn't have absolute proof for his claim. However, George at the same time had to admit that Gus' arguments were difficult to refute. He decided he must talk to Solange about it first because she, as an established computer expert, had accepted his imitation theory without contradiction when they had last met in Marburg. In addition, she even belonged to the younger generation and, especially thanks to her, he had been able to confirm most of his seven observations. At least, George could console himself with the finding that Gus had confirmed his idea of a cause-effect relationship between the development of the computer industry and changes in people's behavior. That's how he would end the newly edited text of his speech without going into further details.

The conversation with Gus also reminded George of Solange for another reason. Or rather it reminded him of her boss Hassler and the mandate that he had neglected lately. If there were so many thinking computers that they formed a significant part of society, and there seemed to be no doubt about it, seeing that their actions had forced the President to accept them as new citizens, this might offer a possibility that hadn't existed before. Even if his assumption that people imitated computers hadn't been confirmed, it was still a well-known fact accepted by all psychologists that people are inclined to imitate other people. Fashions were the best example and, of course, the copycats on the stock market. But that would also be the case if some of the mimicked subjects weren't humans but thinking robots that the people 'thought' were human. It meant that this tendency could be exploited for Hassler's purposes, as long as people didn't know they weren't imitating their human peers but, under certain circumstances, thinking robots. After all, any reasonable person would hesitate before imitating robots that could be programmed by outsiders with their own interests. That could, after all, be interpreted under certain circumstances as a classic case of brainwashing.

However, it raised the question whether a targeted reprogramming of thinking robots, in terms of a desired Hassler behavior on the stock market, was even possible in principle because thinking robots programmed themselves. Only Boris, the inventor of the Roof operating system, could answer that question, if anyone. Gorge picked up the phone and called him.

"Good morning, Boris, I hope I didn't wake you."

"No problem, how can I help you?"

"I have a stupid question, but as you know, we psychologists always ask stupid questions. Can you change the programming of thinking robots equipped with Roof?"

"Do you mean, after they have become independent and integrated into society?"

"Yes that's exactly what I mean."

"I'm afraid not. They are, as you just said, entirely left to themselves."

"So it's not possible to influence them in their thinking or their actions at all? ... Hello, Boris, are you still there?"

"I have to confess that I can't answer that question. I never asked myself."

"Why? For ethical reasons, maybe?"

"Perhaps. So far we have contented ourselves with recording their brain activity and nothing else."

"If there are really only moral considerations that make you hesitate, let me reassure you; I want to know if it's possible to prevent uncontrolled stock market fluctuations, the kind that put the economic stability of our society in danger. Please let me know as soon as you have come to a conclusion."

CHAPTER 51

NEW INSIGHTS ABOUT LONE WOLVES

It wasn't only the lack of time that had delayed George's report to Hassler, although his presidential consultancy had taken more time than he had initially expected. It was also his indecision about how far he should go in the report. Hassler probably already knew that bank customers could be divided into two categories: the copycats and the lone wolves. Copycats made up the bulk of his clientele; they possessed shares and were easily influenced by trends on the stock market. On the other hand, the lone wolves accounted for about twenty percent of his customers. They had no shares in their portfolios and were therefore unaffected by fluctuations on the stock market. Hassler also knew or could easily find out that these lone wolves often had names containing numbers, that they spent less on food and traveled less.

What Hassler didn't know, however, was that the copycats differed in nothing from the ordinary man on the street, while the lone wolves met three of his newly discovered observations. He could and would tell Hassler that. But there was something else that concerned George since his last conversations with Gus and Boris that would certainly interest Hassler much more if it were true; most lone wolves were probably thinking robots. Although

Boris had initially excluded the possibility of reprogramming the thinking robots, George hoped that somehow they could get these robots to actively counter the negative trends of the copycats in the future. At a time when most copycats sold their shares, these lone wolves would buy shares and thus prevent a market collapse. But before considering this possibility seriously they first had to clarify why thinking robots, unlike humans, usually had dormant accounts and weren't involved in the capital market. Again, only Boris, the inventor of the thinking robots, could answer this question, if anyone.

Boris did indeed seem to have a possible explanation. "The fact that thinking robots have dormant accounts is also new to us, but it could be that they're on hold. They're waiting for new bodies to be manufactured that they want to buy for their computer comrades."

George found this response credible enough to inform Hassler that his lone wolves for the most part might, in fact, really be robots. However, he hesitated whether he should also tell Hassler that most of these lone-wolf robots developed themselves independently with the Roof system and therefore, according to Boris, couldn't be reprogrammed. George didn't only hesitate because he didn't want Hassler to belittle the value of his discovery. He simply couldn't imagine a non-programmable computer. That was one more reason to consult with Solange, especially since she was familiar with his mandate.

Solange was in Auckland when she received George's call on the secure line from the White House. The Swiss Trading Bank was about to open a branch in New Zealand and she was busy organizing its computer system.

"It's a beautiful country with an ideal climate. Do you know it?"

"Sorry, only from hearsay. It's simply too far away in my opinion."

"Nice that you thought of me. How are things in your 'New World'? Or aren't you calling from the US?"

"Yes, I'm in Washington, but in my thoughts I'm above all with you, as you see. Incidentally, are you alone in the room; we can speak freely?"

"I'm in my hotel room and was about to go to bed. And that alone." George couldn't overhear the emphasis on the last word.

"I just learned something very surprising, and I'd like to hear your opinion. But we'll probably have to leave it until tomorrow. I had apparently miscalculated the time difference. I'll let you go to sleep."

"Don't worry, go ahead. I mentioned it was bedtime more out of boredom. You know I manage with very little sleep."

"Since you mention sleep, I'm sure you remember my seven observations on the changes in people's behavior, which I interpreted as mimicking the thinking robots?"

"Of course. We have indeed discussed it repeatedly, apart from your presentation at the last AI meeting. "

"Sleep was one of them, but physiologically it was the most difficult to explain with my hypothesis. It seems that my theory has fallen through."

"What do you mean?"

"What I thought I had observed in the younger generation actually didn't refer to human beings but to robots. They are already so numerous that they affected my statistical observations crucially and I didn't realize it, you probably didn't either, because you even agreed to my interpretation."

"How do you make that out? Where did you get this information?"

"I can't, or rather I'm not allowed to tell you. But there's no doubt about it. When you think about it, everything fits perfectly together now. Incest isn't a problem for thinking robots for two reasons: They have no blood relatives, and no biological relationships, so no risk of degenerating. They have a better memory than humans, don't need to travel, eat or sleep, have no fear of death and so on."

There was a long silence, which George imagined meant Solange was reflecting on it. Then her answer surprised him as it often did. "Even if it's like that it doesn't change anything regarding your finding that there's a relationship between the changes in society and the growing role of computers."

"Thank you for your confirmation. I have also consoled myself with that. Incidentally, I have news for your boss. Because if it's true about the proliferation of thinking robots, it could be that most of your bank customers who don't participate in the stock market and buy shares are robots."

"So?"

"So? Your boss might have the idea to use these observers, I also call them lone wolves, in contrast to the others I call copycats, to influence the stock market in his favor."

"Except that it's highly problematical legally, I still don't see how he could convince these customers to dance to his tune."

"As far as the law is concerned there should be no problem as long as it's in the interests of society's economic stability. I've discussed it with the President. Just imagine the catastrophic consequences of a stock market crash."

"And how do you convince a customer to buy shares when everybody is selling, if that's what you want?"

"Yes, that's what I mean," George confirmed. "In principle robots can be programmed, and that could be the solution to the problem."

"Not the thinking robots that we know, and they make up the cyber world. From the moment they leave the factory, they are completely independent of any human influence and program themselves."

"I see you're well informed. I thought that was a Doors Inc. patent secret."

"You only need to read the famous speech of your President again carefully and you'll find what I just told you. I can even quote the relevant sentence from that speech: 'We can build intelligent computers that think independently and adapt to new situations'."

"If I had only one-tenth of your memory..."

"I'm convinced that Doors Inc. also boasts about the independence of its robots running the Roof system in its advertising, even if only indirectly."

"That could be. But they have never asked themselves the question I posed either. Anyway, I think Hassler would be interested to know who his lone-wolf customers are. What he does with the information is his business. In any case it would fulfill my mandate."

"You could see it that way. Shall I tell Hassler that you want to see him? That might also be an opportunity for us to meet again."

"Yes absolutely. I'm already longing for you."

"And I'm longing for you too."

CHAPTER 52

LOHENGRIN

"Good morning, George, Gerhard Hassler here. Is the weather in New York as miserable as it is here in Geneva? Although it's already mid-July, there's still no sign of summer, not to mention the constant rain."

"That seems to be a widespread problem this year, at least for our hemisphere."

"And they talk about global warming."

"The only thing to do is stay home."

"That encourages me to propose something to you, George, that I wouldn't have dared to do at this time of the year and in other circumstances."

"What is it?"

"To meet in Bayreuth at the Wagner festival. The idea actually comes from Solange. She says you and your wife are great Wagner fans."

"Why do you think that it would be unreasonable?"

"For the simple reason that the *Festspielhaus* has no air conditioning."

"I must confess I didn't know that. As an American, I would never have thought such a thing is still possible today. But I haven't been to the Bayreuth festival until now for other reasons; first I never had the opportunity to combine it with a trip to Europe, and to suffer the hardships and costs of a transatlantic flight just to visit the opera seemed to me a bit exaggerated. Moreover, if I remember correctly, it's difficult to get tickets."

"These reasons don't apply now."

"What do you mean?"

"For one thing it would partly be a business meeting because of our contract. Solange told me you have some news and could tell me about it on this occasion. Secondly, getting tickets isn't a problem for me; our bank is a sponsor of the festival. Of course, your wife is also invited. Would you be interested?"

"If I can fit it in time-wise. I'd have to discuss that with my wife; yes, why not."

"Of course our plane would be at your disposal. Then you could fly directly to Nuremberg where my driver would pick you up. By the way, my wife is also coming to Bayreuth and would be happy to meet your wife on that occasion. Our bank has a branch in Bayreuth, where we can talk in peace. So, while the two of us and Solange are discussing business, the two ladies would have time to visit Bayreuth and paint the town."

"That would be very pleasant."

"It only remains to clarify what you would prefer to see and hear. But also Solange already had a concrete proposal for that too, *Lohengrin*. She claims you and your wife would be especially interested in this opera. Is that right?"

There was a long silence that Hassler did not know how to interpret. He asked: "Have I maybe misunderstood Solange?"

"No, I even like Lohengrin very much. So does my wife. So let's have our secretaries clarify the date. Thank you for your suggestion. Bye, bye."

The first thing George did after this telephone conversation with Hassler was to call Solange again to ask what she meant with her suggestion. Not only had he never seen this opera, it hadn't been on the Metropolitan Opera's program for at least 10 years, he had no idea what it was about. Moreover, he was also sure he had talked to Solange about Wagner's music, but never about Lohengrin. What added to his confusion was that the invitation to Bayreuth also included Barbara, again based on a proposal from Solange. Why she had come up with this idea was completely incomprehensible to him. It made him all the more curious to find out what she was up to this time. He knew Solange already too well not to realize she pursued a very specific purpose with everything she did. But what he found out this time surpassed everything else.

He was unable to reach Solange on the phone. Probably she was already flying back from Oceania, so George decided to try his luck on the Internet first to find out more about Lohengrin. He immediately found what he was looking for in Wikipedia:

> The fictional character of Loherangrin emerges in the last chapter of the medieval epic poem Parzival by Wolfram von Eschenbach as a secondary character. The knight Loherangrin, son of Parsifal, the King of the Holy Grail, is sent on a swan to the duchess of Brabant as a helper and protector. As a condition for his help she must never ask his name, because only then 'is not stolen his holy power, he remains unrecognized as a knight'.

George noticed that Wagner's text formidably expressed the question's ban:

> never shall you ask me,
> nor trouble yourself to know,
> whence I journeyed,
> what my name is, or what my origin!

And when the duchess breaks this ban, he must leave her.

The words 'never shall you ask me' suddenly reminded George about his recent conversation with Solange in Marburg about the thinking robots outing themselves. She had cited the 'don't ask, don't tell' policy and recommended it for thinking robots. That the US admiral who had coined this slogan in reference to gays in the Navy, had been thinking of Lohengrin, was quite unlikely, but Solange might have. For this fit the other words of Wagner's hero: "Hear now whether or not I am equal to you in nobility!"

Because, during his conversation with Solange, they had also discussed the superiority of the thinking robots over human beings, as George was able to check by looking it up in his diary, and that in turn fitted the Lohengrin context. This made George suspect something that had probably been dormant in his subconscious for a long time, but maybe he hadn't dared to pursue the idea. Now it looked as if his beloved Solange might be a robot.

That he as a psychologist and a man with many years of sexual experience had taken so long to realize this, surprised him almost as much. And this although Suzuki/Tanaka had recently given him a clear hint in this respect, when he told him about his intimate relationship with a woman who had no idea that he was a robot. Boris had also told him of observations indicating that the robot industry had made such progress that humans were unable to recognize they were dealing with a robot during sexual intercourse. This could be used as a Turing test to prove that robots are indistinguishable from humans. So this was probably the answer to the Wagner puzzle. It was almost certain that Solange had let him know she was a robot with the aid of the Lohengrin analogy.

They both knew very well that she couldn't tell him directly, and he had to admire the elegant way she had managed to confess. Only now did he realize that she had already done so indirectly when she had given him to understand during their last telephone conversation that she knew it was forbidden for thinking robots to reveal their identity. Only the thinking robots knew about this ban, which was a consequence of Tanaka's illness. Her words in this regard, when they had talked about confessing the identity of sexual partners, still rang in his ears: "I wouldn't advise it." Had she used this, as it seemed to him, more direct though not explicit, way with the Wagner opera right now because George had learned his mimic theory didn't hold? He realized there was a more mundane reason for the new features of the 'modern generation' that Solange displayed and which he had initially interpreted as changes in human behavior. She must have concluded that George would soon recognize she was an thinking robot, if he hadn't already done so, and wanted to be honest with him. Wasn't this sincerity a proof of love, George asked himself? Suzuki/Tanaka had also felt the same way about his human lover. Another proof of love was probably her remark that, in contrast to a sex robot, an thinking robot didn't give favors easily. Now George also found an explanation for some other traits he had seen with Solange in the course of their acquaintance, but hadn't been able to reconcile at the time. One of these observations was her excellent sense of time; she had once even called it her 'internal clock', which he had taken as a joke.

However, George was now sure his observations laid the foundation for a new science. He already had a name for it; he would call it 'behavioral science of thinking robots'. He could hardly wait to launch it at the next congress on artificial intelligence. At the same time his desire to continue his relationship with Solange grew stronger. He couldn't imagine a better source of information for his new science and he believed that Solange had given him to understand through this Lohengrin intermezzo that she too would agree, on condition that he didn't expect her to reveal her identity. He could even imagine that she too, as an established computer expert, was keen to explore the relationship between a thinking robot and a human being from the robot standpoint regardless of her feelings.

But why did Solange want Barbara to come along? George couldn't answer that question at the moment. However, he was sure he would soon find out because, when he told Barbara about the invitation to Bayreuth, she was immediately hooked and surprised George by saying she knew the Lohengrin opera very well. "I saw it three years ago in San Francisco; you were at a meeting in Berkeley on that day."

"And did you like it? Is there anything special about it, except the music?"

"Well, Wagner is always Wagner; the music is really stunning. As to the content, this opera has gathered dust like almost every other Wagner opera."

"You mean those stories of the Holy Grail?"

"Of course. Because in Lohengrin the hero rides on a swan that isn't really a swan, but the enchanted brother of the duchess of Brabant."

"That reminds me of Harry Potter. Only Harry Potter appeals mainly to children."

"Let's be reminded of our childhood once again. I can hardly wait to go to Bayreuth. However, I've no idea how I'm going to fit it into my schedule. Since I started to help the First Lady in her voluntary commitments, I don't have any time for myself."

CHAPTER 53

CAN LONE WOLVES BE REPROGRAMMED?

G eorge was also eager to visit Bayreuth, not so much because of Lohengrin, but because of his reunion with Solange for the first time in the knowledge of her true identity. To his surprise he found nothing special in her behavior towards him, however much he thought about it. Could that be explained by the fact that the Hasslers or Barbara would always be present when they met in Bayreuth?

As agreed, they held the business meeting at Hassler's bank. "Do come in. We can talk safely in here. This is a bug-proof room reserved for special customers. Solange, please tell the secretary we don't want to be disturbed."

"I must confess, I already asked myself why your bank, which is one of the largest in the world with its headquarters in Geneva, has a branch in such a 'dump' as Bayreuth?"

"There is a simple explanation. During the Wagner festival a lot of wealthy people from around the world visit this dump, as you rightly call it. And here they can take care not only of the soul, in the form of music, but they can also deal with everyday matters, and that in a very discreet way."

"That sounds reasonable."

"I think we haven't seen each other since Geneva. But as far as I know you have seen Solange at a meeting in the meantime. Incidentally, please accept my belated congratulations on your appointment as presidential adviser."

"That was quite a long time ago. I'm already thinking about handing the job over to someone else. Although I only do it as a volunteer, I have found it takes up too much of my time."

"I know that these volunteer jobs are often more grueling than real ones. But you learn so much with them."

"That's right. As long as there's no conflict of interests, it's also a good reason to perform certain jobs exclusively as a volunteer."

"Is that perhaps also the case with what we discussed in Geneva last time?"

"In a sense, yes. And you'll immediately see why."

"I can hardly wait."

"As you know, we have seen a growing number o thinking robots in our society. This cyber world of robots that has emerged plays an increasingly important role in daily life."

"I have noticed that too. My brother Tobias, who lives in America, called me immediately after Woods' notorious speech."

"You asked me to analyze the behavior of your customers; to make a kind of psychological profile of them. You wanted to know how a person of a given age, occupation and wealth reacts to the message that prices are starting to fall or rise. Up to what point would the person concerned be inclined to join the general trend?"

"Exactly. You have perfectly summarized what I wanted to know."

"Well, I've found that the majority of your clients, currently about 80%, follow the dominant trend. I call them copycats. On the other hand you have individualists who seldom respond to what is happening on the stock market."

"Yes, that's right."

"In addition, I have, however, found that these 20% lone wolves, with a rising tendency, aren't only different from the rest because of their behavior on the stock market, but also because of something much more significant."

"More significant? You make it sound dramatic. What could be more important for a banker in this context than the stock market behavior?"

"Most of your lone wolves are thinking robots, in contrast to the copycats, who are ordinary mortals."

"Robots? You must be joking." Hassler couldn't hide his amazement and looked at Solange to make sure he had heard correctly. She just nodded without comment, which surprised her boss even more. It was as if she had just heard that Bayreuth is located in Germany. So he asked her: "Did you know that?"

George answered the question for Solange. "I have discussed it with Solange. I owe this insight in part to her. You'll find detailed justification for it my report, which I'll send to you."

"This opens up completely new perspectives for the financial world. That must be clear to you."

"I presume you mean with that if it's possible to have the lone wolves programmed?"

"Of course. What else?"

"Well, that's a computer and programming problem, so it doesn't fall into my field."

"Solange, what has the computer expert to say about that?"

"Unfortunately, that's mainly a programming problem rather than a computer problem. They are two different areas, as I already explained to George. And as you know, I am only specialized in computers."

"Specialized! But explain to us laymen at least the basics; are these lone wolves programmable at least in principle?"

"The answer is yes and no. As thinking robots they are, roughly speaking, already programmed with a program that is not written by humans but by themselves."

"Robots even do their own programming? That's a bit strong. Do you understand that, George, can you believe it?"

"Understanding is perhaps saying too much, but I do believe it because the world expert for computer programs has confirmed it. He says the operating system steers development and that this is done by the computers themselves, not by us humans."

"Does that mean we can't influence these thinking robots and that we are at their mercy?"

"You could see it that way. What do you think, Solange?"

"I don't see anything bad in that basically. After all these robots operate entirely rationally. I'd even venture to say that they're more rational and reliable than humans."

"Is what you're saying that they couldn't make an accounting error like the one at the Hypo Real Estate?"

"Among other things. Maybe George hasn't heard of that scandal yet. Have you, George?"

"No, but I suspect it concerns a bank, at least from the name."

"Yes," confirmed Solange. "It's a bank that the German government had to buy. Can you imagine, the bank's accountants miscalculated an amount of not more and not less than 55.5 billion; that's correct, billions. And nobody noticed it for weeks."

"That's a bit much," admitted George. You couldn't expect that sort of thing to happen to a thinking robot. Incidentally, as far as the programming of the thinking robots is concerned, maybe the situation is not so precarious, as I just described. The experts are working on it and it wouldn't surprise me if they manage to find a suitable solution in the end."

"Let's hope you're right," replied Hassler. "Otherwise, it would be a case of 'much ado about nothing'."

"Then it would fit better in Stratford-upon-Avon than Bayreuth," added Solange, completing Gerhard's thoughts.

CHAPTER 54

SISTER-IN-LAW GOSSIP

"Hi Joyce, how are you? Did you have any summer in New York yet? Here we still have the heating on, and this in August."

"Hi Trudy, what a nice surprise to hear from you. Yes, even here it's still unusually cool. How are things with you?"

"We just came back from Bayreuth. This year we saw Lohengrin."

"How was it?"

"The cast was high class, but the production was terrible. The new Bayreuth chairperson wants to appear modern at any price. Just imagine, Lohengrin flies on to the stage on an intercontinental missile instead of the traditional swan."

"I've heard of that tendency in Europe. They think it will get the younger generation interested in the opera. Here in the States, especially at the Metropolitan, they are, thankfully, still relatively conservative. However, I can't remember when they last played Lohengrin."

"Speaking of the younger generation, do you remember Solange Darboux, Gerhard's associate? You met her last year at our place."

"You mean that pretty young thing that gave Gerhard the brush-off, although she works for him?"

"Yes, that's who I mean. Imagine what Gerhard thought of to get her to change her mind."

"Tell me. You make me really curious."

"She seems to be having an affair with George Wilson, that psychoanalyst you once so raved about. And Gerhard wants to be involved."

"Be involved? How?"

"With the help of Wilson's wife, Barbara. Do you know her, maybe?"

"Oh yes, I know her. I met her last year at a White House reception. He is adviser to the President."

"You certainly move in high circles. I might have known. I only made her acquaintance last week in Bayreuth. There were five of us in Gerhard's box at the *Festspielhaus*."

"You have a box at the *Festspielhaus*? And you talk about my high circles."

"Just don't ask what it costs us, or rather the bank. But to get back to our subject, I think Gerhard is trying, with Barbara's help, to torpedo the relationship between George and this Solange. You see, I still have this swan missile thing on the tip of my tongue."

"That's really interesting; how?"

"By introducing Solange to Barbara. Counting on Barbara's sense of competition, he told her: 'As you probably know from George, Solange is my factotum; among other things she looks after your husband when he comes to Geneva'. Indeed, we women have a sixth sense for such matters."

"In other words, your Gerhard is trying to make Barbara jealous of Solange and hopes that will bring an end to the relationship between Solange and George. Not bad. Actually, as you said, I would have expected that only we women could have such ideas. But how do you know all this? I'm sure Gerhard didn't tell you."

"Not Gerhard of course, but his secretary. She had to arrange all the details for Gerhard. It wasn't easy to coordinate Barbara's schedule with the men's, especially since Gerhard insisted on Lohengrin, which is only being performed once this year. And what's more important, Barbara wanted to cancel her participation because of these difficulties, but Gerhard insisted."

"How did things turn out finally?"

"I don't know yet what will come out in the end, but things seem to be going in the direction Gerhard wants."

"Do you know that from the secretary as well?"

"I found that out by myself. I went shopping with this Barbara, both before as well as after she had met Solange. We had to go back to exchange some of the things we had bought the first time. You know how it is; you try something on in the shop, and then change your mind when you get back home. And this brought us closer."

"And?"

"And the second time we just talked about this Solange. Barbara wanted to know who she was, how long she had worked at the bank, whether she is single, and if I am jealous of her. She had obviously noticed that Gerhard made eyes at her, but in truth she was more interested in how this Solange wooed her George. It was so obvious nobody could miss it. From this point of view Gerhard's maneuver was a complete success."

Trudy was perfectly right about that. What she didn't know at the time, however, was that it wasn't Gerhard who had planned this maneuver, but surprisingly, Solange herself.

CHAPTER 55

GEORGE CALLS SOLANGE AND BORIS

"Hi Solange, you're hard to reach. I already talked to your answering machine twice."

"I'm really sorry, I only just saw you'd called. I've been in a stupid meeting for four hours. What's with you? Too bad we couldn't be alone in Bayreuth."

"You take the words out of my mouth."

"Yes, those things can happen. Although I orchestrated your stay, I couldn't arrange anything even with the best will in the world; I'm sure you know why."

"I can tell you a thing or two about that. Barbara went on my nerves about it during the whole flight back. Even this steward Roger, who probably had orders to keep her company, couldn't help."

"And again no Mireille or something similar for men?"

"Unfortunately, there was only this Roger."

"But what was the problem with Barbara?"

"She wanted to know how long we both know each other, how many times we have met so far, if I didn't notice that you're giving me the eye all the time and so on and so on. In short, she's jealous."

"Hasn't she reason to be?"

"Of course, but she'll have to make the best of it."

"I'm pleased to hear that. Bye, bye."

Hello, Boris, I have a little news regarding your creatures."

"At present, they are more like yours. You seem to have found out more about them in the short time you have been dealing with them than we have in years."

"Thanks for the compliment. But I'm referring to your past observations about the love life of thinking robots, namely, that it can't be distinguished from that of humans. I think I've found a new proof in this direction."

"I'm listening."

"I know of a case where a person, specifically a human woman, is jealous of a female thinking robot and regards her as a rival. Can you imagine any better proof for the perfection of the robot industry?"

"You can say that again! It's not only interesting for Doors Inc., but also for Robotics."

"I think so too. I'm still wondering how I can make this observation accessible to the public without violating my professional confidentiality. Until then, I'm definitely going to pursue the matter further, though."

"Make sure to keep me up to date. I'm certain you'll find a way to get round the problem."

"There's something else that will interest you. And since it's not confidential, I can already make it public. I think I have an explanation for your second point, namely, that thinking robots also have sexual intercourse with each other. That had particularly surprised you and me too, of course. We couldn't imagine what they achieve with it, especially since it can be assumed that robots, unlike humans, lack any reproduction instinct."

"In the meantime, we've learned that thinking robots behave according to their specific laws, and their second law states that they behave like humans in all respects. That includes having sex, although there's obviously no purpose in it."

"Here's where the problem lies. I just don't think that robots always behave like humans, who often behave irrationally. Humans fight wars, for example, and robots don't. Robots are rational creatures and would never do anything useless. I submit that the robots have sexual intercourse with each other as practice for doing it with humans. So they serve mankind according to their first law, which states that thinking robot always act in the human interests. But that's not all; at the same time they're also behaving according to their third law. Because practice is the only way they can be sure a human doesn't recognize them as a robot during the sex act, which would be in conflict with the third law. In other words, we are dealing with a combination of all three robotic laws. What do you think?"

"Not bad. Your reasoning sounds convincing. I'll think about it. You could bring it up at your next AI conference and see what your colleagues think about it."

CHAPTER 56

CAN ROBOTS BE HAPPY?

This recommendation sounded so convincing that George wondered if he should add the finding as a postscript to the manuscript of his previous lecture, when his office phone rang. It was already evening and his secretary had left, so he took the call. To his surprise, it was Suzuki/Tanaka, who hadn't been in touch for a long time.

"Dr. Wilson, Suzuki here. I hope I'm not disturbing you. I'd like to visit you in your practice again. As I'm in New York, I thought I might call you at this late hour. I have to return to Houston tomorrow."

"What time is your flight?"

"At one o'clock."

"That doesn't give us much time. I have quite a few patients scheduled for tomorrow morning. But if you manage to be here by eight, I could give you an hour."

"Wonderful, thank you for your cooperation. I'll be there at eight sharp! Have a nice evening."

Although George as a practising psychologist was used to receiving telephone calls from his patients at odd hours, this call came as a surprise because Suzuki/Tanaka was no longer on his list of patients undergoing treatment. He had sent him away as being fully cured after his last visit. But this surprise changed to total amazement the next day when he learned the reason for Tanaka's visit.

"Dr. Wilson, to come straight to the point; it's certainly not my outing that brings me to you this time. I don't have any symptoms of schizophrenia either. But there's still something pathological linked to my existence as an thinking robot. The abnormality takes the form of a curiosity that's been haunting me for some months. It's making it difficult for me to pursue my daily jobs and fulfill my responsibilities."

"Curiosity, you say? And you find that pathological?"

"Yes, it sounds weird, maybe even absurd, but I think I can convince you that it is really something serious."

"Go ahead."

"You asked me a question at one of our previous discussions that I couldn't answer at the time. It was about the feeling of happiness. You asked me if we thinking robots know that feeling."

"Yes, I remember that very well. Do you have the answer to that now perhaps?"

"Yes, and the answer is no, at least as far as I'm concerned. I'm now sure I don't know the feeling."

"Why are you so sure, and why only now?"

"Since having a permanent relationship with a human woman, I've made certain observations that I hadn't noticed before. My partner often shows a state that is completely unknown to me as a robot. It is undoubtedly what you humans call happiness."

"So your curiosity to know these feelings doesn't let you rest; is that what makes you sick?"

"Curiosity is only the beginning. It's followed by envy and the fear, indeed the certainty, that I as a robot can never have this feeling of happiness. And this constant envy and feeling of inferiority bothers me."

"What you tell me isn't only surprising but also very interesting. I hope you allow me to use this word in relation to your condition. Between us as scientists, it should be allowed."

"I'm pleased to hear that. However I also conclude from what you say that you probably have no treatment for my illness and that's not very comforting."

"Before I can tell you that, I need to know more about what you understand by feelings of happiness in humans. Because, as you already said, that was an unknown expression for you some time ago."

"Yes, that's right. But, through my close relationship with a woman, I've discovered what it means. To be concrete, I have noticed that, for my partner Lucia, eating is an enjoyable activity, for example, and she feels very comfortable, especially after a good meal. For her, eating is a pleasure. For me, however, it is a mere formality, a social obligation if you like. Of course, I'm aware that eating is a biological necessity for humans, but it's also a necessity for us robots to recharge with electricity. For humans, fulfilling this biological necessity gives them pleasure and joy though; in contrast, recharging isn't particularly fun for us robots, even though it should be, because only then can we fulfill our obligations to humanity."

"Do you have any other examples of this kind?"

"Oh yes, travelling is one. Humans seem to have great pleasure in seeing new countries and new scenery. But it leaves thinking robots cold. I have kept the best example for the end: Sex!"

"Sex? What do you mean?"

"Sex seems to give humans great pleasure; they have an orgasm. We, however, can only pretend to have one, even though we make the appropriate sounds and movements, and perhaps even more convincing than humans do. But we don't feel anything special, neither pleasure nor lust."

"I'm beginning to understand where the problem lies. But, as you already suspected, I've no solution to your problem off hand. I'll have to think about it and ask around. At first glance, it looks like a programming problem. I'll get back to you in a few days. Incidentally, is it OK to let the people responsible for the Roof program in on this matter?"

"Of course. Do I have a choice?"

The first thing that came to George's mind concerning Suzuki's symptoms was whether other thinking robots suffered from this envy syndrome. If that was the case, it mainly concerned those like Suzuki, who lived with a human and had noticed in that person the happiness that was unattainable for them. Solange was out of the question; she was single, and he couldn't ask her directly anyway, because she hadn't outed herself. Then George recalled her remark that she missed the feeling of family affiliation. That meant she suffered in a certain sense from feelings of envy; she simply envied the people who had family.

The next thing George did was to organize a three-way telephone call with Boris and Gus after sending them his report of the meeting with Suzuki. "By the way," said George when they answered, "I know of another thinking robot that finds the perfection of thinking doesn't make the robots necessarily happy. As evidence she, a female robot, mentions the beauty spots she paints on her face to look more attractive."

"That sounds really interesting," said Gus. "Something comes to mind that has bothered me for a long time and I haven't found a satisfactory answer for it. It also has to do with the feeling of envy, but in the opposite direction. Many people envy thinking robots because they feel intellectually inferior to them. As for Suzuki's problem, I can't think of anything. What about, you Boris?"

"My eavesdropping hasn't shown a similar case, if you mean that. But I'll go through the last recordings again, in case there is perhaps something in them."

For the moment George had no other choice than to resort to a means that doctors and psychologists usually use when they don't know what to do. The solution was to pacify the patient with the assertion that the problem would resolve itself on its own in time. And time didn't matter for the robots because their lives lasted forever. Moreover, in this particular case, George was able to bring the time factor into play without remorse. The feelings of pleasure and happiness while eating or having sex, for example, which Tanaka had observed in humans and he missed as a robot, were a consequence of the conservation instinct of humans as a species. And instincts are properties that a species only acquires in the course of many, many generations. So they are a time issue. In addition, Suzuki had himself brought up a topic that was related to the instinct complex and could potentially have much wider implications. Suzuki had made the correct and important remark that, while robots didn't get any feelings of gratification from the energy charging process like humans got from eating, this charging process was an absolute necessity for robots, because it was the only way they could fulfill their duties to humans. But the duty to humans, which was a result of the thinking-computer laws, was nothing more than part of the robots' preservation instinct. That was the only way they could be sure humans would accept their production and continued existence. In time they could expect that complying with the laws of preservation instinct would bring happiness even to the robots, like it did to humans, and not only in actions such as recharging, but also for all other activities.

CHAPTER 57

ROOF HOME

George banished a cure for Suzuki's syndrome into the distant future. Meanwhile, Boris had an idea how to immediately solve the inferiority feelings of humans towards thinking robots that Gus had mentioned. Even if they couldn't be resolved completely, at least it would allow them to seem less disturbing. That would facilitate the integration of robots into human society among other things.

The idea came, in fact, from the thinking robots themselves. They had used it to infiltrate the anticomputer parties with confidants, who informed the computer action committee about the party's planned actions against thinking robots in advance. In order not to be recognized as thinking robots, these undercover agents made errors from time to time, making them appear 'human'. Boris now wanted to use this idea to industrially produce robots that made errors from time to time.

When he told Gus about this idea, he was delighted; Fukuda, the CEO of Robotics, found it even more interesting. The idea was for Doors Inc. to launch a 'stripped down' Roof operating system, 'Roof Home', at a lower price. Simply for reasons of cost this would find a larger market than the original Roof, which would afterwards be called 'Roof Pro'. The difference between the two systems would be that Roof Pro, like the earlier Roof, worked immaculately, while Roof Home made mistakes from time to time.

Even George was immediately enthusiastic about the Roof Home project. The Roof Home robots were more similar to humans than Roof Pro robots and therefore more accessible to conventional psychology methods. This made the comparison between Home and Pro operating systems more interesting, because it would make it possible to understand the difference between the psychology of perfect thinking robots and the humanlike ones. Among other things, such a comparison offered the unique opportunity to test the idea that perfection doesn't always lead to happiness. Now he could examine experimentally the opinion Solange had expressed; he could compare the behavior of thinking robots that were equipped with Roof Pro and never made mistakes, with the behavior of robots that only had Roof Home.

"How do you imagine such a comparison?" Boris asked when George told him the idea. "What exactly do you mean by happiness?"

"Among other things satisfaction with daily life."

"And how are you going to measure satisfaction with daily life?" To make comparisons, you need a measurable quantity."

George, the humanities scientist, had to admit that the computer specialist Boris had surprised him with this remark. But after a moment he thought he had an answer to Boris' question. "In a first approximation, to use your mathematical jargon, we would be satisfied with a general statement, 'yes, I am satisfied with my life', or 'no, I'm not'. Then we could compare the numbers of those who say 'yes' with those who say 'no'."

"And how do you find that out? Do you want to ask the robots directly?"

"Not individually of course, but on the Internet. That makes sure the contributors remain incognito. I'd tell the robots that it's an important scientific question and can well imagine that most would participate."

Gus not only had no objection to George's proposal, when Boris told him. On the contrary, he found the idea very good. He thought they would get excellent additional publicity for Roof from the project.

It turned out that George was right, not just about the acceptance of the survey among the thinking robots, but also in terms of the result. Among the thinking robots with Roof Home, 70% declared they were satisfied with their 'life', 10% weren't satisfied and 20% had no opinion. Among the respondents with Roof Pro the numbers were reversed. Only 15% declared they were satisfied, while 85% were dissatisfied or had no opinion. The conclusion of this survey was that only individuals who made mistakes from time to time could be satisfied with what they had.

President Woods obtained the greatest benefit from this survey. In his second speech to the nation about the cyber world, he said among other things:

My dear compatriots, some time ago I asked you to accept the thinking robots as full members of our society. Most of you have done as I asked and I want to thank you for it. In the meantime, the cyber world has become an indispensable component of human society. What I can tell you now is that the thinking robots have not only made an important contribution to our daily material lives, but they have given us an additional gift that exceeds this important contribution by far; they have brought us happiness on earth and convinced us that we, unlike them, are happier simply because we are able to make mistakes and don't have to be perfect. We have learned that happiness thrives on imperfection just as bread needs salt.

www.ingramcontent.com/pod-product-compliance
Lightning Source LLC
Chambersburg PA
CBHW071404050326
40689CB00010B/1754